Value Stream Management for Lean Healthcare

Four Steps to Planning, Mapping, Implementing, and Controlling Improvements in All Types of Healthcare Environments

By Don Tapping
Sue Kozlowski, MSA, MT(ASCP)SBB DLM, CSSBB(ASQ)
Laura Archbold, RN, BSN, MBA, and
Todd Sperl, Master Black Belt

ISBN 978-0-9792887-8-4

08 07 06 05 04 03   5 4 3 2 1

MCS Media, Inc.
888 Ridge Road
Chelsea, MI 48118
United States of America
Telephone 734-475-4301
E-mail: info@theleanstore.com

Cover concept and art direction: Jody Williams
Page design: Jody Williams
Content edit: Chris Tapping and Nina Rodriguez

Library of Congress Cataloging-in-Publication Data

This publication is designed to provide the most up-to-date, accurate and authoritative information for the improvement of healthcare processes and practices. It is sold with the understanding that neither the authors, editors, nor the publisher are engaged in providing legal, accounting, or other professional service. If legal advice or other expert assistance is required, the services of a competent professional consultant should be sought.

All MCS Media, Inc. books are available at special quantity discounts. Please contact The Lean Store, info@theleanstore.com or 734-475-4301, for additional information.

Contents

Overview

Topics Include:

- ✦ **Publisher's Message**
- ✦ **Special Thanks**
- ✦ **The Purpose of this Book**
- ✦ **Healthcare Professionals Who Could Benefit from this Book**
- ✦ **Islands of Care**
- ✦ **Learning Features**

Publisher's Message

"The simultaneous occurrence of events which, taken individually, would be far less powerful than the result of their chance combination. Such occurrences are rare by their very nature, so that even a slight change in any one event contributing to the perfect storm would lessen its overall impact" is the definition of perfect storm, based on Sebastian Junger's novel and screenplay, *The Perfect Storm*. Healthcare has its own version of a perfect storm: The many events occurring in the past, all contributing to the situation it finds itself in today. Many experts call this "the healthcare crisis" and are in agreement that it is not due to just one event. It is this "simultaneous occurrence of events" (i.e., increased utilization on providing the latest (and most expensive) technology, shortage of healthcare professionals entering the field while many are retiring, escalating litigation costs, payment gateway inefficiencies through Medicare, Medicaid, PPOs, HMOs, etc., more informed and educated patients, the 20-30 year-old hospital facilities requiring new construction to meet the Baby Boomer demand for services, etc.) that is coming together today challenging the healthcare industry to respond with improved patient care and safety.

As this perfect storm is looming on the horizon, or, for many facilities, is already there, it would be wise to look for ways to lessen its impact as much as possible. A business tool referred to as Lean (i.e., continuous improvement tools and concepts based on the Toyota Production System) can be used to lessen these effects by engaging the front-line worker in improving all aspects of healthcare services through a very simple practice known as the elimination of waste.

Continuous improvement, as outlined in this book, provides its own version of a perfect storm, but in this instance, the resultant combination of forces is good. The compilation of the teachings of Taiichi Ohno, founder of the Toyota Production System; Henry Ford, industrialist; Edward Deming, quality leader, to name a few throughout the years have provided significant pieces to the continuous improvement movement known as Lean. Lean is the engagement of the process worker (i.e., front-line) in finding a better or more efficient way to do something. It is through this elimination of process waste and variation that new standards of value-added services can be created allowing for a more streamline, cost-effective operation. Lean provides many tools that can help with this entire process, which to be effective, must fully be embraced by management. Lean and all its tools will be thoroughly explained throughout this book. Current quality/continuous improvement programs (i.e.,Total Quality Management (TQM) or Six Sigma) can be supplemented with this Lean direction to accelerate improvements.

"She's comin' on, boys, and she's comin' on strong," radioed Captain Bill (played by George Clooney in the movie, The Perfect Storm) on the sword fishing boat named Andrea Gail off the coast of Nova Scotia on October 31, 1991, just before he and his five crew members disappeared without a trace. This book introduces, in detail, the Lean version of a perfect storm to assist the healthcare industry in efforts to provide a better outcome than the Andrea Gail did for her crew on that fateful October date.

To quote an old adage, "Fight fire with fire".

Don Tapping

Special Thanks

St. John Health and Trinity Health must be acknowledged for their willingness to share best practices on what is required to implement a successful Lean-Sigma program. St. John Health is based in Warren, Michigan and provides services throughout southeastern Michigan with 7 hospitals, and over 100 surgery, ambulatory, physician practice, and long-term care facilities. They have over 18,000 employees. Trinity Health, a world-class healthcare system, is the fourth-largest Catholic healthcare system in the country. Based in Novi, Michigan, Trinity Health operates 44 acute-care hospitals, 379 outpatient facilities, 26 long-term care facilities, and numerous home health offices and hospice programs in seven core states with tens of thousands of employees. Both organizations are aggressively committing the necessary resources to improve healthcare in terms of quality, cost, and patient-service delivery for their communities with a Lean-Sigma focus. Therefore, without their willingness to share their best practices, this book might not have been written. The following are their messages and brief bios of their Lean-Sigma leaders.

St. John Health's Journey toward Lean, Six Sigma, and Quality

On October 31, 2003, St. John Health began its deployment of Six Sigma. Within two years, the system was ready to add the Lean approach due to the need to engage the process worker in all aspects of the continuous improvement cycle. St. John opted for naming their continuous program "Operational Excellence". All leaders were trained in the Lean management philosophy and skeptics were turned into believers when they saw how Lean "Rapid Improvement Events" (Kaizen Events) could create positive change for patients and providers alike. St. John has currently deployed and integrated their Operational Excellence program into their daily operations, so that each manager is responsible and accountable for results achieved through the use of Lean tools and concepts.

Susan F. Kozlowski, MSA, MT(ASCP)SBB DLM, CSSBB(ASQ) was one of the first Lean Six Sigma Black Belts at St. John Health. After completing numerous projects in areas of inpatient flow, bed management, the Emergency Department, Surgical Services, and Registration, Sue then served as the Coordinator for the St. John Health Lean Six Sigma Leadership Education program, certifying over 350 leaders within two years. Currently, Sue is the Manager of Performance Improvement at Henry Ford Hospital in Detroit, helping to implement Lean flow for inpatient throughout. Sue's background is in clinical laboratory operations and she is Adjunct Associate Professor in the Eugene Applebaum College of Pharmacy and Health Sciences at Wayne State University. She is a highly-rated speaker at national meetings for topics related to laboratory services, management practices, and Lean-Six Sigma. Certified as a Black Belt by the American Society for Quality (ASQ), Sue is an active member and has served as a judge for the International Team Excellence Awards.

Trinity Health's Journey toward Lean, Six Sigma, and Quality

The Mission, Values, and Vision of Trinity Health continue to call on us to fulfill the healing ministry of Jesus by serving others in these challenging times to transform healthcare delivery. Reduced reimbursement or payment for care, increased regulations, and the rising numbers of people who are uninsured and vulnerable, are just a few of the many issues that pose serious challenges. Our organization brings together physicians, nurses, clergy, and staff whose talent and energy drive a sustainable healing ministry of remarkable skill and scale. By combining expertise and resources, Trinity Health has the capacity to fund community benefit programs, capital investments, and information technology. Since 2003, Trinity Heath has used Six Sigma and Lean methods to identify and drive out unnecessary cost and sources of dissatisfaction among patients, associates, and medical staff members. Teams of trained Process Excellence experts create data-driven, customer focused process improvements that result in lasting enhancements to patient care, customer service, and financial performance today.

Laura Archbold, RN, BSN, MBA, Master Black Belt, is a Senior Process Excellence Consultant at Trinity Health. She used her 25-plus years of experience as an operating room nurse to effectively lead Six Sigma projects regarding surgeon preference cards, the accuracy of surgical instrumentation, the reduction of surgical cancellations, and the redesign of a surgical preparation center. Laura was the lead Lean facilitator in Trinity Health's Orthopedic Care Transformation project. Laura conducts Process Excellence training and supports organizational assessments and projects across Trinity Health, including such projects as Genesis Readiness (implementation of an electronic health record), Length of Stay reduction, best practice patient designation, medication reconciliation, and OB workflow documentation. These efforts are targeted to improve both clinical operations improvement and organizational performance and effectiveness. Laura serves as an examiner for the Michigan Quality Board and is a member of ASQ.

Case study contributors

Todd Sperl is a Master Black Belt/Lean Sensei and led the deployment of Lean-Six Sigma across St. John Health. His experience ranges from facilitating large, complex organizational transformation initiatives to achieve significant and measurable results, to leading numerous smaller type improvements. Currently Todd is Managing Partner at Lean Fox Solutions, LLC, a healthcare consulting firm where their vision is to improve the patient care experience. Todd can be contacted at tsperl@leanfoxsolutions.com.

Michael Blatchford is a Chartered Process Engineer who has spent 16 years in various industries with a focus on implementing Lean principles. The last 5 years Michael has focused on implementing Lean in Australian and New Zealand hospitals and dental surgeries. Michael is part of The Health Roundtable, an organization set up in 1995 by the Australian and New Zealand public hospital's CEOs to promote innovation, collaboration, and benchmarking. Michael can be contacted at mblatchford@bigpond.com.

Pieter Walker has over 17 years experience in leadership training, strategic planning, change management within both the public and private sectors specializing in healthcare. Pieter is Chairman of the Board for Ceytro (Sri Lanka) and also connected to The Health Round Table and The International Round Table which collaborates with over 110 teaching hospitals from around the world. Pieter can be contacted at pieter.walker@healthroundtable.org.

The Purpose of this Book

Value Stream Management (VSM) is a proven, effective, and disciplined step-by-step methodology for understanding and applying the principles and practices of the Toyota Production System (i.e., Lean) to improve processes within an organization. The Toyota Production System is known for its world-class practices of having efficient processes due to well-adhered standards, while empowering employees to find and eliminate waste. These types of efforts are also referred to as Lean. We have found continued success in applying the Value Stream Management methodology in hospitals, clinics, and labs, as well as physician groups and nursing homes. You will be introduced to many of these successes throughout the book as topical anecdotes. Following the *Value Stream Management for Lean Healthcare* methodology will improve overall facility (hospital, clinic, ministry, house, etc.) efficiencies, as well as, most importantly, patient care and safety. It should also be noted that the content in this book will support any and all Lean - Six Sigma projects. (*Six Sigma is a sophisticated, statistical-based problem-solving methodology that requires a certified Black Belt or Green Belt to conduct the training for effective implementation.*)

The VSM process is similar to treating a patient. It requires people (i.e., healthcare providers, aides, technicians, administrative support, etc.) and vendors (suppliers for medical equipment, pharmaceutical companies, etc.) working together to effectively yield the benefits of Lean throughout the entire supply chain. As the treatment of a patient is individually tailored, Lean must also be tailored to the facility, department, and/or process that requires improvement.

In this book you will learn how to:

✦ Apply the Value Stream Management methodology to specific projects within your healthcare facility
✦ Educate staff on the fundamentals of Lean so that Lean can be part of everyone's daily activities
✦ Create a business case to inform the staff on the need for Lean
✦ Determine where wastes exist in processes and facilitate how to eliminate them through Total Employee Involvement (TEI)
✦ Create current and future state value stream maps, as well as a detailed plan for implementation
✦ Accelerate improvements activities by selecting the right quality improvement or Lean tool(s) for a project
✦ Improve patient (direct care), as well as non-patient (non-direct care), processes
✦ Document improvement activities to convey to management the success Lean can have on improving the bottom-line, quality, and patient care and safety
✦ Use Lean tools to ensure improvements are sustained (i.e., controlled) over time
✦ Conduct a Kaizen Event

Value Stream Management for Lean Healthcare will provide you with a step-by-step methodology to implement Lean. It will be up to management to commit the necessary resources (i.e., training, materials, and meeting times) and be actively involved for the Lean or Six Sigma projects to have the opportunity for success. *Serious effort is required!*

Value Stream Management for Lean Healthcare has been arranged into four main chapters: Assess, Diagnosis, Treat, and Prevent. These chapters will provide the skeletal framework on how the Lean tools and practices can be effectively applied in your Lean journey. Just as patients' care requires a thorough history and physical exam to assist in determining a plan of care for the patient; likewise, this book will provide a similar approach for the treatment and care of your facilities' "process ailments".

Healthcare Professionals Who Could Benefit from this Book

Healthcare professionals with any experience in previous TQM, Lean, or Six Sigma training will benefit from this book. Or, if the Lean concept is new to you, this book will teach you an approach that will enhance your abilities to lead and/or participate more effectively in all future continuous improvement efforts.

The following healthcare professionals who would benefit from reading this book and applying the methodology are:

Top management (Chief Medical Officer, Chief Executive Officer, Chief Financial Officer, Director of Medicine, Director of Nursing, etc.) must have a general *understanding* of Lean and how it can impact their organization. This group is responsible, as well as others, for creating the long range strategic direction for the institution. Individuals in this group will typically become the **Team Champions** *(the person(s) who have the authority to commit organizational resources) for the improvement initiatives.* This group must provide the following:

1) The allocation of time for the various staff members to attend meetings to learn, brainstorm, and implement improvements
2) The necessary roadmap (i.e., methodology) for departmental heads to follow when implementing an improvement project to ensure a standard approach is followed
3) Individual enthusiasm to the various departmental managers and process owners by visiting the area and commenting positively, reviewing progress reports and providing feedback, requesting mini-presentations at certain milestones of the project, etc.
4) The long term vision and the supporting short-term strategies to attain the vision
5) Measurements or targets (i.e., derived from the Balanced Scorecard) for each department
6) Communication channels to allow departments (and other facilities within the system) to share their successes and to promote optimal flow and process improvement

These actions will allow project teams to be confident that top management is in full support of their efforts for improvement. ***The most appropriate sections to read for this group would be pages 7,18-21,34,37,57-61,55,58,68-69,153-156,184,193,196,201,206,214,226,228-233,236-239,242,244-279, and 282.***

Departmental heads (Quality Assurance Managers, Billing/Coding Managers, Charge Nurses, Nursing Managers/Supervisors, Human Resource Managers, Training Directors (i.e., Lean or Six Sigma Coordinators), Facility Managers/Engineers, etc.) must have a *thorough and practical understanding* of Lean. Their responsibilities will include providing the necessary training on how the Lean tools can work (apply) in their areas. The individuals within this group will likely be the team leader and/or process owner for a specific project. This group must provide the following:

1) A keen understanding of the Lean tools and concepts to communicate to their staff
2) Training to their staff on the Lean tools and concepts
3) The business case for their department relating how improvements link to the strategic direction of the facility and its positive impact it will have on their daily work activities
4) Communication and negotiation skills to referee cross-departmental resource priorities
5) Support to the staff through positive coaching and involvement

This workbook supports these actions because it provides the detailed framework (i.e., the Value Stream Management process) for exactly what needs to be done when implementing a Lean initiative. ***The most appropriate sections to read for this group would be EVERYTHING! This is the operational group that must not only lead the change but fully understand the Lean tools and subsequently embrace the methodology.***

Staff (physicians, nurses, technicians, aides, ancillary personnel, i.e., admissions, billing, records, etc.) must have a *working understanding* of Lean. This group must provide the process "knowledge" required to effectively solve problems. Without this group's "buy-in" of the solution, any improvements or changes will not be sustained, regardless on how impressive the improvements initially appear on paper. This group must provide the following:

1) A desire to improve their process or work area
2) An open mind that process change will be for the better in terms of patient care and safety, as well job satisfaction
3) Reliable knowledge on how their current processes run
4) Ideas on how the process can be improved

This workbook will provide numerous Lean healthcare examples (i.e., case studies) to further assist this group's overall understanding of how Lean can be applied in healthcare. ***The most appropriate sections to read for this group would be pages 7,13-15,35-36,56-58,82,88,103-106,121,126-129,132,152,167-170,184,188,192-193,196,206,212-214,226, and 228-231.***

Islands of Care

The healthcare system is comprised of many parts, with many seemingly well connected, while others are not. To determine value from the patient perspective all these parts (i.e., various healthcare services), also referred to as Islands of Care, will most likely require some type of process improvement. Patients today are more of a healthcare partner (and less of just a patient awaiting orders). For example, if a patient requires extended care from a hospital stay, then all the approvals, transportation, insurance info, etc. needed for a well-coordinated long term treatment facility should be coordinated in a stress free manner. However, in many instances the patient is not stress free. The solution is to better synchronize communications and processes between and within these Islands of Care. This will help to eliminate the bottlenecks (non value-added activities) that cause stress for the patient while at the same time improving hospital efficiencies.

Islands of Care
Bridging the Continuum of Care for the Ultimate Patient Experience

Long Term Treatment Facilities

Improved Proceses
- Laboratory
- Radiology
- Physician Support
- Pharmacy Record
- Medical Record
- Billing

Lean Tools

Urgent Care Centers

Improved Proceses
- Laboratory
- X-Ray
- Link to PCP
- Pharmacy Record
- Billing

Lean Tools

Physician Offices and Clinics

Improved Proceses
- Laboratory
- Radiology
- Medical Record
- Surgical Boarding
- ED/Direct Admin
- Pharmacy Record

Lean Tools

Retirement Homes

Improved Proceses
- Physician Support
- Behavioral Medicine
- Home Care Treatment
- Medical Record
- Billing
- Pharmacy

Lean Tools

Home Care Treatment

Improved Proceses
- Laboratory
- Medical Record
- Billing
- Link to PCP

Lean Tools

Senior Services

Improved Proceses
- Physician Support
- Pharmacy Record
- Link to PCP
- Billing

Lean Tools

Behavorial Medicine

Improved Proceses
- Laboratory/Toxicology
- Medical Record
- Clinical/Day Programs
- Link to PCP
- Billing

Lean Tools

Funeral Homes

Improved Proceses
- Link to PCP
- Medical Record
- Link ot Med Examiner
- Legal Record

Lean Tools

Outpatient Diagnostic Center

Improved Processes
- Laboratory/Toxicology results to PCP
- Medical Records
- Billing

Lean Tools

Physical/Occupational Therapy

Improved Proceses
- Link to PCP
- Medical Record
- Billing

Lean Tools

Hospitals

PCP= Primary Care Physician
Note: Value streams and processes listed above are not all inclusive.

Learning Features

The following book features should assist you in learning and implementing *Value Stream Management for Lean Healthcare*. They are:

   Overall Layout
   Forms, Worksheets, and Checklists
   Readiness Guides
   Case Studies
   Key Terms
   Useful Appendix
   Glossary
   Index

Overall Layout

The four main chapters have been arranged into Assess, Diagnosis, Treat, and Prevent. A similar four phase approach has been used successfully for nearly 60 years in the manufacturing industry for process improvement and problem solving and is known as the PLAN-DO-CHECK-ACT (PDCA) cycle, also referred to as the Deming cycle. Just as a circle has no end, the PDCA cycle should be repeated again and again to continually improve and refine a process. The Assess, Diagnosis, Treat, and Prevent phases should be used similarly in applying Lean tools and practices.

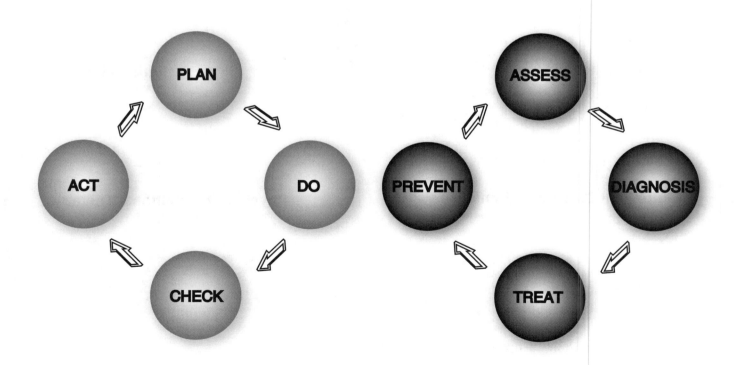

PLAN-DO-CHECK-ACT (PDCA) PHASES

ASSESS-DIAGNOSIS-TREAT-PREVENT PHASES AS RELATED TO VALUE STREAM MANAGEMENT FOR LEAN HEALTHCARE

The four phases are:

Assess. This is the most critical step in Lean healthcare. In medicine, professional skills are used to assess and evaluate a patient. In Lean, similar assessment skills are used to evaluate an area or process and prepare it for detailed analysis. This involves teamwork and management involvement from the beginning. Each member of the team will play a vital role, which is to bring different skills to the table. In this chapter you will learn how to establish an effective team, collect the appropriate data, determine which project or area requires immediate improvement efforts, and understand the current process (i.e., value stream or process map).

Diagnosis. Just as stethoscopes, oxygen saturation monitors, labs, etc. assist in determining a diagnosis of a patient, Lean tools are similarly used to identify and gather information to further analyze a process. This involves continued reliance on teamwork, as a diagnosis is often reached using a multi-disciplinary approach, thus allowing for a statement or conclusion to be drawn concerning the nature or cause of the area or process requiring attention. This will provide the bridge from assessing an area (previous phase) to ensuring the correct treatment (next phase) is taken. In this chapter you will learn how certain Lean tools will correlate measurements to improvement initiatives, conduct a Waste Walk (audit), and decide on which may be the best data collection methods to use, to name a few.

Treat. This involves the application of a Lean tool to a process or area. In medicine, the ultimate goal is to make the patient well. In Lean, the goal is to attain a state of process wellness that allows for continuous improvement (i.e., the elimination of waste). In this chapter you will learn the Lean tools of 5S, takt time, pitch, standard work, leveling, mistake (or error) proofing etc. to name a few.

Prevent. The old saying "An apple a day keeps the doctor away" is analogous to maintaining a healthy (i.e., Lean) process once it has been improved. In medicine, often rehabilitation, life style change, continued medications, yearly checkups, etc. are used to ensure that the ailment the patient experienced does not reappear. In comparison, this applies to process improvement. This is achieved through controlling the improvements implemented in the previous phases through effective measurements, visual controls, Total Employee Involvement (TEI), and reward and recognition from management. In this chapter you will learn how to create Storyboards and Paynter Charts, as well as how to create a visual control system.

The tools and concepts explained in each of the chapters (phases) have been implemented successfully throughout healthcare facilities in the US, Canada, Australia, New Zealand, as well as many other countries throughout the world. However, it must be stated that each facility, clinic, and team project is unique. Teams must adapt and use the appropriate tool given the situation and not be so structured into which phase a particular concept or tool belongs. The Greek word: *arete* (uh-REE-tay) means habitual excellence and is synonymous with Lean. Lean is about applying common sense approaches to solving your problems while striving for process excellence. If you keep that in mind, as well as these four phases, you will have a successful Lean journey.

Forms, Worksheets, and Checklists

Throughout this book there will be sample forms, worksheets, and detailed checklists to reinforce the information presented. The forms and worksheets are available in Microsoft Excel at www.theleanstore.com, under Etools/Forms and Worksheets.

Readiness Guides

A Readiness Guide concludes each phase. It consists of a series of questions to prepare you for the next phase. It will serve as a review for that chapter as well.

Case Studies

The VSM four phases are explained in detail throughout this book using the Oakview Hospital Emergency Department (ED) case study (as denoted by the lightly-shaded areas and pages). Additional (mini) case studies are presented in each of the sections, as well as more detailed ones in the Appendix. All the case studies are presented to demonstrate the VSM process and the various applications of the Lean tools.

Key Terms

Definitions of key terms are displayed in italics providing a visual cue for that key term or concept. They are also found in the Glossary.

Useful Appendix

The Appendix includes: more detailed case studies, Kaizen approaches to implementing Lean, integrating EMR/EMS into your projects, applying 5S to your Desktop (PC), etc.

Glossary

Lean term definitions will be provided in the back of the workbook for a quick reference.

Index

The index will provide a quick access to a specific topic or tool.

Chapter 1: Setting the Stage for Lean Healthcare

Topics Include:

✦ The Healthcare Crisis
✦ The Evolution of Healthcare Quality: Quality Assurance, Total Quality Management, Quality Campaigns, Six Sigma, and Lean
✦ Why Lean Healthcare?
✦ The Value Stream
✦ The Value Stream Management Process
✦ Types of Kaizens

The Healthcare Crisis

While various issues are contributing to the perfect storm, including the economy, legislature, regulatory requirements that constantly evolve, this book would like to address four issues. The four issues are:

1. Increasing costs
2. Nursing/staff shortages
3. Diminishing/limited funding from federal, state, and local agencies
4. The "Baby Boomers" retirement years

1. Increasing costs

"Medical tourism" is a very real threat to the current healthcare system in the U.S. For example, a bone-marrow transplant costs approximately $2.5 million in the United States. Doctors in India can do it for less than $26,000 with the same quality outcomes. Heart-bypass surgeries cost anywhere from $60,000 to $150,000 in this country. In Asia, the average cost is $10,000. Other less-serious procedures - tummy tucks, face lifts, breast implants, LASIK eye surgery, even MRIs and dental work (i.e., crowns, bridges, tooth implants) - can also be performed overseas at a fraction of what they cost here in the U.S. Patients, as well as insurance agencies, are looking at overseas options for obtaining services for themselves or their members.

Healthcare cost has become a large part of most countries Gross Domestic Product (GDP) and will continue to increase. It has become a global issue. Here in the U.S., as well as Canada, the healthcare industry is under tremendous pressure to contain costs to ensure patient services remain within their border. Even though the U.S. has the latest medical technologies, while having one of the highest standards for patient care and safety with people from all over the world seeking treatment, the demand for these services does come with a heavy price. Healthcare costs are increasing at double digit rates each year and that is straining the U.S. economy, as well as others. Hospitals, labs, clinics, and home healthcare organizations throughout the U.S. (and world) are looking to control this escalation of cost while at the same time attempting to maintain and improve the standards of care. Many have found an answer through a methodology of continuous improvement that has been successful in the manufacturing industry. This new and exciting method is referred to as Lean, or better known as the Toyota Production System. This (along with programs such as Six Sigma) has, and will continue to become a key methodology for the healthcare industry in reducing costs.

Healthcare costs on all fronts, from prescription co-pays to organ transplants, are being transferred to the consumer (patient) who may or may not have adequate coverage. Mothers, having just given birth, are being sent home within 24 hours due to insurance companies' cost containment measures in reducing the length of days allowed to stay in the hospital. Yet, costs for these types of services are escalating with no end in sight.

The primary factors contributing to these increasing costs in healthcare are:

Insurances. Healthcare insurance costs are increasing and so are the co-pays and deductibles. Although co-pays represent a small percentage of the overall insurance cost, they give the consumer some insight into the increasing costs that must be absorbed by the employer to provide employee coverage. Medicare/Medicaid programs greatly impact healthcare costs/revenues.

Facility Overhead. The majority of hospitals are twenty to thirty years old. Organizations (i.e., healthcare systems) are currently either building new facilities or completing extensive remodeling to accommodate the expected healthcare needs of the Baby Boomer generation. They must also attract highly qualified professionals to remain competitive in services, education, and research. The overhead related to this service is a significant cost factor.

Malpractice premiums. Doctors (and, at times, nurses) must carry expensive malpractice insurance due to excessive litigation.

Competitive healthcare. Doctors, nurses, technicians, aides, and staff administrators must be paid competitively to successfully staff organizations. Also, hospitals are aggressively competing for patients through all types of multi-media marketing avenues.

Infrastructure Changes. Billing and coding, scheduling, laboratory tests, information technology, and human resources may present inherent inefficiencies due to the increase in the supporting information required by insurance and governmental agencies.

Decreased Funding. The decrease in federal, state, and local funding for public and mental health facilities increases the financial burdens on the already-stressed hospital staffs.

Rapidly Changing Technology Requirements. Advancements in pharmaceutical and medical technology require extensive research and development, thereby, contributing to the higher cost of healthcare. Hospitals must also purchase the latest, most advanced equipment to compete in attracting the most qualified physicians and staff.

2. Nursing/staff shortages

Nurses are a major part of the healthcare team in a hospital. They have been educated and are responsible for: direct patient care, patient and family education, patient advocacy, charting, and collaboration with other healthcare team members.

Nurses (and staff) are under enormous pressure to provide this care. They are responsible not only for direct care for patients but also for providing increased documentation as the result of EMR systems that are not Lean. Many organizations have redundant systems in place with both electronic and paper processes in place, contributing to massive amounts of rework and defects to protect the institution from litigation. They also experience resource capacity issues (i.e., lack of aides, technicians) which places more work on them. This prevents nurses from what they were educated to do - administer direct patient care. Nurses (and staff) desire to provide high quality care. With all of this occurring, nurses are feeling frustrated and leaving traditional nursing jobs to enter home healthcare, teaching, administration, sales, and other area specialty jobs. As this employment trend continues new, qualified nurses must be found to replace them.

The average age of a healthcare professional is nearing 50. This, coupled with the shortage of providers and day to day staffing demands, makes it difficult for organizations to provide patients with effective and efficient, quality care.

Contributing to the employee issue is the availability of needed supplies. Nurses and other caregivers can spend an inordinate amount of time searching for supplies and equipment (which can easily be improved using the Lean tool known as 5S, as explained beginning on page 160).

3. Diminishing/limiting funds from federal, state, and local agencies

There are populations (i.e., immigrants, working poor, indigent, homeless, and elderly) having limited or no access to healthcare facilities but still requiring care (i.e., the underserved). These facilities, already under financial burdens, are still providing services to these groups. For example, Trauma 1 centers must treat anyone entering their emergency rooms. The treatment (and associated costs that may not be recovered) for these services is no different than for someone who has adequate coverage, and causes a tremendous drain on a fiscal 'thin-ice' budget. EMTALA (The Emergency Medical Treatment and Active Labor Act) impacts the bottom-line of a hospital as it does not limit coverage. EMTALA is a statute that requires hospitals and ambulance services to provide care to anyone needing emergency treatment regardless of citizenship, legal status or ability to pay. There are no reimbursement provisions. As a result of the act, patients needing emergency treatment can be discharged only under their own informed consent or when their condition requires transfer to a hospital better equipped to administer the treatment. This purpose, however, does not limit the coverage of its provisions and virtually applies to all hospitals in the U.S., with the exception of the Shriners' Hospital for Crippled Children and many military hospitals.

4. The "Baby Boomers" retirement years

The Baby Boomers, individuals born between 1946 and 1964, make up one of the largest and most prosperous generations in U.S. history. As a group, they have enjoyed a higher income during their working years than any preceding generation. As they move out of the workforce and into retirement over the next 15 - 20 years, these boomers will begin to draw on their savings, private pensions, and also will become eligible for benefits from government programs such as Social Security and Medicare.

The impending wave of retirements of these Baby Boomers has become a source of concern for two reasons. First, the population of retirees will accelerate more quickly than the taxpaying workforce at a time when average benefits per retiree are expected to continue rising. This will place a severe (and mounting) budgetary pressure on the federal government. Second, many researchers have questioned whether a significant portion of the Baby Boomers have accumulating enough wealth to pay for an adequate retirement - let alone what their healthcare costs will be. Not only could inadequate savings leave Boomers poorly prepared, but it could compound the government's budgetary problems by limiting the growth of investment, productivity, and wages (which drive federal revenues). Baby Boomers, regardless of whether they will have enough of a private savings plan, or if the federal programs are sufficiently funded, or a national healthcare insurance program comes to fruition, will require an increase in services at all levels of the healthcare continuum.

There are no quick fixes for addressing these areas; however, we can find some insight into what happened with the Japanese car industry from a similar situation. In the 1960s, the quality of Japanese cars and products were questionable. Their cars (as well as other manufactured products) were of poor quality. The Japanese automotive industry leaders, in particular, the Toyota Motor Corporation, decided to improve quality of their product while at the same time realizing they had to compete with the global car manufacturers of General Motors, Ford, and Chrysler. Through years of studying the manufacturing best practices of Eli Whitney and Henry Ford, to name a few, Toyota combined what they had learned with their culture of employee involvement and participation, as well as their inherent requirement to do more with less (due to not having the vast economies of scale and raw materials the US manufacturers enjoyed). After approximately 30 years, this culmination of knowledge and practices became known as the Toyota Production System or Lean. The Toyota Production System (i.e., Lean) is currently known as one of the premiere business models in how to effectively and continually reduce costs while improving customer satisfaction. Over the past thirty years, U.S. manufacturers have adopted Lean as one of their business strategies allowing them to reduce waste, reduce costs, improve quality, and improve customer and employee satisfaction.

These four issues of increasing costs, nursing/staff shortages, diminishing/limited funding from federal, state, and local agencies, and the "Baby Boomers" retirement years (not entirely inclusive of what ails the healthcare system) can be addressed by using the Value Stream Management process. VSM focuses on identifying and eliminating waste of all kinds. All healthcare professionals must believe that the current system can be improved. Healthcare personnel must diagnose their processes using a Lean approach and begin to heal what is ailing. In doing so, patient care will be improved and costs will be reduced.

The U.S. is not alone in having healthcare problems. From China, the *People's Daily* (2008-03-13):

> The government of Hong Kong Special Administrative Region (HKSAR) Thursday launched a healthcare reform consultation to seek public views on the future development of the city's healthcare system and financing arrangements.
>
> While Hong Kong's health indicators rank among the best in the world, Chief Secretary for the Administration of HKSAR Henry Tang said, in face of an aging population and rapid advance in medical technology, the HKSAR government has the responsibility to join hands with the community to solve the problem of ever increasing medical costs. He said proposals of the consultation document are aimed at maintaining the quality healthcare service, enhancing the efficiency of the healthcare system, promoting competition in service delivery, while at the same time improving health through preventive care, and ensuring that no one would be left unattended.

Many of the ideas in the article reflect the same challenges facing other countries in their efforts to improve healthcare. The conclusion is that no country has the answer or is immune to external or internal issues facing them. But, there is an answer for this healthcare crisis in reducing costs, improving staff and patient satisfaction, and above all, improving patient care. This is achieved through creating more efficient patient and non-patient care processes by reducing waste. This is accomplished through implementing *Value Stream Management for Lean Healthcare.*

The Evolution of Healthcare Quality: Quality Assurance, Total Quality Management, Quality Campaigns, Six Sigma, and Lean

"First, do no harm."
Hippocrates

Quality improvement is one of the desired goals that Lean strives to achieve. It does no good to improve processes if quality is sacrificed. Lean is an extension of this quality improvement movement. The following brief history will provide some insights on how the healthcare industry has progressed in their improvement strategies over the years by using a variety of techniques and systems in attempting to advance the overall healthcare system.

Quality Assurance

From the beginning of time, the intention of well-meaning healthcare providers was to help and not harm those for whom they cared, starting with Hippocrates (460- 370 BC) on the island of Cos, Greece. Hippocrates, known as the "Father of Medicine" in the Age of Pericles, had quality at the forefront of healthcare. He was the first physician to reject superstitions and beliefs that credited supernatural or divine forces with causing illness. His disciplined and intellectual approach revolutionized medicine in ancient Greece, thereby making the practice of medicine a profession. The notion of "First, do no harm" from Hippocrates continues today. Other examples of how quality evolved are as follows.

Florence Nightingale (1820-1910) was known as a caring nurse for the poor and indigent in London, England. She became famous for her work in the Crimean War caring for the soldiers, as well as starting the Nightingale Training School for the training of nurses. Known as the founder of modern day nursing, she wrote several books, most notably, *Notes on Nursing, What It Is, What It Is Not, Florence Nightingale - to her Nurses*, that were instrumental in calling attention to the importance of cleanliness and sanitation to decrease death rates in hospitals.

Dr. Ernest Codman, a surgeon, compared surgical death rates at Massachusetts General Hospital with those in other Boston-area hospitals in 1910 and is often credited with initiating quality in healthcare.

In 1951 the Joint Commission of Accreditation of Hospitals (JCAH) was formed to:

✦ Stimulate continuous improvement inpatient care processes and outcomes
✦ Increase efficiency/reduce costs
✦ Strengthen the public's confidence
✦ Improve the management of health services
✦ Provide education on better/best practices

In 1975, the Quality of Professional Services standard was published, requiring that hospitals demonstrate that the quality of patient care was consistently optimal by continually evaluating care through reliable and valid measures. This would remain the healthcare quality mantra for many years. The standard also required explicit, measurable criteria to be used in retrospective, outcome-focused, time-limited audits of the care at a facility. Early medical record audits in healthcare focused on morbidity and mortality reviews. Retrospective audits, as well as quality assurance with its ongoing monitoring and evaluation, became fixtures in healthcare, adding particular topics as the need arose.

Changes and improvements in healthcare quality methodologies occurred slowly. In 1979, the Joint Commission, as an independent and non-profit organization, added a quality assurance chapter with standards. These standards emphasized the creation of a coordinated, organization-wide quality assurance program that focused on problems, which when resolved, would significantly impact patient care outcomes. Further revision to these standards in 1985 replaced the problem-focused approach with systematic monitoring and evaluation of important aspects of patient care. This standard would ensure that continuous performance data collection with appropriate problem solving would improve care and "assure" quality. Unfortunately, little direction was given to healthcare professionals as to how to correctly identify important aspects of care and how to select and gather appropriate data.

In 1987, the Joint Commission changed its name to the Joint Commission on Accreditation of Healthcare Organizations (JCAHO) and launched its *Agenda for Change*, in an attempt to link the accreditation process with an effective means to stimulate continuous improvement in healthcare. The *Agenda for Change* included the following:

- ✦ An emphasis on the use of quality improvement (QI) tools to effectively assess and improve performance
- ✦ A redirection of Joint Commission standards
- ✦ Improvement of the survey and decision-making process
- ✦ Elimination of irrelevant and redundant standards

The *Agenda for Change* drastically changed the assessment process of healthcare organizations from a review of their structures and capabilities to how well care was actually provided. In addition, the *Agenda for Change* brought forth quality assessment and improvement standards in place of the traditional quality assurance standards. These new standards expanded on the strong foundation quality assurance provided, such as using reliable data for monitoring, while attempting to remove some of the negative connotations of quality assurance. From quality assessment and improvement, healthcare attempted this transition to total quality management.

Total Quality Management

Total Quality Management (TQM) came to healthcare in the late 1980s as a result of American industries' focus on Japan's successes with quality. *TQM is a comprehensive and structured approach to organizational management that seeks to improve the quality of products, services, and customer satisfaction through ongoing refinements.* TQM is based on quality management from the customer's point of view; therefore, to make TQM succeed, an organization must know what its customers want and need. TQM originated in manufacturing but has been applied to many different types of organizations, such as hospitals, schools, hotels, and churches. TQM processes are divided into four sequential steps: Plan, Do, Check, and Act (the PDCA cycle).

Walter A. Shewhart, a statistician at Western Electric, developed this cycle in 1931. (It was later popularized by one of his students, Edward Deming.) In the *planning* phase, people define the problem to be addressed, collect relevant data, and ascertain the problem's root cause. In the *doing* phase, people develop and implement a solution, and decide upon a measurement to gauge its effectiveness. In the *checking* phase, people confirm the results through before-and-after data comparison. In the *acting* phase, people document their results, inform others about process changes, and make recommendations for the problem to be addressed in the next PDCA cycle.

At first, the application of TQM to healthcare made sense and generated a great deal of excitement. But healthcare's experience and success with TQM, like that of many other industries, was short lived. A survey conducted of hospital leaders representing 3,303 hospitals in 1993 by Shortell, found that 69% of those hospitals included in the survey had at least begun the implementation of TQM. Despite the initial enthusiasm for TQM, many hospitals were never able to figure out how to implement it permanently. Others spent considerable time and money to develop, implement, and support the ongoing maintenance of TQM and yet, over time, TQM lost its luster for these organizations and was forgotten about.

Why wasn't TQM successful in healthcare? In some organizations, TQM experienced sudden death as frustrated quality professionals and healthcare administrators quickly abandoned their efforts. In other organizations, TQM's demise occurred slowly and painfully as attempts were made to keep it alive as hope continued for its recovery and sustained livelihood. TQM's failure in healthcare may be contributed to several factors, including:

- ✦ TQM was a costly investment
- ✦ Concepts and tools were new and unfamiliar
- ✦ Hierarchical bureaucracies acted as a hindrance (senior management not involved)
- ✦ Senior management knowledge and expertise in TQM was insufficient
- ✦ TQM was time consuming and laborious
- ✦ Middle-management resisted it
- ✦ Employees' training and support was inadequate
- ✦ Trained experts became scarce due to attrition and lack of ongoing training
- ✦ Leadership was unable to correlate TQM initiatives to the strategic plan
- ✦ Information systems were inadequate
- ✦ Management environments were controlling versus empowering

Though all of these factors contributed to the failure of TQM in healthcare, the major reasons for its failure may have been insufficient senior management support, involvement, and commitment; lack of direction on how to implement TQM; and lack of a sense of urgency in respect to the challenges faced by healthcare compared to those being faced today. Successful implementation of TQM required a long-term commitment to stay on course without seeing immediate results. TQM did not provide immediate problem resolution and those looking for quick fixes declared TQM a failure and pulled the plug without giving it sufficient time to show results. Despite TQM's failure, healthcare continued moving forward utilizing bits and pieces of what survived the TQM movement, such as the PDCA cycle, teams, and the use of Quality Improvement (QI) tools. TQM, in and of itself, did not fail; it failed (on a continuum) in healthcare.

Quality Campaigns

In 1996, the Institute of Medicine launched an effort on assessing and improving the nation's quality of healthcare by their released reports - *Too Err is Human: Building a Safer Health System (1999)* and *Crossing the Quality Chasm: A New Health System for the 21st Century (2001)*. This brought attention to many of the quality ailments within the healthcare system.

 Dr. Donald Berwick, one of America's leading patient safety advocates, is a clinical professor of pediatrics and health care policy at Harvard Medical School, and is the founder, president, and CEO of the Institute for Healthcare Improvement. From IHI's website About Us: "The Institute for Healthcare Improvement (IHI) is an independent not-for-profit organization helping to lead the improvement of healthcare throughout the world. Founded in 1991 and based in Cambridge, Massachusetts, IHI works to accelerate improvement by building the will for change, cultivating promising concepts for improving patient care, and helping healthcare systems put those ideas into action." Dr. Berwick, in the mid-1990s, launched the Save 100,000 Lives Campaign in efforts to save lives that were to be lost from mistakes made within the healthcare system. He later built upon that campaign's 3000-hospital participation with the 1,000,000 Lives Campaign, as well as the 5,000,000 Lives Campaign (from harm). This newer campaign focused on allowing the hospitals that participated to share their results and have everyone benefit from each other. His leadership and direction has brought to the forefront the issues of patient care and safety in the healthcare industry. The IHI is but one organization that is committed to the advancement of healthcare's best practices in the U.S. (Note: Canada has a program called Safer Healthcare Now, a Canadian College of Health Service Executives' (CCHSE) National Awards Program that recognizes individuals and teams that demonstrate significant progress, investment, commitment and validation in the area of healthcare). And then, in the late 1990s, Six Sigma appeared.

Six Sigma

Six Sigma is defined as a customer-focused, statistically based process improvement methodology for reducing defects based on process improvements. The ideal of Six Sigma is 3.4 defects or errors out of every million-defect opportunities for error. Related measurements and statistics are used extensively to identify variation and the root causes of problems. Cross-functional teams are led by a certified Six Sigma Black Belt or Green Belt and are deployed to improve processes and successfully achieve pre-set targets that positively impact the bottom-line. In short, Six Sigma uses facts and data to achieve the needs and desires of the organization's external and internal customers. Six Sigma, strives to use data to assist in the identification and elimination of waste.

The process improvement methodology or roadmap of Six Sigma is referred to as the D-M-A-I-C process. D-M-A-I-C stands for: Define, Measure, Analyze, Improve, and Control.

The phases are:

Defining phase is where the problem to be addressed and the objectives to be obtained are clearly defined.
Measuring phase includes the identification of performance requirements, data collection, and validation that a problem exists.
Analyzing phase is when data is collected in a measurement system and then analyzed to identify the root cause(s) of variations.
Improvement phase is the development and implementation of solutions to remove the cause(s) of variation.
Control phase establishes standard measurements to sustain the improved performance.

Six Sigma entered the healthcare field in approximately 1999 and, for some organizations, has worked to improve both the clinical and non-clinical processes. Six Sigma builds on the principles of TQM and has been referred to as "TQM on steroids". Some differences in Six Sigma and TQM include:

Six Sigma	TQM
D-M-A-I-C provides a step-by-step guide	TQM does not include an instruction manual
Problems are selected based on their relationship to strategic priorities and potential impact to the bottom-line	Less focused approach to problem selection; goal is improvement in all areas without guidelines for problem resolution
Focus is cross-functional	Focus is departmentalized
Focus is on error reduction	Focus is on incremental improvement
Structured use of highly trained individuals	Less formalized training requirements

Understanding these differences may increase the odds of Lean - Six Sigma success when implemented in healthcare.

Lean

The references to the word Lean, the Toyota Production System, waste elimination, and process/continuous improvement are used synonymously throughout the world. *Lean is defined as all the tools and concepts, along with the philosophical approach derived from The Toyota Production System, that works to eliminate all waste or non value-added activities from a process while improving flow.* The continued focus on the elimination of waste should be a daily, hourly, or minute-by-minute review by all employees within an organization. Lean is a long-term commitment for positive change within an organization, not something that occurs overnight or even in one year.. Lean is not meant to eliminate people, but to use them more effectively. With that thought in mind, work elements or staff duties may need to be modified to accommodate this waste-free (Lean) environment. Lean can greatly assist a facility to remain competitive while at the same time developing a motivated work force through TEI.

Lean tools are used to:

+ Identify and eliminate waste quickly and efficiently
+ Increase communication at all levels of the organization
+ Reduce cost, improve quality, and meet service and care obligations in a safe environment
+ Facilitate incremental improvements throughout the organization as well as larger cost reduction or patient care type improvements tied to the Balanced Scorecard
+ Improve customer (patient), staff, and employee satisfaction

Lean is truly a compilation of world-class practices as described in the following simplified points:

1. In 1896, Sakichi Toyoda invented Japan's first power loom called "the Toyoda Steam Power Loom." Automation continued to progress with this loom with improvements such as the use of: broken pick automatic stop units, warp transport units, and cloth winding units, etc. (to name a few). These looms were inexpensive and made of durable mixed metal and wood construction. They made a major contribution to the mechanization of Japan's textile industry. Sakichi Toyoda later evolved the Steam Power Loom into an automatic loom in 1902, allowing for it to visualize defects and stop the machine whenever a thread would snap. This was the beginning of the Lean tools known as visual controls, quick setups, and mistake proofing.

2. In 1913, Henry Ford started mass production of the Model T car, using the continuous flow assembly line (conveyor belts). Henry Ford created production efficiencies through standardizing the work methods as well as product - "You can have any color car - as long as it's black". This was the beginning of the Lean tools known as continuous flow and standard work, however it was ignoring the voice of the customer.

3. In the late 1940s, Japan, and specifically the Toyota Motor Corporation, desired to compete in the American automotive market. Japan automotive companies could not mass produce on a level to compete with the United States. Therefore, to be competitive they had to find ways to do more with less and a group of Toyota engineers visited the U.S. to experience and learn more about automotive manufacturing. During their

time in the U.S. the engineers visited an American supermarket. They were very impressed with the supermarket's system of replenishment of first-in first-out (FIFO) (food items were stocked from the back so that the older items would be purchase first). This was all controlled by a simple card attached to one of items on the shelf (and when purchased signaled the store owner to order more). This simple card (or now referred to as a **kanban**) *serves as a visual signal to a process that replenishment is required.* This was the beginning of the Lean tools known as the supermarket pull system and kanbans.

4. In the 1950s, Edward Deming, while working under General Douglas MacArthur as a census consultant to the Japanese government after World War II, famously taught statistical process control methods to Japanese business leaders. The Japanese industry and business leaders were eager to learn any and all methods to improve quality for their products. This was the beginning of the Lean tools known as simplified problem solving and quality control.

5. In 2001, a Lean implementation methodology (i.e., Value Stream Management) was published as a structured Lean approach based on studies of the Toyota Production System for Lean implementation. Value Stream Management allowed kaizen workshops (teams focused on the implementation of a Lean tool or concept within a specified time period) to be integrated into a structured plan for improvement, along with the appropriate measurement systems. This was the beginning of a disciplined, step-by-step approach to the implementation of Lean.

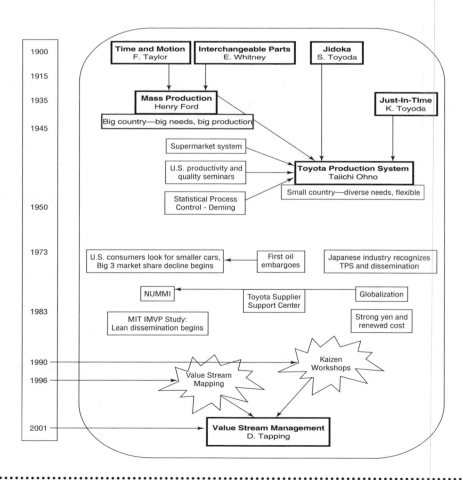

In late 1980s, early 1990s, and to this day customers were and are demanding price reductions. The Traditional Thinking model had been when an organization continually increased prices to its customers (Cost + Profit = Price).   As raw material prices for manufacturing goods were increasing correspondingly with healthcare cost and employee wages, the only way to satisfy the customer's demand for price reductions and keep their business was to lower costs internally (the - Cost part of the Lean Thinking formula). Toyota also developed this cost-reduction or Lean Thinking philosophy. Market conditions (the constant in the equation) set the selling price. Focusing on internal costs where Price - Cost = Profit, becomes a philosophical (Lean) approach and leads the drive to improvement initiatives. This "new" customer will not pay for waste in the processes and is very astute in determining what they are willing to pay for a product or service.

The following illustration demonstrates Traditional Thinking versus the Lean Thinking model.

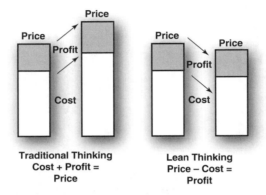

Successes in the global manufacturing world are now being achieved using the same Lean tools in all types of industries; healthcare, financial services, construction, armed services, etc. with great success.

The Toyota Production System is often displayed as a house, with the foundation comprised of people and tools, while the concepts of Just-In-Time and Jidoka (Building Quality In) support the overall goal of customer satisfaction through superior performance in quality, cost, and delivery of a product or service. For healthcare, it is very similar, with ultimate patient care and safety as the goal.

In conclusion, the Toyota Production System is a compilation of world-class practices adapted from the United States, Germany, and Japan. For example, today in Japan they refer to Just-In-Time as "JIT" - an American acronym. Similarly, takt time, a German word, refers to "beat" or "rhythm." It is not important as to which word came from where, it is most important to understand what Lean can do for you. These concepts will be explained later on in this book.

Keep in mind, that is has been stated by the management and employees of the Toyota Motor Corporation, that they have been at Lean for over 60+ years...*and they are just beginning!*

How TQM, Six Sigma, and Lean are Similar?

The specific tools of Lean are discussed in subsequent chapters. In reality, there are more similarities between TQM, Six Sigma, and Lean than there are differences. In fact, many of the same elements are found in all three as shown in the following chart.

Elements of Quality Improvement Methods	TQM	Six Sigma	Lean
Long-term commitment	✓	✓	✓
Effort is organization-wide	✓	✓	✓
Quality Improvement tools are utilized	✓	✓	✓
Problem-solving is conducted by teams	✓	✓	✓
Employees are involved and empowered	✓	✓	✓
Actions are taken to avoid mistakes and prevent defects - root cause(s) eliminated	✓	✓	👍
Objective measures are used	✓	✓	✓
Variation in processes is reduced	✓	👍	✓
Involvement of leadership is critical	✓	✓	✓
Focus is on the customer	✓	✓	✓
Work is viewed as processes	✓	✓	✓
Decisions are based on data	✓	✓	✓
Statistical methods are utilized	✓	👍	✓
Actions are taken to standardize work	✓	✓	✓
Waste is removed from the process and employee's jobs are easier and safer	✓	✓	👍
Goal is continuous improvement in all work	✓	■	✓
Requires no additional resources or substantial training to do	✓	■	✓

✓ Denotes similar quality
👍 Denotes slight advantage

Six Sigma and Lean philosophies and concepts build on TQM. Why then, with all the similarities, did TQM not succeed in healthcare while Six Sigma and Lean are demonstrating drastic improvements and successes? Why are Six Sigma and Lean seemingly easier to implement than TQM? The answer lies not in the similarities between TQM, Six Sigma, and Lean, but in their differences.

How Six Sigma and Lean Differ from TQM?

Six Sigma and Lean, although based on TQM principles, have distinct differences from TQM which are making their implementation in healthcare easier and much more sustainable. One difference is the rapidity of positive results. Six Sigma and Lean are producing improvements more quickly with positive effects to the bottom line, while TQM tried to incrementally improve the entire organization.. With such a large scope, improvement efforts made using TQM tended to be minor and less visible to the organization while Six Sigma and Lean's improvements are more drastic and foster an infectious desire for more improvements. TQM tended to be compartmentalized with narrow results while Six Sigma and Lean are cross-functional with improvements permeating department boundaries. TQM came without specific guidelines in exactly how to do it, making implementation difficult. Six Sigma and Lean, more appropriately, are accompanied with very user-friendly how-to-guides, allowing for a greater ease of implementation.

Six Sigma and Lean may be experiencing greater success than TQM for other reasons, including a focus on the improvement of processes that have a positive impact on patient care and safety, as well as the reduction of stress for the employees. Some of these successes are:

1. Improved clinical outcomes
2. Improved customer satisfaction
3. Improved employee satisfaction
4. Improved throughput
5. Reduced cycle/lead times

6. Reduced production/overhead costs
7. Reduced error rates
8. Reduced waste
9. Safer work environments
10. Positive change in corporate cultures

We have looked at similarities and some differences between TQM, Six Sigma, and Lean. Now let us take a closer look at the differences between Six Sigma and Lean.

How Lean and Six Sigma Differ?

Although Six Sigma and Lean have many similarities, there are major differences that make each unique. Six Sigma and Lean are both very effective means to improve quality, but have different approaches to getting the job done. The primary differences between the two are shown below.

Six Sigma	Lean
Longer duration to complete project	Relatively short duration for eliminating waste
Hierarchical structure for oversight	Less need for hierarchical structure and oversight
Requires extensive training for individuals to attain certification levels (e.g., Black, Green, or White Belt status)	Less extensive training for the learning, implementation, and maintenance
Projects/teams must have a management sponsor and project manager	Anyone can make quick improvements with knowledge of the process - no one is working in a vacuum
Selected projects tie to strategic priorities of the organization	Goal is to eliminate all waste throughout the organization
Projects are not considered successful unless there is a positive impact to the bottom line	Projects that eliminate non value-added activities (waste) are considered successful
Heavy reliance on statistical methods	Lean can be successful without statistics
Sophisticated problem solving approach utilizing complex tools	Practical approach to problem solving utilizing user-friendly tools
More difficult to teach, understand, implement, and maintain	Easier to teach, understand, implement, and maintain

The merits of either method in healthcare can be argued based on organizational culture and needs, and personal experience. Many healthcare organizations have successfully implemented Six Sigma and have improved quality. On the other hand, many healthcare organizations have successfully implemented Lean and also have improved quality. In fact, many organizations have successfully combined both programs. Both Lean and Six Sigma effectively decrease process variation and can work very well together or independent of each other. However, the focus of this book is to provide the reasons and tools for the application of Lean in healthcare. (This is not to state that Lean should be the only program "in town", but that it should be considered a major portion of any business improvement methodology, whether it be Six Sigma or some other type program.)

So Why Lean?

There are basically three reasons why Lean can be used with confidence. First of all, the training requirements and implementation time for Lean are minimal. Basic concepts of Lean can be taught very quickly and improvements can be implemented the same day. For example, when an individual understands that some of their daily activities are non value-added or waste; activities such as excess time spent walking, waiting, and moving, immediate changes can be made to improve the process. Waste reduction will become automatic for people as they become aware of waste. Improvements are continuously made at all stages of work. Often, the completion of one Lean or Kaizen Event stimulates the participants to think of other areas for improvement.

Secondly, Lean's application in an organization is broad. Attempts are made to eliminate waste in all areas. With Six Sigma, projects are more narrowly focused and are highly recommended to have a direct correlation to strategic priorities and the bottom line. *The application of Six Sigma in healthcare was proven more difficult than the application of Lean. It is often difficult to directly correlate a clinical process with a bottom line result and obtain the data required to continuously monitor the improvements of a clinical process through an empowered staff (i.e., process ownership).* Lean, on the other hand, has successfully and quickly been implemented in all areas of healthcare, but also with bottom line and strategic implications while engaging the staff. One community hospital in the Midwest area trained over 300 people in Lean and completed 57 Kaizen Events in less than a year with great results in all performance measurements. There are tools, such as 5S, that can get everyone engaged and in the right mindset for applications of Lean. *5S is a workplace organizational program that assists to improve efficiencies by having items (work, equipment, charts, labs, supplies, electronic files and folders) in the most convenient location for easy access.*

The third reason is that improvements made, while utilizing Lean concepts, positively impact all areas of healthcare including safety, patient/customer satisfaction, employee/staff satisfaction, and clinical outcomes, as well as the bottom line. Customers (i.e., patients) are more satisfied with the decreased wait times, reduction of duplicate documentation, and fewer errors or mix-ups. This elimination of waste impacts the bottom line by decreasing the number of required resources to complete the same amount of work. Employees are empowered to change work they are directly involved in, to making their work more effective (less waste) while becoming more rewarding. Clinical outcomes are improved as the variation in processes is eliminated and work is standardized.

Healthcare has gone through an evolution of process improvements. It must be acknowledged that Lean should not be considered just another program of the month; it is much more than that. Lean, and its problem solving counterpart of Six Sigma, offers the healthcare community the opportunity to obtain long term, sustainable results. Lean must be introduced and supported by top management, but, more importantly, Lean ideas must be implemented by the staff whom have the desire to improve.

Why Lean Healthcare?

As previously mentioned in The Healthcare Crisis section of this book, healthcare industry leaders have realized that improvements throughout the system must become a priority. The healthcare system as it exists today must improve. The consumer has become increasingly aware of hospital's inefficiencies through avenues such as U.S. Department of Healthcare & Human Services (HHS.gov) and their hospital compare website (www.hospitalcompare.hhs.gov). The tremendous concern for patient safety and care, as well as healthcare premium cost escalations, nursing/staff shortages, and diminishing/limited funds from federal, state, and local agencies are fundamental reasons improvements in healthcare are necessary. The General Motors Corporation reported that healthcare expenditures equate to $1,525 per car produced in 2003. This cost is more than the steel to make the car! This significant portion of the healthcare cost for a product is continually gaining international attention due to its growing percentage of what comprises the total cost of that product (or service). It is within that cost structure that Lean will provide a means by which waste can be eliminated (which will reduce costs overall) while improving patient care and safety, profitability, and staff job satisfaction. The national numbers for overall waste in healthcare is estimated between 30 and 40%. However, some insist the number is more like 60%!

Lean is centered on eliminating waste through continuous improvement while always keeping the customer (internal or external, i.e., patient) in mind. Waste is defined as non valued-added activities that the customer is unwilling to pay for. Non valued-added activities are the inefficiencies within the process. The service or product provided to the customer must be what the customer is willing to pay for (value-added). For example, when a patient had been seen by a doctor, had an X-ray taken, had blood drawn, etc. are all considered value-added activities. On the other hand, patients do not want to pay for non value-added activities such as omissions of lab work resulting in redoing tests, waiting (for anything), duplication of service (paperwork, labs, X-rays, etc.). The functions of patient charting, transporting a patient, billing and coding, etc. may appear as non value-added, but are not because they are necessary to ensure total patient satisfaction and safety. However, for example, excessive delays for a patient to be transported can be considered waste. Therefore, as we discuss eliminating waste (or non valued-activities), be careful to not refer to ancillary services and non direct patient care as non value-added activities. They are essential services required for patient safety and care.

The ultimate customer in healthcare is the patient, considered typically as the external customer. Internal customers can be other staff, departments, vendors, or other healthcare providers that too must improve their processes for further satisfaction and care for the external customer. Physicians are becoming more engaged in this type of work and see themselves as the ultimate customer of hospitals - who brings the patients? To understand the Value Stream Management process you must first understand the value stream. The value stream is the "nervous system" of Lean.

The Value Stream

A **value stream** is defined as the actions (both valued-added and non value-added) that are necessary to deliver a product or service to a customer. A value stream may include a single process comprised of many activities or a linked series of processes.

A stream is the flow of water from a source, a mountain runoff or lake, through various land formations, to an ocean, lake, or sea. For organizations, this stream is a flow of work from an upstream (request for service) down through the river (processes), into the ocean, lake, or sea (service delivered).

Most rivers have bends and other hindrances where the water does not flow as smoothly.

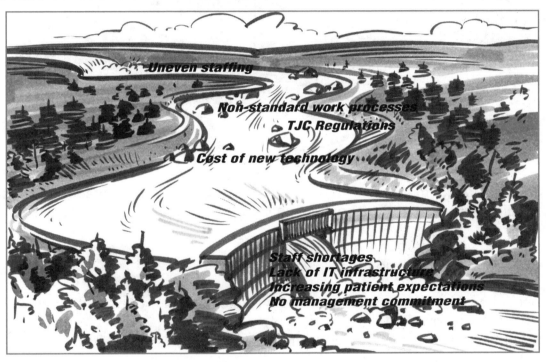

Examples of some hindrances in healthcare, or in any other industry, may be::

+ Culture of organization or department
+ "It's not my job" attitude
+ Lack of vision or purpose from upper management
+ Lack of capable processes and standards
+ Fear of change
+ Not trained properly
+ Financial constraints
+ Lack of departmental communication and co-ordination of care or information (departmental silos)
+ Governmental regulations
+ Legal constraints
+ Safety concerns
+ Certification/licensing requirements

These hindrances can cause and/or contribute to non value-added activities. The goal of Lean and/or Lean-Sigma in healthcare is to eliminate those activities or wastes and provide to the customer with only what they are willing to paying for, the value-added activities. The elimination of waste will cause a smoother work flow (i.e., patient, information, services) with no (or minimal) hindrances.

The Value Stream Management process will allow a facility to create, manage, and sustain value stream "rivers of patient care and non-patient care services" improvements with little or no hindrances.

Value Stream Management will do the following:

- ✦ Focus the improvement efforts toward a single customer or patient process (one ship or boat going down the river, not a fleet)
- ✦ Prevent scope creep (i.e., getting off track)
- ✦ Allow for departmental areas to be improved with minimal resource allocation
- ✦ Allow resource coordination/allocation across the organization
- ✦ Allow for a means of moving from the current state to the future state through Lean tool application and proper communication
- ✦ Provide a structure for the process owner with the necessary skills to initiate Lean-Sigma projects more frequently
- ✦ Allow Lean to be understood in everyday terminology

The Value Stream Management Process

Value Stream Management Process for Lean Healthcare is a methodology comprised of four phases. The four phases are:

1. Assess
2. Diagnosis
3. Treat
4. Prevent

Even though each phase is separate, there is an overlap on the Lean tools being used. For example, Data Collection is explained in the Assess phase; however, some Data Collection will most likely be done in each of the phases. A Team Charter (a document indicating the team's purpose and deliverables) is prepared in the Assess phase and as more information becomes available, it would then need to be updated. The case studies and the improvement tools explained in this book are organized around these four phases as it is a familiar model for healthcare professionals.

Value Stream Management can be applied to an entire value stream or an individual process within the value stream.

The entire Value Stream....   **...or an invididual process or area.**

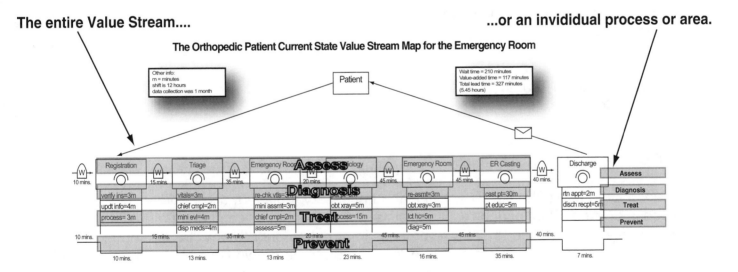

The Oak Valley Health Systems will serve as the teaching example on how each Lean tool can be applied given the conditions of the case. Every possible situation cannot be explained through this one case study. Therefore, additional case studies will be presented throughout the book to provide additional understanding of a particular tool or concept. Also, the Appendix contains more detailed case studies to further assist your understanding on how Lean can be implemented in healthcare.

The Four Phases

The Lean journey is similar to the treatment of a patient. It requires people (healthcare providers and staff) and support from various departments and ancillary staff to effectively apply the Lean concepts and tools. As the treatment of a patient is individually tailored, Lean must also be tailored to the facility, department, and/or process in which it will be used. The four phases can be implemented by conducting a Kaizen Event (see next section - Types of Kaizens) or through some other type improvement program.

The *Assess Phase* (Chapter 2) is the most critical step in Lean healthcare. This phase will explain the various tools that must be used so that everyone can understand how the current process is running. In medicine, professional skills are used to assess and evaluate a patient. If an assessment is not accurate then all other phases will not be accurate. This would result in no improvement or the worsening of a situation. In Lean, similar assessment skills are used to evaluate an area or process and prepare it for detailed analysis. This phase, as well as the others, requires teamwork. Each member of the team plays a vital role, each bringing to the table different skills to help improve a process or area. In this phase, the following tools will be explained:

Management Commitment - Stakeholder Involvement
The Balanced Scorecard
Performance Measurements
Project Prioritization Worksheet
Distribution Report
Takt Time
Cycle Time
Basics of Good Teams
Team Ground Rules
Effective Meetings
Value Stream Mapping
Flowcharts (or Process Maps)

The *Diagnosis Phase* (Chapter 3) explains the necessary tools that allow additional analysis of the process or area. Just as lab results assists in determining or confirming a diagnosis of a patient, Lean tools are used to analyze process information prior to any "treatment" of the process. This phase allows a statement or conclusion to be drawn concerning the nature or cause of the area or process requiring attention. This phase will provide the transition from assessing an area or process through further analysis and understanding to be sure the correct treatment (or action) is taken. In this phase, the following tools will be explained:

Waste Overview
The Elevator Speech
How to Conduct a Waste Walk
Data Collection
Brainstorming, Cause and Effect Diagram, and 5 Why Analysis
Financial Analysis

The *Treat Phase* (Chapter 4) is the actual training and application or implementation of the Lean tools. Just as therapy (physical, speech, or occupational) is used for treatment after the assessment and diagnosis of a patient to a specific care pathway, so too in the Lean process, treatment involves additional Lean tools to make positive change in the process. In medicine, the ultimate goal is to achieve wellness for a patient. In Lean, the goal is to attain a state of continuous improvement (or process wellness) that meets the needs of the patient (or customer).

In this phase, the following tools will be explained:

> 5S
> Just-In-Time (Continuous Flow, Pull System, and Kanbans)
> Pitch
> Work Load Balancing
> Standard Work
> Physical Layout
> Leveling
> Mistake Proofing
> Visual Production Board
> Impact Map
> Gantt Chart

The *Prevent Phase* (Chapter 5) will explain how to control and sustain improvements over time. It will also provide the avenue in which to disseminate the Lean project into other areas. Just as "An apple a day, keeps the doctor away", this phase implies the sustaining of the new, healthier process. Lean tools are applied to ensure Total Employee Involvement (TEI) and that improvements are sustained over time. This phase will also provide ideas on how to expand the knowledge gained from one Kaizen Event to all areas of the hospital and/or other hospitals within a system.

In this phase, the following tools will be explained:

> Lean Chronicle
> Paynter Chart
> Run Chart
> Visual Control
> Storyboard
> Yokoten

After each phase, a Readiness Guide will be provided. The Readiness Guide is a checklist for you to review, ensuring you have a good understanding of the tools and concepts contained in the chapter prior to proceeding to the next phase.

The Value Stream Management process is implemented through different types of Kaizen Events (or similar-type programs).

Types of Kaizens

Kaizen is derived from the word "kai" which means to "take apart" and "zen" which means to "make good". Kaizen is also synonymous with continuous improvement.

Kai - zen

"Take apart"   "Make good"

Kaizen can be major organizational improvements directed to an entire value stream (i.e., integrating two business units' processes) or it can be something very simple (i.e., placing a Post-it Note on a signature page to make sure a document is signed in the right location) - and everything in-between.

There are mainly two different types of kaizens to assist you in your entire improvement initiatives, the Kaizen Event and the Idea Kaizen.

The Kaizen Event

*The **Kaizen Event** is a focused group of individuals dedicated to applying Lean tools to a specific area within a certain time period.* There are three phases to conducting a Kaizen Event.

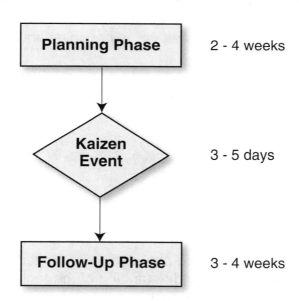

| Planning Phase | 2 - 4 weeks |

| Kaizen Event | 3 - 5 days |

| Follow-Up Phase | 3 - 4 weeks |

The following few pages are general guidelines for the various activities that would comprise a week-long Kaizen Event. This information should be customized and adapted to your improvement project guidelines.

Note: The Kaizen Event, and its associated activities, can be spread out over a period of 2-4 weeks (or longer), as long as the appropriate time is allocated for each meeting and the team is committed.

Planning Phase

The Planning Phase is the most important phase. Everyone must be aligned on the specifics of the project as well as ensuring alignment to the Balanced Scorecard. The following charts can be used as a guide when proceeding through this phase.

Kaizen Event Preparation Schedule
The Kaizen Event Preparation Schedule should be used by the team leader/facilitator, Lean Sensei, Black or Green Belt, or whomever is facilitating the continuous improvement event. The success of a Kaizen Event depends on the detailed planning that is done beforehand. Place a checkmark (✔) by those items that have been completed.

3 Weeks Before Event

☐ 1. Select area and topic.
☐ 2. Meet with sponsor (champion), process owner, financial leader, and any other key associates to:
    - Prioritize value streams that relate to the Balanced Scorecard
    - Secure full time participation by team members for the event
    - Ensure sponsor is availalbe for the kick-off meeting and the report outs (if applicable)
    - Discuss objectives and scope of the project
☐ 3. Ask these questions:
    - Will this team improve the process/functional performance?
    - Are the resources being focused on the right priorities?
    - What is the business case for analyzing and improving this value stream?
☐ 4. When filling out a Team Charter, ensure:
    - Facilitator is assigned
    - Additional expertise (i.e., Lean Sensei, Black or Green Belt) is available (if appropriate)
    - Team member roles are defined (scribe, timekeeper, tech rep, etc.)
    - Boundaries of the project are clearly defined
    - Customers of the process are clearly identified
    - Suppliers to the process or area are clearly identified
    - Dates have been established and agreed to
☐ 5. Secure conference room for the event. The room should be:
    - Located as close as possible to the process area that is being worked on
    - Available for the duration of the event
    - Large enough to conduct simulations (if required in the training)
☐ 6. Obtain all necessary supplies, such as:
    - Post-it Notes   - Flip charts and markers   - LCD projector
    - Butcher paper roll   - Access to copy machine   - Copies of training
    - Catering requirements   - Materials (pocket guides, handbooks)   - Snacks ☺

Deliverables

☐ 1. Team Charter created.
☐ 2. Metric/goal initially agreed upon.
☐ 3. Date(s) of the event determined.
☐ 4. Invitation sent to team members that includes date, location, event particulars, and Team Charter.
☐ 5. All necessary supplies (training materials) have been ordered.

Comments/Notes:

_____

_____

Kaizen Event Preparation Schedule

The Kaizen Event Preparation Schedule should be used by the team leader/facilitator, Lean Sensei, Black or Green Belt, or whomever is facilitating the continuous improvement event. The success of a Kaizen Event depends on the detailed planning that is done beforehand. Place a checkmark (✔) by those items that have been completed.

2 Weeks Before Event

- [ ] 1. Review the 3 Weeks Before Event list.
- [ ] 2. Gather data/identify sources that would be on a current state value stream map.
      - Obtain financials, flowcharts, etc. of the process(es)
      - Run reports of data of current process or collect real time (if applicable)
- [ ] 3. Determine current customer steady state demand (takt time).
- [ ] 4. Determine key individuals needed to support the event as on an ad hoc basis (facilities, IT, HR, etc.). Communicate with them appropriately.
- [ ] 5. Review the Team Charter with sponsor and process owner. Discuss schedules, measurements, targets, and deliverables on the proposed event.
- [ ] 6. Review Lessons Learned, Sunset Reports, Kaizen Event Evalution Forms from any previous events that may impact this event.

Deliverables

- [ ] 1. Team Charter completed and agreement reached on specific deliverables.
- [ ] 2. Sponsor scheduled for kick-off meeting and report outs.
- [ ] 3. Date(s) of the event determined.
- [ ] 4. All team members notified.
- [ ] 5. Data collection started.

1 Week Before Event

- [ ] 1. Review 3 Weeks Before Event and 2 Weeks Before Event list and resolve open issues.
- [ ] 2. Hold final preparation meeting with process owner.
- [ ] 3. Review metrics and goals with process owner for final agreement.
- [ ] 4. Update Team Charter, if necessary.

Deliverables

- [ ] 1. Team member participation verfied.
- [ ] 2. Team Charter released to all team members.
- [ ] 3. Materials acquired.
- [ ] 4. Room and catering verified (those snacks ☺).

Comments/Notes:

_____

_____

One of the most important parts of this Planning Phase is to ensure the sponsor (champion) and process owner (departmental head or supervisor/manager) are in complete agreement as to the scope of the project and resources required, as well as having the appropriate team members available.

The following process flowchart will further assist you in preparing for the appropriate type of Kaizen Event.

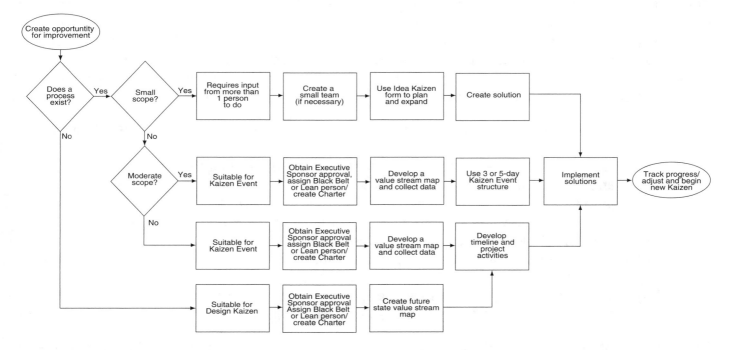

There may be Kaizen Events that require considerable IT support and/or external resources to be used. If this is the case, assemble the team and meet on a regular basis and attempt to put a time frame (not more than 1 year) on the entire project, often referred to as a Design Kaizen. When enough information is present to implement change, then follow the standard procedures for conducting a Kaizen Event. Some examples may include projects such as: the roll-out of a new software scheduling system and/or EMR/EMS (Electronic Medical Records/System) to the physician's offices, the relocation of departments to a new building, etc.

Kaizen Event

This phase is the time allocated for: training on the Lean tools, conducting the value stream mapping exercise or updating the map, observing the process if not done previously, making changes to the physical layout, creating standards, testing the improvements, and making recommendations to management for enterprise-wide implementation. This is considered the *Just Do It* part of the Kaizen Event. Most hospitals dedicate a block of time for this part, typically 3 to 5 days. The schedule can be as follows:

Day 1 am: Review Team Charter and Data Collected, Discuss Business Case, Initiate Lean Training
Day 1 pm: Continue Lean Training (include a simulation) - Data Collection
Day 2 am: Value Stream Map Current State
Day 2 pm: Conduct Waste Audit and Create Future State Map
Day 3 am: Detail Activities Required for Implementation of Future State Map
Day 3 pm: Create Worksheets, Forms, Checklists, etc.
Day 4 am: Implement, Adjust, Measure, and Observe
Day 4 pm: Implement, Adjust, Measure, and Observe
Day 5 am: Prepare Report Out to Management
Day 5 pm: Report Out to Management, Team Recognition

Each of these half-day segments have additional activities that need to be completed. For example, Day 1 am: would include such topics/activities as:

✦ What is Lean (its origination with Eli Whitney and Henry Ford, as well as its history as the Toyota Production System)
✦ Why is Lean and/or Six Sigma needed now (list various issues confronting healthcare as a whole as well as local competitors e.g., that new facility that is advertising about their CyberKnife knife, etc.) - creating the business case
✦ Examples of Lean and/or Six Sigma successes from other healthcare facilities
✦ Description of the main Lean tools of 5S, takt time, continuous flow, standard work, mistake proofing (and others that you feel would be appropriate) - while not overwhelming the team with too many tools
✦ Explain the 7 (or 8) types of waste and conduct a Waste Walk (of some other waste activity) to relate wastes to their work
✦ Discuss the long term approach regarding Lean - what must be embraced by the staff for any changes to be sustained
✦ Discuss the importance of teaming and conduct a fun activity demonstrating its impact
✦ Review the Team Charter and any supporting data

Note: Many of these activities can be completed prior to the Kaizen Event.

It is highly recommended that a Lean simulation be conducted at some point during the training.

It is the purpose of this book to provide you with the checklists, forms, worksheets, and examples to assist you in progressing through a similar-type workshop.

At the end of each day the team should report out to management on the progress-to-date. These meetings ensure good communication to everyone involved, as well as providing the opportunity to discuss issues that may have been encountered during that day. Management should be prepared to react and/or make a decision regarding barriers presented.

The following is an example of a Kaizen Event Daily Review providing the team and management a standard report for which to base discussions.

Kaizen Event Daily Review

The Kaizen Event Daily Review allows for a team to list their accomplishments, as well as their areas of concern, that should be reviewed by the team champion on a daily basis. Many times there will be a report-out at the end of the day in which all leadership of the organization are invited to attend. This review allows for immediate communication as to the project's status.

By: Date:

Team Name or Value Stream:

Measurements	Metrics						
	# Before	Day 1	Day 2	Day 3	Day 4	Day 5	Target

Accomplishments:	Concerns:	Plans:

Follow-Up Phase

Many Kaizen Events will be localized to a specific area or process, mainly for evaluation to determine if enterprise-wide implementation is warranted. The specific area or process improved must be monitored post Kaizen Event to ensure the improvements are sustained over time. *A Kaizen Event Scorecard is used to summarize and keep track of Kaizen progress over time.*

The following is an example of a Kaizen Event Scorecard.

Kaizen Event Scorecard

The Kaizen Event Scorecard is meant to regularly convey the results of the improvements. In doing so, it will provide the team with the necessary data in which to make corrections if trends are negative and the improvements are not going as expected. The Scorecard will also provide management with the improvement team's progress-to-date.

Event Name: Site/Location: Date:

Value Stream Impacted: Process Owner(s):   Team Members:

Team Champion/Sponsor: Team Leader:

Metrics

Measurements	# Start of Event	# End of Event	7 Day Date: ____	14 Day Date: ____	30 Day Date: ____	60 Day Date: ____	90 Day Date: ____	Target

Overall Evaluation:

R Y G	R Y G	R Y G	R Y G	R Y G

Key:

■ Performance Meets or Exceeds Target (Green)

▨ Performance is Short but close to Target (within 10% of Target) (Yellow)

▢ Performance is Significantly Unfavorable to Target (below 10% of Target) (Red)

If the measurement is not meeting target(s) the below 3 W's of information (What, Who, and When) must clearly indicate how you plan to meet or exceed target.

What (tied to Measurements above)	Who	When	Comments/Status

Comments/Notes:

A project may not be totally completed during the specific Kaizen Event time period due to circumstances and issues arising from what is found out during the week-long event. Therefore, continue to submit the Kaizen Event Scorecard to management (or just the team sponsor) on a regular basis. Continue to meet with the team on a weekly basis until the project is completed. If another team is responsible for enterprise-wide implementation, ensure that selected team members are part of the new team. In conclusion, recognize and reward all team members.

Submit a final report when the Kaizen Event is completed.

Recommendations on conducting Kaizen Events:

- ✦ Complete all three phases
- ✦ Keep Kaizen Events focused on what is being measured - "you treasure what you measure"
- ✦ Ensure 5S is part of any/all Kaizen Events
- ✦ Ensure good communication from management and request support, if needed
- ✦ Keep all employees informed of the progress

The Planning Phase and the Follow-up Phase are just as important as the Kaizen Event.

The benefits of Kaizen Events are they:

- ✦ Allow for quick implementation of Lean tools and concepts
- ✦ Train employees in detailed application of Lean tools and concepts
- ✦ Improve work flow
- ✦ Improve productivity
- ✦ Improve measurements from the Balanced Scorecard (or other Key Performance Indicators)
- ✦ Create awareness on the importance of continuous improvement
- ✦ Provide employees with the confidence that Lean (change) can work

The following is an example of a 5 day, Monday - Friday, Kaizen Event. Many of the activities listed can be done that day, or the previous day. This will depend on the organizational resources and capacity, as well as the facilitator's Lean and/or Sigma project experience. Use the following as a strawman in creating a 5 day Kaizen Event for your facility.

Kaizen Event Daily Schedule - Days 1-3

The Kaizen Event Daily Schedule is a guide to ensure each of the items listed below are reviewed by the team each day during the week-long Kaizen Event. Use this as a guide, as each project will require some adaptation and customization on the use of the Lean tools.

Project Focus: **Dates:**

Day One
- ❏ Review team goals and objectives; train on Lean tools; review 5 day event schedule
- ❏ Review "before" data, documentation, and data collection tools
- ❏ Determine takt time/cycle time calculations; Standard Work Sheet, work layout; 5S
- ❏ Create process map or value stream with sticky-notes for current processes
- ❏ Take a "Waste Walk" if needed to further identify opportunities; take "before" photos
- ❏ Identify value-added vs non value-added steps
- ❏ Select non value-added wastes to attack
- ❏ Develop future state process or value stream map
- ❏ Meet with stakeholders and review progress, ideas
- ❏ Team recap of WWW (Who, does What, and When); create daily plan for Tuesday
- ❏ Daily Report-Out to management

Day Two
- ❏ Review findings/decisions from Day 1; review Day 2 plan
- ❏ Create solutions for new process
- ❏ Create plan for new process and/or work layout
- ❏ Meet with stakeholders and review progress, ideas; solicit concerns, comments
- ❏ Notify ancillary support groups of needed efforts/materials
- ❏ Draft standard work (i.e., Standard Operating Procedures (SOP))
- ❏ Develop training protocol for affected stakeholders, determine start time
- ❏ Develop communication plan for site/stakeholders
- ❏ Team recap and WWW; create daily plan for Wednesday
- ❏ Daily Report-Out to management

Day Three
- ❏ Train stakeholders on new physical (or work) layout and standard work
- ❏ Assign a team member to each stakeholder
- ❏ Run new process; collect data; adjust as necessary
- ❏ Fix problems immediately
- ❏ Create visual controls
- ❏ Work on 5S and safety issues
- ❏ Create/post Key Messages and appropriate tools
- ❏ Revise communication plan for site/stakeholders
- ❏ Team recap and WWW; create daily plan for Thursday
- ❏ Daily Report-Out to management

Notes

_____

_____

_____

Kaizen Event Daily Schedule - Days 4-5+

The Kaizen Event Daily Schedule is a guide to ensure each of the items listed below are reviewed by the team each day during the week-long Kaizen Event. Use this as a guide, as each project will require some adaptation and customization on the use of the Lean tools.

Project Focus: **Dates:**

Day Four
- ❏ Continue training stakeholders on new work layout, process via standard work procedures
- ❏ Continue to run new process; fix problems from Day Three
- ❏ Review "after" data, documentation, and tools (same as "before" in Day One previous category)
- ❏ Take after area pictures and team photo
- ❏ Conduct debriefing session with stakeholders
- ❏ Develop weekly measurement plan
- ❏ Make plans to meet with process owner/sponsor on weekly basis to review metrics

Day Five
- ❏ Compile data from improvements
- ❏ Propose plan for sustaining and controlling improvements made (detailed as possible)
- ❏ Create plan for enterprise-wide roll out along with resources required (costs, equipment, manpower, etc.)
- ❏ Prepare final presentation
- ❏ Give final presentation to management
- ❏ Reward and recognize team members

Day Five +
- ❏ Monitor and control through visual measurements
- ❏ Report with 7-14-30-60-90 day measurements and adjust if necessary
- ❏ Submit Kaizen information via a Sunset Report (or Yokoten) and make available electronically for shared knoweldge

Notes

_____

_____

_____

Idea Kaizen

*The **Idea Kaizen** is a quick and easy method to document and solve a simple problem. This is an on-the-spot type problem solving method and a problem resolution activity requiring minimal resources and (typically) no management approval.* The Idea Kaizen is similar in nature to an idea submitted in an organizational Suggestion Program. The main difference is that in the Idea Kaizen employees are empowered and encouraged to make the change themselves, if at all possible. These changes (or improvements) should not have any negative impact on other parts of the organization.

It is the employees doing their job, working that process level detail (i.e., providing a service or processing information), day in and day out that have the best ideas on how to reduce and eliminate waste, however, they may not be aware of the impact that waste has in their process. The Idea Kaizen is meant to engage those employees to gain additional ownership of their processes through self-initiated improvements (and waste elimination). Once Idea Kaizens become a way of life for all employees within an organization, then a true continuous improvement culture will have emerged.

Note: Some Idea Kaizens may require a Kaizen Event. The important aspect of the Idea Kaizen is to document improvement ideas as they occur when they are fresh on that person's mind. Many times Idea Kaizen forms will be made available throughout a Kaizen Event. As the team progresses through understanding and applying the Lean tools to their targeted area, process, or value stream, this may stimulate improvement ideas that are beyond the scope of the current project. Therefore, use the following Idea Kaizen form to capture these "other" improvement ideas for sooner-than-later implementation.

Idea Kaizen Form

Name:_____   Department:_____

Upstream Customer:_____   Downstream Customer:_____

The Idea Kaizen is a quick and easy method to document and solve a simple problem. This is an on-the-spot type problem solving method and a problem resolution activity requiring minimal resources and (typically) no management approval. However, management should be made aware of the improvements.

Step 1: Describe the Problem.   Date:_____
Include photos, charts, and graphs, if necessary.

Step 2: Describe the Action to be Taken.   Date:_____
Include photos, charts, and graphs, if necessary.

Step 3: Follow-up. Did the Action Work?   ❑ Yes ❑ No   Date:_____
Include photos, charts, and graphs, if necessary.
Additional Notes:

The following chart summarizes the qualities of the Idea Kaizen and the Kaizen Event.

Idea Kaizen	Kaizen Event
✔ On-the-spot type solutions ✔ Similar to submitting an idea in a company's Suggestion Program ✔ Few resources required (time, people, etc.) ✔ Not requiring value stream mapping ✔ Not as structured ✔ May be a "quick-fix" ✔ Not as detailed ✔ Common sense solution ✔ Requires only the individual (or 1 other person) for implementation ✔ May require a Kaizen Event	✔ Requires a cross-functional team ✔ Typically identified as a waste on a value stream map ✔ Structured process ✔ Lean tools utilized ✔ 3 to 5 days to complete ✔ Identifies root cause(s) ✔ Requires good data collection ✔ Can be tied directly to Balanced Scorecard and Key Performance Indicators ✔ Requires up-front planning ✔ Requires post-event follow-up

Kaizens, whether it is a full blown week long Kaizen Event, or that simple idea that one person implements, are meant to create empowerment of the workforce in creating improved standards of care and safety while reducing waste (and costs).

When introducing Lean or Six Sigma to any group in healthcare, remember that one of the reasons that they are in healthcare is because they have the desire to help people. Past improvement activities may or may not have been done with the focus and commitment that Lean provides. It is up to the process owner, team champion, and/or Lean Sensei or Six Sigma facilitator to tactfully and respectfully acknowledge past practices and focus the team in finding new opportunities to reduce the non value-added activities (i.e., waste). This can be accomplished through a Kaizen Event or Idea Kaizen (or the improvement methodology that the organization is currently using).

Whether the Value Stream Management, Six Sigma, Lean, or PDCA methodology is used to determine and/or prioritize your improvement projects, it is a good idea to create a visual map, "the big picture", so everyone can "see" and therefore better understand the various processes that comprise the major patient flow pathways. As displayed in the following illustration, healthcare facilities are a complex combination of inputs, measurement systems, people, processes (pathways, protocols, etc.), functional areas (departments), and their resultant outputs. These all must work together for a patient to have the proper healthcare experience.

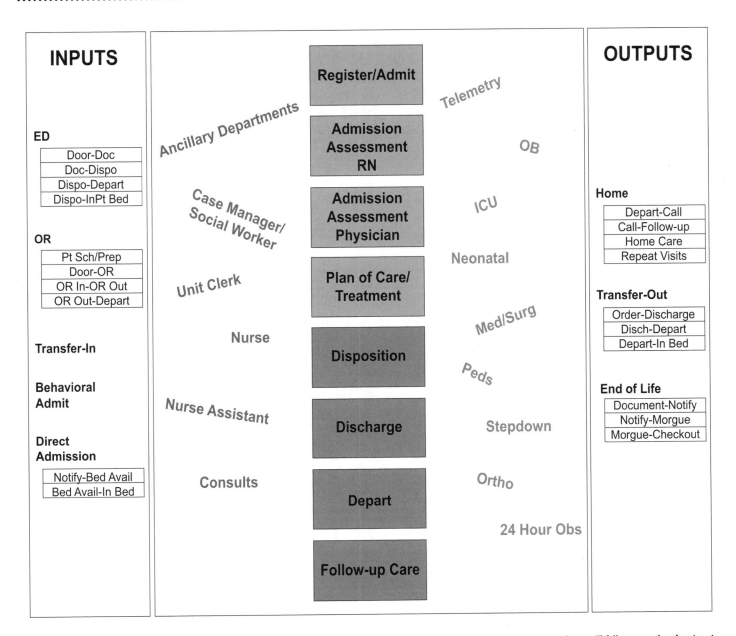

INPUTS

ED

Door-Doc
Doc-Dispo
Dispo-Depart
Dispo-InPt Bed

OR

Pt Sch/Prep
Door-OR
OR In-OR Out
OR Out-Depart

Transfer-In

Behavioral Admit

Direct Admission

Notify-Bed Avail
Bed Avail-In Bed

Ancillary Departments

Case Manager/ Social Worker

Unit Clerk

Nurse

Nurse Assistant

Consults

Register/Admit

Admission Assessment RN

Admission Assessment Physician

Plan of Care/ Treatment

Disposition

Discharge

Depart

Follow-up Care

Telemetry

OB

ICU

Neonatal

Med/Surg

Peds

Stepdown

Ortho

24 Hour Obs

OUTPUTS

Home

Depart-Call
Call-Follow-up
Home Care
Repeat Visits

Transfer-Out

Order-Discharge
Disch-Depart
Depart-In Bed

End of Life

Document-Notify
Notify-Morgue
Morgue-Checkout

After looking at all these processes and sub-processes, the question may arise, "Where do I start since there are so many areas that could be improved?" To that question, we, as authors, suggest you learn from the following case study, understand the four-approach methodology, read the additional case studies, use what makes most sense for your organization, and then begin a project using what you have learned. Undoubtedly, each Kaizen Event or improvement project will itself improve as you gain additional experience.

Chapter 2:
Assess

Topics Include:

- ✦ Introduction to Oak Valley Health System Case Study
- ✦ Management Commitment - Stakeholder Involvement
- ✦ The Balanced Scorecard
- ✦ Project Prioritization Worksheet
- ✦ Distribution Report
- ✦ Takt Time
- ✦ Cycle Time
- ✦ Basics of Good Teams
- ✦ Effective Meetings
- ✦ Value Stream Mapping
- ✦ Flowcharts (or Process Maps)
- ✦ Readiness Guide for Assess

The Lean tools and concepts contained in the next four chapters will be thoroughly explained, as well as referenced to their application in the Oak Valley Health System case study (as denoted by the lightly-shaded areas and pages). This should provide you with enough in-depth knowledge to apply that tool or concept to your healthcare process.

Introduction to the Oak Valley Health System Case Study

Oak Valley Health System (OVHS) is located in a Midwestern metropolitan area with a population of a little over one million people. OVHS consists of five hospitals, twelve urgent care and specialty clinics, as well as satellite laboratories, home healthcare and hospice care services, and all are within a thirty mile radius of the city.

Oak Valley's mission statement is:

"The Oak Valley Health System is committed to providing personal and high quality state of the art care with compassion and community focus."

A few community issues facing OVHS include:

✦ A competitor health system opened a new triage clinic within its Emergency Department three months ago while another competitor has been aggressively advertising their new CyberKnife
✦ The local teaching hospital received funding to establish a new birthing center
✦ A local organization recently announced plans for adding 500 new jobs within the next 18 months
✦ Two new retirement communities were recently approved by the city's zoning board and are to be built in the next three-to-five years

A few internal changes facing OVHS include:

✦ The Electronic Medical Records (EMR) system has been implemented in three of the five hospitals and is scheduled to be fully installed in all hospitals within the year
✦ The use of hospitalists and the current arrangement with the physician groups
✦ To address the nursing staff shortage, the hospital system recently partnered with a local university and established a work co-op program for its nursing students
✦ The laboratory in each hospital is making major equipment changes to take advantage of robotic specimen handling
✦ The contract for all Radiology work has recently been given to a new group, resulting in some friction within the departments
✦ Each hospital will designate one unit as a "short-stay" unit for observation patients and other patients with stays expected in the 1 - 2 day range

Oakview Hospital

Oakview Hospital, the largest facility within the Oak Valley Health System, is located just outside the city limit. It is referred to as the "hospital in the woods" due to its location of buildings surrounded by large, broad-leaved oak trees. It is a 340 licensed-bed, full-service hospital having specialties that include emergency medicine, orthopedics, cardiology, oncology, neurology, surgery, gastroenterology, physical therapy, behavioral medicine, and pediatrics. Oakview also has a critical care unit that is a Level 1 Trauma Center, a Chest Pain Center, a Stroke Center, a Physical Rehabilitation Center, and a Birthing Center. Oakview Hospital's management team is under pressure from System level senior leadership to improve performance on all levels.

For the past three years OVHS has rolled out a Six Sigma program entitled Operational Excellence and has had some limited success at each of their hospitals. Recently the CEO of Oakview Hospital, John Abrahms, MD; the Vice President of Quality Assurance, Mary Hart MSN; the Chief Nursing Office, Judy Dean; and the Director of Operational Excellence (Six Sigma Master Black Belt), Sue Richards, attended a Lean Healthcare Conference at a local university. Dr. Abrahms, Ms. Hart, Ms. Dean, and Ms. Richards determined that the Lean tools and practices referenced at the conference would be a valuable addition to their Operational Excellence program.

Note: It is important to understand that the tools and concepts referenced in the Oakview Hospital ED case study were used more than once during the overall ED project. Not every aspect of the case study could be explained in this book.

Management Commitment - Stakeholder Involvement

Process improvement projects will not be successful (sustained and controlled) if managers (and stakeholders) are not aligned with the team objectives from the beginning to the end. Healthcare roles vary in the type and level of support they provide for any process improvement program. The list below, while not all inclusive, indicates the various healthcare staffing levels and their corresponding levels of support.

Title/Position - top management
President, CEO, CFO, CMO, CNO, All VPs, Directors, etc.

Required Level of Support
- ✦ Develop and communicate the long term vision for healthcare services
- ✦ Review aggressively the Balanced Scorecard
- ✦ Allocate resources to improve Balanced Scorecard numbers to appropriate targets
- ✦ Place an emphasis on staff development, training, and career development
- ✦ Understand the importance of Lean as a long term business improvement methodology that does not have an end in sight - a continuous journey
- ✦ Embrace improvement projects by requesting report outs regularly
- ✦ Advocates that change will be for the better

Title Position - middle management
Managers, Supervisors, Team Leaders, Unit Coordinators, Six Sigma Black Belts, Lean Coordinators, etc.

Required Level of Support
- ✦ Actively engage improvement activities that support the Balanced Scorecard
- ✦ Balance daily activities in providing patient care while allowing time for improvements
- ✦ Believe that change can be for the better
- ✦ Know, understand, teach, and apply Lean tools
- ✦ Energize employees through active participation in a Kaizen Event
- ✦ Develop quick adapters of change to further accelerate improvement projects
- ✦ Use daily measurements to monitor performance
- ✦ Capture organizational process knowledge through work standardization

Title Position - staff or process worker (typically the person that has the closest contact with the patient) (not all ancillary employees have direct contact with the patient, but do provide support) RNs (non-management), Technicians, Aides, Administration Support, Clerks, etc.

Required Level of Support

✦ Contribute ideas that will improve the overall patient care experience and quality of care, as well as those ancillary (administrative) services
✦ Support peers when change is difficult for them
✦ Participate in team meetings
✦ Adhere to new standards that have been created

These are just a few overall activities for each group. In summary, top management must provide the overall vision and direction for the organization while Lean (improvement) ideas typically should come from the process workers. Managers must provide that bridge to link the two, as well as contribute their ideas.

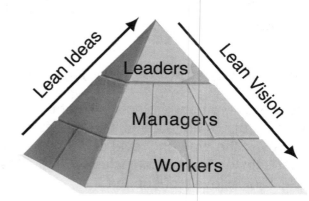

The stakeholder, the employee that is working the process and thinking "What's In It For Me?", must be convinced that Lean, and the subsequent change that the process or area will require, is good for them. This is just as important as management commitment. The Balanced Scorecard and its roll-out of a departmental measurement system (i.e., the Goal Card) will assist organizations in providing communication between top management, middle level managers, and the process worker.

The Balanced Scorecard

The Balanced Scorecard *(or sometimes referred to as a Balanced Score Sheet, Quality Dashboard, etc.) enables an organization to measure itself at every level against a corporate vision and/or industry benchmark and is linked to the strategic plan.* An industry benchmark is a peer or competitor standard by which one can be judged. The Balanced Scorecard is an evaluation of the current state of non-financial - and at times - financial measurements of an organization. Just as a patient has vitals signs of blood pressure, respiratory rate, etc., so too must hospitals monitor their "vital" signs of (Door to Discharge, Door to Inpatient Bed, Patient/Staff Satisfaction, Surgical On-Time Starts, Patient Throughput, Total Patient Days, Case Mix Adjusted Length of Stay, Growth, etc.). In Lean, it is critical to have an effective system of measurements to guide the continuous improvement initiatives. The Balanced Scorecard is a tool to document these measurements associated with those specific categories and thereby identify negative trends in time to take corrective action prior to a crisis situation. The categories and measurements from the Balanced Scorecard typically require further stratification to be translated into departmental/team performance measures.

Note: Balanced Scorecards can be developed for an entire healthcare system or for an individual hospital. Typically, System Scorecards will drive the individual hospital's Scorecard to more specific areas and departments. Hoshin kanri is a method devised to capture and cement strategic goals, as well as flashes of insight about the future, as well as develop the means to bring these into reality.

Purpose of the Balanced Scorecard

The Balanced Scorecard is a visual sheet displaying up-to-date performance measurement data of an organization on a one page (8.5" x 11.0") document. Performance measurements (or also knows as Key Performance Indicators or KPIs) are agreed upon numbers by an organization that will reflect how well the organization is meeting its overall goals. KPIs are typically long-term considerations for an organization. They have the following purpose:

- ✦ Focus on measurements and what is important to the organization
- ✦ Communicate organizational intent
- ✦ Involve everyone in improvement (directly or indirectly)
- ✦ Balance operational performance measures so organizational growth can occur
- ✦ Support the good of the organization over the particular interests of specific functions
- ✦ Create a binding purpose
- ✦ Drive continuous improvement initiatives

A unique feature of the Balanced Scorecard is that management (at the System level or at the hospital level) will have one sheet to monitor performance for the entire organization. This score sheet should have the following data:

- ✦ Key Performance Indicator, by category
- ✦ Champion or manager responsible
- ✦ Previous one or two year's average score (if available by quarter)
- ✦ Industry benchmarks
- ✦ Monthly scores (actual and target)
- ✦ Year-to-date (average)
- ✦ Target (monthly)

The Scorecard enables a management team to meet on a regular basis, at least monthly, and review their performance for the entire organization. If measures are within the "target" range, there may be opportunities to share how/why everything is on target. Resources typically will be committed only when a measurement is out of the target range or a negative trend is occurring for two consecutive months.

Color codes (or shading) of the measurements on the Balanced Scorecard are used to identify areas of concern. For example:

Red: indication that the measurement is below a certain percentage of the benchmark number (e.g., more than 10%) and immediate action is required
Yellow: indication that the measurement is within a certain percentage of the benchmark number (e.g., less than 10%) or the last two months have demonstrated a negative trend and is an indication for concern
Green: indication that the measurement is acceptable to the organization and best practices should be shared with other facilities within the System

The "balanced" part of the Balanced Scorecard represents the notion that measurements should be focusing on all aspects of an organization, not just one. It takes a balanced view of internal and external measures to give the entire picture of an organization.

The Balanced Scorecard usually offers five perspectives:

1. Financial measures (satisfying the shareholders)
2. Internal processes (key internal processes - quality and efficiencies)
3. Patient and staff needs and expectations (satisfying the customer)
4. Human Relations (including safety and ergonomics)
5. Growth and profitability

A Balanced Scorecard system avoids measures that make one function look good at the expense of another. One of the best reasons for measuring something is because of the following sayings "what gets measured gets done" or "you measure what you treasure." Just playing golf without keeping score may be fun, but if someone desires to improve their game, then keeping score is important. The same holds true for measurements within an organization, in that, these "scores" must be kept to assist the facility into overall improvements.

Why Balanced Scorecards are Important

Systems lacking Balanced Scorecards often experience large performance gaps between their strategic objectives and actual execution: the strategic direction has been determined, but the organization is not heading that way and efficiency is probably not optimal.

As strategic objectives are deployed into an organization, more specific measurements (daily or process level) must be created (and measured) that will connect the departments and continuous improvements teams to these overall objectives. This will create the alignment necessary for any hospital to fully engage the improvement process.

The Balanced Scorecard is:

✦ Linked/aligned to the strategic plan
✦ A structured measurement process
✦ Easy to understand
✦ Used at all levels
✦ Standard measurements
✦ Measurements that can be managed by good data collection
✦ A living document that evolves as the organization moves along its continuous improvement journey

Deploying a Balanced Scorecard will assist managers in creating a structure for measurement and feedback and thus be used to drive departmental measurements. The departmental measurements also need to be tracked (measured and subsequently improved upon).

How to Implement Balanced Scorecards

Implementing Balanced Scorecards is an ongoing process, not a one-time event. When performed well, the Balanced Scorecard system combines thoughtful management vision with careful employee fact-finding. The result is a management system based on performance measures that will guide the organization toward its intended destination.

The steps in implementing Balanced Scorecards are:

1. Identify the core management team
2. Understand and refine the organizational strategy
3. Determine the levels for measurement
4. Identify goals (targets) for each measure
5. Create the Balanced Scorecard
6. Build the Departmental/Team Goal Card
7. Monitor the Balanced Scorecard

Each of these steps will be discussed in detail.

Step 1: Identify the core management team

The core management team is the group of senior executives of the organization and other key leaders who will launch and oversee the Balanced Scorecard system. The core management team has members with authority and responsibility for running the organization, including daily operations.

One problem in conventional organizations is that the wrong people - people without proper knowledge or understanding of the processes being evaluated - make the important decisions. The Balanced Scorecard solves this problem by including people at all levels of the organization to obtain a clear picture of what is currently happening. The main body of this group may include the following people:

+ The Chief Executive Officer (C.E.O.) of the facility (or System)
+ The Chief Medical Officer (CMO)
+ The Vice Presidents (VPs)
+ The Chief Financial Officer (CFO)
+ The Chief Nursing Officer (CNO)
+ The Directors and/or Managers of the departments
+ Representatives (front-line) employees from various functional areas

Step 2: Understand and refine the organizational strategy

The second step in implementing a Balanced Scorecard is to review the organizational (or corporate) strategy - and perhaps refine it. If a growth strategy has not been articulated, or if it needs to be updated, this is the time to do so before any measurements are tied to it.

Some common measurements may include areas such as:

- ✦ Patient/family satisfaction
- ✦ Financial (business) growth
- ✦ Internal process improvement - related to quality, core measures, regulatory compliance, etc.
- ✦ Human Relations (or staff satisfaction)
- ✦ Profitability
- ✦ Emergency Services
- ✦ Surgical Services
- ✦ Morbidity/Mortality Rates

A well-written strategy opens the door to determining performance measures. These categories will coincide with similar type measurement categories identified in Step 3.

Step 3: Determine the levels for measurement

The Balanced Scorecard system works best when top-level strategic measures are translated to staff-line performance measures. This can be done with three levels of measurement: Hospital (or System) (Level I), departmental (Level II), and operational (Level III) type measurements.

Level I measurements are derived from the strategic direction of the organization. They are defined by top level management (CEO, CMO, COO, CFO, Chief Nursing Officer, VPs, etc.). **If there is a System level of metrics, the Level I metrics may be identical to the facility-specific targets; or each facility may create its own version of metrics per standardized criteria as appropriate for unique patient types, services, and geographic locations.** These measurements should be reviewed at least monthly, but ideally weekly. If weekly meetings are not feasible then a "flash report" for patient volumes, revenue, etc. should be distributed weekly; but cycle times and most other metrics then are calculated and reviewed monthly. *A flash report is the weekly communication of the Balanced Scorecard's critical measurements to management allowing them to keep abreast of the trends, as well as call attention to any significant changes that may require immediate action.*

Level II, or the departmental measurements, are derived from Level I. Some of these may be identical or slightly more detailed than those from Level I. These are departmentally driven and will determine where resources need to be focused for improvement at the operational level. Level II value stream maps usually prove most useful in determining Kaizen projects or focused areas for improvement.

Do not concern yourself so much as which is Level I and Level II. The important aspect of these two level measures is to guide the organization to commit the appropriate resources in the needed areas that require the most attention for improvement. By using Balanced Scorecards, leadership can identify trends early and assign appropriate resources to eliminate or prevent a trend from turning negative. Therefore, the more attuned the measurements are to the day-to-day operations, the sooner appropriate actions can be taken. A main factor for Lean success is to establish a system to prevent negative trends from occurring.

Here is an example how Level I and Level II measurements can work.

Level I for System (or hospital): A healthcare system has multiple facilities that report their overall numbers in common categories, such as: Financial (such as Total admits, Total Outpt Visits, Cost per Case, Cost per Visit, Operating Margin, Net Revenue, Case Mix Index); Quality (such as Methicillin-resistant Staphylococcus aureus (MRSA) patients, adverse effects, falls, medication errors, decubitus, post-surgical infection rate, number of codes); Service (such as cycle times, registration errors, inappropriate patient transfers, ED patients "Left Without Being Seen" or left "Against Medical Advice"); and Satisfaction (for Customers, Staff, and Physicians); usually there are five to seven overall categories defined for this level.

Level II: Each department's staff must consider the Level I Balanced Scorecard when developing their departmental measurements. This "departmental scorecard" can be identical to the Level I main categories with sub-categories; or, more likely, will include some department-specific items. For example, in the ED, the following measurements may be identified as: Door-to-Doc (from when the patient arrives to the ED to when they are first seen by the doctor), Doc-to-Dispo (from when the patient is first seen by the doctor to when their disposition has been determined), and Dispo-to-Depart (from when the disposition has been determined until treatment has been completed in the ED or the patient is admitted for continued care) cycle times, ED Volume, ED Admits, Return visits for same complaint, etc. Operating Room Level II measurements may include the following: on-time first case starts, on-time subsequent case starts, close-to-cut for room turnover, on-time case completions, overtime for anesthesia staff, overtime for nurse staff, etc.

Additional measures for either Level I or Level II are:

Financial: Overall net revenue growth, cost of care experience (across continuum), operating margin, cost per case for inpatients, revenue per case, cost per encounter for outpatients, case mix index, % paid overtime, Length of Stay, uncompensated care, bad debt, reimbursement %, Medicare %
Quality: % Adherence to practice guidelines (or clinical bundles), use of dangerous abbreviations, medication errors
Service: Appointment timeliness, missed appointments, on-time appointments for outpatient visits, community sponsored activities per quarter
Customer Satisfaction: Patient satisfaction, patient satisfaction mean score, complaints
Associate Satisfaction: Work Environment Survey, WES mean score, voluntary turnover, vacancy rate, physician satisfaction, physician satisfaction mean score
Leadership Development: Internal promotion rate, leadership class attendance, 360 survey mean score, % top performance evaluation score, employee involvement in Lean events, percentage of staff trained in Lean healthcare

To drill down even further, Level III or operational measurements can become a team's measure for a Lean project, with specifically defined targets.

Examples for Surgical Services

Financial: Cost per case (total, labor, supplies/equipment), revenue per case, revenue per physician, overtime by job title, contribution margin, instrument loss rate
Quality: Surgical site verification/time outs, post-surgical infection rates, surgical complications, % unplanned post-surgical admissions, adverse event log
Service: First case on-time starts, case turn-around time, ED-to-OR time for surgical consult cases, avg time to board, % boarding discrepancies, % emergency boarding requests
Customer Satisfaction: Same as Level II, at dept. level
Associate Satisfaction: Same as Level II, at dept. level
Leadership: Same as Level II, at dept. level

Examples for ED:

Financial: Cost per case, revenue per case, overtime by job title, physician billables, time to close chart, rate of admission, % payment of deductibles/copays on site
Quality: Abandoned rate (seen by doctor, left before being discharged), ED referrals to network physicians, ED repeat visits for same complaint
Service: Left Without Being Seen, avg time Door-to-Doc, avg time Doc-to-Dispo, avg time Dispo-to-Depart, avg time Dispo-to-Admit
Customer Satisfaction: Same as Level II, at dept. level
Associate Satisfaction: Same as Level II, at dept. level
Leadership: Same as Level II, at dept. level

Examples for Billing and Coding:

Financial: Avg bill per case by DRG (Diagnosis-Related Group), avg time to code chart, potential lost revenue (incorrect/incomplete documentation), cash balances, charges, accounts receivable, collection ratios
Quality: Rejection rate by reason, compliance, % reimbursement, clean claim rate
Service: Avg time to code chart
Customer Satisfaction: Same as Level II, at dept. level
Associate Satisfaction: Same as Level II, at dept. level
Leadership: Same as Level II, at dept. level

Examples for Facility Management:

Financial: Cost per square foot (labor and other), utility costs, facility costs as a percent of operating cost
Quality: Problem log, equipment failure reports, improper processing reports, facility condition index
Service: Avg time to respond to requests, avg time to request completion, complaints, work orders overdue, inventory levels for specific items
Customer Satisfaction: Same as Level II, at dept. level
Associate Satisfaction: Same as Level II, at dept. level
Leadership: Same as Level II, at dept. level

The System (or Corporate) level measures are usually characterized as "output" measures. For example, a financial output measure might be "Growth". A quality output measure might be "On-Time Starts for OR."

All organizations are unique and should design the appropriate measurement levels to serve their needs. If three levels are not enough - add one. If three levels are too many - take one away.

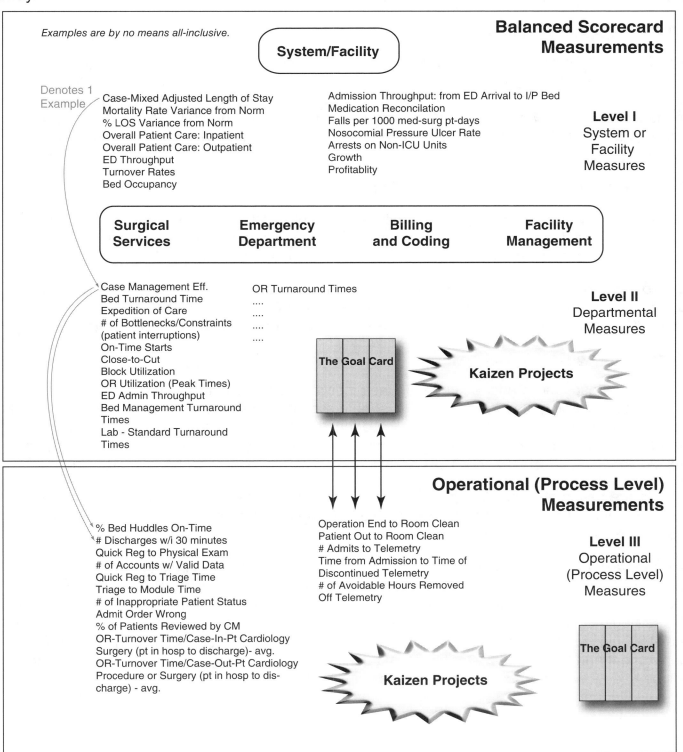

Step 4: Identify goals (targets) for each measure

It should be emphasized that by setting a goal and measure for an organization, it also is setting a performance standard. The Balanced Scorecard provides a system to measure and monitor that performance - and to take action. After having established a corporate direction by articulating a strategy and subsequent goals, and then making that direction operational through defining the measurements, it is time to create the Balanced Scorecard.

Step 5: Create the Balanced Scorecard

The Balanced Scorecard is the primary tool used by the core management team. It is one sheet that monitors the performance of the organization. It will be used to review the overall performance of the organization on a regular basis, often weekly. It should be shared with department managers and improvement team leaders (i.e, the departmental heads). There are many vendor-type Scorecards available for purchase, however, an Excel spreadsheet can be just as effective.

Step 6: Build the Departmental/Team Goal Card

Once an organization or facility has established the high level goals, it is then time to translate those goals into departmental goals that the staff can then impact through continuous improvement efforts. This can be accomplished through the active deployment of Goal Cards.

Do not underestimate the importance of creating this Goal Card or something similar. If Level I and II measures, or goals cannot be translated into operational process level or Level III measurements, then the best Lean or Six Sigma projects will be compromised.

Understanding Goal Cards

People feel responsible and take pride in their individual work when they have control over the processes governing their jobs. There must be a system in place to assure that the process that the employees are working on is what is important to the organization in terms of profitability and quality of care. This alignment, and the setting of personal and team goals, is the first step in developing a high-performance, TEI type workforce - a culture of continuous improvement.

People are best motivated by setting their own goals as long as there is some direction from management. The Goal Card involves everyone in the organization in aligning the Balanced Scorecard measurements into daily, operational measures for improvements.

*A **Goal Card** is a tool for individuals, teams, and departments that outlines the specific actions that will contribute to continuous improvement initiatives derived from the Balanced Scorecard (Level I and II measures) over a particular time period, usually one year.* The Goal Card aligns the strategic direction of the hospital or System to operations. It allows employees to embrace the strategic direction of the organization by creating a visual contract defining the goals of a department and the individual (or team) that contributes to it. Many times a value stream map will be used to visually assist in making this alignment.

Strategic planning sessions are typically held at the beginning of the year to determine the Balanced Scorecard data for Level I and Level II measures. Once this is completed, Goal Cards should be printed and distributed to the departmental managers/supervisors. The departmental managers and supervisors should then meet with their respective staff to determine their goals, sign the Goal Card, and then determine appropriate resources to meet those goals. This typically will require one or more Kaizen Events to be scheduled.

The Goal Card should be posted in a common area. Multiple Goal Cards can be used within a large department to further segment the various functions. Also, smaller independent facilities, with less than 100 employees, can have each staff member fill out a Goal Card.

A typical Goal Card measures 8" x 11" and is made of card stock. It is folded into three sections, allowing for six panels on which to display information as shown in the illustration below.

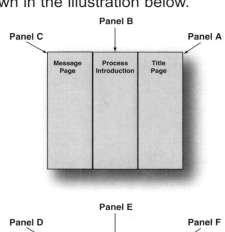

Management prepares the three exterior panels. Panel A is the front of the card when folded and acts as the title page. Panel B introduces the process of the Goal Card and is usually written by the senior manager in the organization. Panel C is the back page and will contain references to the strategic plan and is written by the President, CEO, and/or COO of the organization.

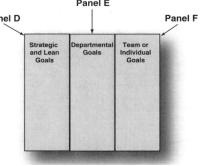

Departmental team members will gain a consensus and prepare the three interior panels. Panel D will contain the facilities' or Systems' strategy and goals (Level I). Panel E will convey the Lean-Sigma goals, the business unit goals (Level II). Panel F will be the place where each team or individual can list their team goals (Level III measurements/goals).

Note: The purpose of a Goal Card is to ensure improvement efforts are a continued focus and not just when a trend turns negative or a problem arises. The Value Stream Management methodology can be used in both circumstances.

Process improvements and effective teaming do not occur by accident. Success comes from a constancy of purpose towards improving services. Goal Cards provide for clear communication of the strategy and goals for the organization and department. It also signifies how everyone must work together to achieve those goals. When everyone understands the process and is engaged, the likelihood for success is that much greater. By using the Goal Card, managers can effectively motivate and monitor the staff through relevant performance measurements as tied to the Goal Card.

The most important aspect of the Goal Card is to align the upper level measurements (Level I) to specific departmental/team and/or individual measurements (Level II and/or Operational) so resources can be properly allocated. The following illustration is used to clarify the Goal Card and the various levels of measurement.

System Strategic Goals	Hospital Strategic Goals	Departmental Goals
Level I Measurements	Level I Measurements (with possible modifications)	Level II Measurements (also may include some Level III)

The following is the Goal Card for Oakview Hospital's ED.

Message from the President
Oak Valley Health System

Oak Valley Health System will achieve success when we are able to provide efficient, clinically-effective care in a way that meets – and exceeds - our patients' needs. Our strategic plan is based on the need to maintain an operating margin that will sustain our capital investment plan, as well as our employee investment plan – our ability to pay well, provide great benefits, and develop and retain our talented employees.

Clinical quality care will be the foundation of our success, as we provide the most effective care for our patients in the most appropriate in-patient or ambulatory settings.

Lastly, we will build on our reputation for clinical excellence, patient satisfaction, and process efficiency, for improved excellence within our regional area.

Please join us on this journey to excellence!

Bruce Stubbs, MD
President & CEO, Oak Vally Health System
Janice Rathborne, MSN
Vice President, Patient Services
Dave Hendrix, MBA
Chief Financial Officer
Carrie Millhouse
Vice President, Human Resources
George Thomas, MD
Chief Medical Officer
Vanessa Williams, PhD
Director of Quality Improvement

Message from the President
Oakview Hospital

We look forward to the next year with excitement on the following initiatives:

- the acquisition of St. Mary Health Alliance
- the continued roll-out of EMR/EMS to the physician groups in our area
- the opening of the new birthing center
- the acquisition of a new CyberKnife
- Integration of a new Radiology group

These, and other projects, only can happen with the full cooperation of our entire healthcare team of physicians, nurses, aides, technicians, as well as administrative and auxillary staff. It is with this group at Oakview that will allow us to continue to provide the quality care for the patients in the community we serve.

We are on our third year of focused continuous improvement program of Operational Excellence. We are totally committed to its success. It is through the use of this Goal Card that has assisted us to remain competitive and be in a position of continued growth. Much of this can only occur if the organization is in total alignment.

Your past support in meeting the goals you set forth in the Goal Card is appreciated and I know you will continue that type of support in the coming year.

Sincerely,
John Abrahms, MD
President & CEO, Oakview Hospital

Oak Valley Health System

The Oakview Hospital Goal Card
"the hospital in the woods"

"The Oak Valley Health System is committed to providing personal and high quality state of the art care with compassion and community focus."

✚ Oak Vally Health System Strategic Goals

The following goals represent the direction of OVHS. We need to focus our efforts in these areas to provide the infrastructure required to serve our patients and community in the short and long term.

Finance Goals
Operating Margin %:	5.0
Adj Cost per Equiv Admit	7500

Quality
Bundles, % of 100%	100
Mortality Rate, Var from Norm	< -1.0
Falls per 100 Pt Days	< 2.5

Service (Cycle Time)
ED % of Admitted Pts Meeting Target (4.5 hrs)	85
ED LOS for Admit Patients (hrs)	4.5
OR % On-time Case Starts	85
LOS, Med-Surg (Days)	3.5

Satisfaction
Inpt Satisfaction	4.0
ED Satisfaction	4.0
OR Satisfaction	4.0
Physician Satisfaction (quarterly)	4.0
Employee Satisfaction (quarterly)	4.0

✚ Oakview Hospital Strategic Goals

In support of the strategic goals of OVHS, we will continue to focus our efforts to improve our goals as they are aligned with the system goals.

Finance Goals
Operating Margin %:	4.0
Adj Cost per Equiv Admit	7500

Quality
Bundles, % of 100%	100
Mortality Rate, Var from Norm	< -1.0
Falls per 100 Pt Days	< 2.5

Service (Cycle Time)
ED % of Admitted Pts Meeting Target (4.5 hrs)	85
OR % On-time Case Starts	85
LOS, Med-Surg (Days)	3.5

Satisfaction
Inpt Satisfaction	4.0
ED Satisfaction	4.0
OR Satisfaction	4.0
Physician Satisfaction (quarterly)	4.0
Employee Satisfaction (quarterly)	4.0

✚ ED Goal Card

Value Statement

"The process for admitting a patient has two goals: efficiency in the process and the patient in the right bed the first time. We need to move our admitted patients as quickly as possible to a more clincially appropriate care setting, one that meets the needs of the patients and their families in a less crisis-driven environment."

Team/Department/Individual Goals:

ED Adm Pts LOS <= 4.5 hrs, improve from 6 hrs (25%)
Dispo-to-Admit Cycle Time <= 1.5 hrs, improve by 50%
ED Patient Satisifaction, improve by 50%
Bed/Clothing check >= 95% complete, improve by 50%
Admit Order to Bed Assigned <= 30 min, improve by 50%
Bed Assigned to Pt in Bed <= 30 min, improve by 50%

Signatures:

Dave Beck	Judy Carne
Anne Calley	Mary Beth Ginsey
Bill Hagan	Tonya Burns
Sue Burns	Mary Marton-Hayes
Margaret Rodriguez	Sarah Schultz
Ben Kingsley, MD	Lisa Helms
Rodney Backus, MD	Mary Potts-Genfrey, MD
Kathy Janeway	

The ED staff realized that if the ED Adm Pts LOS and Dispo-to-Admit cycle times were reduced, it would have a positive impact on the Balanced Scorecard measurement of ED % of Admit Pts Meeting Target of 4.5 Hours (page 73).

The Financial goals for operating margin % may not the same for the System as it is for the hospital. Since each facility or hospital in a System may have different core competencies, markets, and/or levels of service, they likely well have different goals to meet.

Step 7: Monitor the Balanced Scorecard

Monitoring Balanced Scorecards must be systematic and organized. It requires the following:

- ✦ Regular meetings by the core management team
- ✦ Cross-functional review teams on the departmental level
- ✦ Regular reviews on the operational level
- ✦ A meeting schedule (when meetings will occur)
- ✦ A standard review agenda (how review will proceed)
- ✦ A standardized reaction plan for when targets are not being met

For example, one organization created the following structure:

1. The core management team met every Tuesday morning from 9:00 a.m. to 9:30 a.m. to review goals and corporate measures, only spending time on outstanding action items and measures. Acknowledgement and progress was reported for those measurements that were not meeting the target.
2. Departmental teams met on the first Wednesday of every month for ½ hour. They also dealt with outstanding action items and measures that did not meet standard targets. In addition, they addressed issues given to them by the core management team. However, no actual problem solving was performed in that meeting. Additional improvement teams were selected by this group to address any problems and negative trends as well as report any progress made toward improving those trends. Team Leaders for the continuous improvement or Lean project would give a brief presentation (less than 5 minutes) at these meetings throughout the scope of any project.
3. Operational or unit teams met daily for 15 minutes at the end of their shift. This was not only to monitor and review daily performance and capture information, but also to identify problems that required attention as well as announce any team improvement activities forthcoming.

Monitoring and visually reporting progress indicated by the Balanced Scorecard and the Goal Card creates a culture of sharing, teamwork, recognition, and mutual responsibility.

Checklist for Creation of a Balanced Scorecard

1. Identify the "balanced" categories that you will use (many if not all of these should be used).
___ Financial	___ Productivity
___ Patient Satisfaction	___ Supplier Quality
___ Quality	___ Satisfaction (Patient, Staff)
___ Growth/Innovation	___ Other: _____

2. Choose the appropriate key performance indicators (metrics) for each category.

3. Choose a champion or process owner for each Key Performance Indicator.

4. Gather baseline data from the past one to two years (or what is appropriate) for each performance indicator. Determine on how often you will monitor and review data (weekly, monthly, etc.).

5. Identify a target measure (goal) for the category.

6. Identify the "best measure" for your industry (if available).

7. Create a Balanced Scorecard and align the Balanced Scorecard to operational improvements through the use of a Goal Card.

Review Points Regarding Balanced Scorecards and Goal Cards

✦ *Select important measures.* It is meaningless to create a feedback system that does not contribute to the growth of the organization and/or to the departmental/team goals. Measures must contribute to the bottom line and have meaning to a person's daily work. If these measurements do not provide that meaning, then they will not affect performance.

✦ *Involve individuals in building the Goal Cards.* If measures are forced on people, they are less likely to improve performance due to a lack of understanding and buy-in. Managers often choose the wrong measures because they do not have all of the facts needed to make good choices and may not have solicited input from their employees. Also, if workers choose measures without management input then there may not be the organizational alignment necessary for supporting the overall direction of the organization. The way to get the "best" of both worlds is to employ a technique called "catchball". Catchball is a process in which ideas are "tossed" back and forth between the two groups until a consensus is reached.

✦ *Track desirable behavior.* Traditionally people do not share information unless there is a problem. Therefore, feedback is usually negative. But work can be fun and motivating when the numbers are stated positively. For example, rather than "OR Surgical downtime," track "OR Surgical Uptime." Instead of measuring "absenteeism," the measure should be "attendance." For "defects or mistakes" perhaps the measure should be "percent perfect."

✦ *Share organization information - A shift in philosophy.* Regardless of the form that the Scorecard and Goal Card takes, the visual communication of performance is essential. This is often a major change for organizations who have kept organization statistics "secret" from employees. However, if employees are expected to take responsibility for their actions, then the goals of the organization must be transparent to everyone.

✦ *Make scores visual.* The Balanced Scorecard, as well as the Goal Card, should be made visible and posted in a common area within the department. They can also be displayed on the intranet, or with some IT support, within a key click away. All types of measurements displayed should be kept up-to-date.

✦ *Ensure ownership.* Each category within the Balanced Scorecard should have a process owner. Process owners should work with the various departmental managers to ensure their departmental goals (i.e., Goal Cards) are in alignment.

✦ *Determine correct number of categories and measures.* It is difficult to put an exact number for the number of categories that should be contained in a Balanced Scorecard. Usually it is between 6 and 10. Each category should have 3-5 (or so) measurements associated with it. (Goal Cards usually contain 3-5 type departmental measurements.)

Finally, to get started on creating/updating a Balanced Scorecard and its supporting Goal Card, consider the following:

- ✦ Create a core management team
- ✦ Review the Organizational Strategy and ensure that it has a Lean, Lean-Sigma, or continuous improvement component
- ✦ Ensure that the strategy contains performance goals
- ✦ Determine the levels of measurement for the departments and operational units that will be measured (in essence, create an organizational structure for measurement)
- ✦ Identify corporate measures
- ✦ Create the Balanced Scorecard and share it with all departments and units
- ✦ Ensure each department creates their Goal Card based on the Balanced Scorecard (corporate should have these printed up ahead of time with appropriate logos, etc.)
- ✦ Determine meeting schedules for every department to work on their Goal Cards improvement activities
- ✦ Monitor Balanced Scorecards to a standardized schedule to guide departmental goals

Keep in mind that all types of measurements should be carefully reviewed on a periodic basis. When business conditions change, ensure the appropriate measurement category is updated. (For example, if a hospital is acquired as part of the system, ensure that their data is included as soon as possible.)

The following is the Balanced Scorecard for Oakview Hospital. It is typical of many Balanced Scorecards being comprised of the four main categories of Finance, Quality, Service, and Satisfaction.

Oakview Hospital Balanced Scorecard

Category	System - Level I				Hospital/Facility - Level I								
	Owner	Target	FYTD	Last Month	Owner	Target	FYTD	Last Month	Feb	Jan	Dec	Nov	Oct
Finance	**R.D.**				**R.R.**								
Operating Margin %	J.D.	**5.0**	4.2	**3.8**	A.C.	**4.0**	3.2	3.1	3.8	3.2	3.3	3.7	3.5
Adj Cost per Equivalent Admission	S.H.	**7500**	8575	9010	D.R.	**7500**	7025	6995	7525	7025	6995	7555	7025
Quality	**M.H.**				**D.E.**								
Bundles, % at 100%	M.R.	**100**	88	85	A.G.	**100**	88	86	96	94	87	92	88
Mortality Rate, Var from Norm	H.H.	**< -1.0**	-.66	-.77	I.R.	**< -1.0**	-.75	-.80	-9.0	-.75	-.80	-9.0	-.75
Falls/1000 pt days	R.W.	**<2.5**	2.4	2.3	D.T.	**<2.5**	2.3	2.0	2.4	2.3	2.0	2.2	2.3
Service (Cycle Time)	**C.T.**				**H.A.**								
ED % of Admitted Pts Meeting Target of 4.5 Hours	**T.O.**	**85**	**72**	**61**	**T.J.**	**85**	**76**	**76**	**70**	**61**	**58**	**66**	**65**
OR % On-time Case Starts	R.W.	**85**	83	81	S.H.	**85**	87	90	85	87	90	85	87
LOS, Med-Surg (Days)	H.D.	**3.5**	3.7	4.2	S.E.	**3.5**	3.4	3.6	3.5	3.4	3.6	3.5	3.4
ED LOS for Admitted Patients (Hours)	**J.T.**	**4.5**	**6.0**	**5.8**	**M.R.**	**4.5**	**5.2**	**5.8**	**6.0**	**6.0**	**6.4**	**5.9**	**6.2**
Satisfaction	**T.C.**				**M.G.**								
Inpt Satisfaction	L.M.	**4.0**	3.7	3.4	T.H.	**4.0**	3.9	3.7	3.8	3.9	3.7	3.9	3.9
ED Satisfaction	**A.F.**	**4.0**	**2.8**	**2.7**	**K.T.**	**4.0**	**2.4**	**2.3**	**2.4**	**2.3**	**2.3**	**2.1**	**3.2**
OR Satisfaction	Y.C.	**4.0**	3.9	3.9	Y.Y.	**4.0**	3.9	3.8	4.0	3.9	3.9	4.0	3.9
Physician Satisfaction (quarterly)	B.W.	**4.0**	3.8	3.9	D.Y.	**4.0**	3.7	3.6	4.0	3.7	3.6	4.0	3.7
Employee Satisfaction (quarterly)	S.R.	**4.0**	3.8	3.7	J.R.	**4.0**	3.5	3.2	3.4	3.3	3.3	3.5	3.4

Legend

 Meeting target, (within 10% of target)

Not meeting target, (>10% off target)

Through recent Press Ganey patient and employee satisfaction surveys, as well as their Balanced Scorecard review, there were a number of areas identified as requiring immediate attention from the executive leadership team of the hospital, some of which are as follows:

1) **ED% of Admitting Patients Meeting Target of 4.5 Hours** had not been met for the past 6 months. Also, the **ED LOS, Admitted Patients (Hours)**, which is linked to the **ED % of Admitting Patients Meeting Target of 4.5 Hours**, has not been met during the same period of time.
2) **ED (Patient) Satisfaction** had not met the organizational goal for the past 6 months.
3) **Employee Satisfaction** has been low, which was common throughout the hospital.
4) **Operating Margin %**, as well as **Bundles, % at 100%**, were also concerns and required plans to address the issue.

Dr. Abrahms, Ms. Hart, Ms. Dean, and Ms. Richards all believed that if Lean were implemented in a systematic method and *with the right support*, Lean improvements (1 - 4 from above) would lead to a competitive edge in the market. Lean would also improve their productivity and profitability, as well as patient care and safety. They also agreed that the ED would be a good place to begin to incorporate Lean in their Operational Excellence program.

Incorporating Lean within their current program, they expected the following outcomes:

✦ Overall reduction in operating cost (reduction of waste)
✦ Improved staff utilization
✦ Improved patient care and safety
✦ Improved staff satisfaction
✦ Improved scores on their patient satisfaction survey
✦ Improved Length of Stay (by getting patients Into their units sooner will get them onto their care pathway sooner)

The Balanced Scorecard is the starting point for Value Stream Management for the Assess phase. It is an evaluation of the current "state of facility health" and will be the driver for all Lean projects.

Project Prioritization Worksheet

As stated previously, the Balanced Scorecard should identify major areas (i.e., value streams) where improvement efforts will need to be focused. However, there may be times where the management group (or continuous improvement group) will require additional guidelines in selecting the appropriate project (or further refine specific high level value stream areas, i.e., Level I and Level II measurements) to obtain the most "bang for the buck " in determining resource allocation. In these cases it would be beneficial to create a Project Prioritization Worksheet. *The **Project Prioritization Worksheet** is a listing of the main areas of concern relative to the significant factors that are important to the organization.*

The following steps should be used as a guide when creating and using a Project Prioritization Worksheet:

1. Identify area(s) throughout the organization that need improvement (from the Balanced Scorecard (Level I or II, Voice of the Customer surveys, value streams, etc.). **Voice of the Customer** *is a process used to capture (via direct discussions, interviews, surveys, focus groups, observation, reports, logs, etc.) customer (internal or external) requirements and then providing the customers with the best in-class service.*

2. List the important factors that should be considered for overall organization improvement.

3. Place a checkmark in the appropriate categories.

4. Gain a consensus on completing the worksheet.

5. Total the points for each area/process.

6. Determine the area/process with the highest total number of points.

7. Review the list with the team and use this as a basis for project selection, or use this to create a new value stream map.

The Project Prioritization Worksheet is a good tool to use to align (and assist) the department or group on the focus of an improvement project, and most importantly, to ensure all departments will be represented on the improvement team. Distribute the completed worksheet(s) to the appropriate departments/areas that were listed on the worksheet to begin communications. You cannot communicate too often to an area, department, or process worker of what is to come!

Ms. Hart and Ms. Dean were to be the team co-champions, with Ms. Richards as the team facilitator. The three of them met to further explore the main processes/departments and their impact on key factors to ensure the correct team members were to be assigned. The information also assisted in creating an initial Team Charter. They wanted to provide as much information on the importance of this project when meeting with their team for the first time.

The following is their Project Prioritization Worksheet.

Project Prioritization Worksheet

Purpose: To assist in prioritizing the main projects/areas that require Lean tools and practices.

Who should fill it out: This worksheet can be filled out from either the top management team (or members from it) or compiled from the results of a survey.

Directions: The best way to use this tool is to follow these steps:
1. List all Areas/Processes that require immediate improvement (1).
2. Place a checkmark in each Area/Process applicable to the category (2) - (10). The Areas/Processes may have multiple selections. Select the top three to five.
3. Tally the points for each row (11). Use the data to select core team members and create the Team Charter.

*Do not attempt to weight categories as that may cause more confusion than it is worth. Gain a consensus on each category.

(1) Areas/Processes	Categories									(11) Total Points
	(2) Impacts Customer or Patient	(3) Affects Safety	(4) High Volume	(5) Over Budget	(6) Demand Exceeds Capacity	(7) Customer or Patient Dissatisfier	(8) Supplier Dissatisfier	(9) Staff Dissatisfier	(10) Problematic Never Goes Right	
Pt Arrival	✔	✔			✔	✔		✔		5
Registration								✔		1
Triage				✔	✔	✔		✔		4
Bed Assign								✔	✔	2
Ns Assess		✔		✔		✔				3
Phys Assess	✔	✔			✔					3
Lab		✔				✔		✔	✔	4
Radiology		✔				✔		✔	✔	4
Other Anc						✔		✔	✔	3
Pharmacy		✔						✔	✔	3
Disposition	✔	✔	✔		✔	✔	✔			6
Instructions		✔	✔		✔	✔		✔		5
Depart	✔	✔	✔	✔	✔	✔	✔		✔	8

Distribution Report

*The **Distribution Report** is a historical listing on the volume of work or service completed within a specific time period for a department.* The Pivot Table function within Microsoft Excel is a good tool to use to create a Distribution Report. At least 3 months of data would be appropriate. Longer time periods can be used to accommodate known changes (departmental consolidations, seasonable variations, acquisitions, etc.). After the raw data has been collected, a Distribution/Volume Report can be created to further identify specific value streams and assist in the selection of core team members.

Sue, with her background in data collection, created a Distribution/Volume Report listing all the patient services that the hospital offered, and then asking each ancillary department whether they participated in those services. This information would be presented at the first team meeting to convey just how many functions were performed across all services - and would also be used to assist in team selection. The following is a Distribution Report or Volume Report indicating the number of patients seen by the various departments/clinics in Oakview Hospital. This report confirmed that ED had the highest volume of patients per month and would provide a good opportunity to commit the necessary resources for an improvement project.

Distribution/Volume Report

Department Oakview Hospital   **Data Collection Dates** March 1 - 31

Type of Data Collection
✓ Historical (database retrieval)
  Direct Observation (real time)
  Voice of the Customer (survey)

Department (reasons why pts come to the hospital	Pts/month	Registration	OP Scheduling	Transport	Housekeeping	Medical Records
IP visit/surgery	457	X		X	X	X
OP Surgery	140	X	X	X	X	X
OP Laboratory	230	X				X
OP Radiology	160	X	X		X	X
Clinic visit	178	X	X		X	X
ED visit	**2950**	**X**		**X**	**X**	**X**
Outpt Pharmacy visit	124					X
OP Phys/Occ Therapy	85	X	X		X	X
Community classes	425				X	X
Pt visitors - # of visits	1156					

Oakview Hospital's ED, as well as all EDs, have a variable stream of arrivals day and night. Sue continued to analyze ED patient data in 4 hour increments to further understand the ED patient demand as how it is distributed throughout a 24-hour period. The following is the data collected from 15 days in 4 hour blocks of time. This data could have been segmented further into critical patients entering ED, non-critical, or some other category, to further refine the value stream.

Mary, Judy, and Sue decided on the team: the ED nursing manager and process owner, Margaret Rodriquez; ER nurses, Bill Hagan and Anne Calley; ER admin clerk, Sarah Shultz; transporter, John DuBois; IT representative, Randy Simmons; and ER physician, Dr. Ben Kingsley. This would be the initial core team, and if other people were needed, they would be called upon (sometimes referred to as an extended team member).

Distribution Report

Department ED   **Data Collection Dates** March 1 -15

Type of Data Collection
- ✓ Historical (database retrieval)
- Direct Observation (real time)
- Voice of the Customer (survey)

Time Periods	March 1	March 2	March 3	March 4	March 5	March 6	March 7	March 8	March 9	March 10	March 11	March 12	March 13	March 14	March 15	Totals	Patient Volume Average Per 4 Hours
0000 - 0400	4	3	2	5	4	4	4	3	2	4	5	4	5	5	6	60	4
0400 - 0800	7	7	8	12	10	7	9	9	10	12	9	8	8	10	9	135	9
0800 - 1200	14	15	20	15	17	18	16	20	18	17	20	15	14	17	19	255	17
1200 - 1600	18	22	28	27	28	29	30	28	27	26	27	28	30	22	20	390	26
1600 - 2000	40	32	35	32	30	28	26	35	38	31	33	28	30	28	34	480	32
2000 - 0000	14	18	18	16	19	16	14	17	14	17	18	15	18	20	21	255	17
															TOTAL	1575	

Takt Time

A Distribution Report or something similar can be used to determine takt time. *Takt time is a function of time that determines how fast a process must run to meet customer demand.* Takt time only takes a few minutes to calculate, but may take hours to create the Distribution Report. Takt time accomplishes the following:

- ✦ Aligns internal work rate to customer (or patient) demand rate - similar to a metronome keeping pace for someone playing a musical instrument or a drill sergeant calling out his "cadence" to ensure everyone marches in order
- ✦ Focuses awareness on the customer
- ✦ Sets a standard rate for all staff to meet and be measured against

There are three steps in calculating takt time for a value stream.

1. Gather appropriate data on customer demand and determine the volume of work (i.e., information from the Distribution Report).

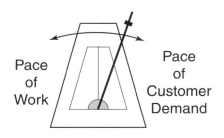

Pace of Work   Pace of Customer Demand

2. Determine total available work time. For example, if Radiology is only open from 0700 to 1900 pm that would be 12 hours. On the other hand, ERs are open 24 hours/day, 7 days a week. If you have varying hours within the value stream, you can do the following:

   a. Create separate takt times for each process or segments of time as categories from the Distribution Report.
   b. Create takt time using the lower number of hours available for each category.

The net available work time is the total available work time minus time for meetings, breaks, and any other non value-added activities and/or any time that the process is not available.

$$\text{Takt time} = \frac{\text{Available daily work time}}{\text{Total daily volume required}} = \frac{\text{Time}}{\text{Volume}} = \frac{T}{V}$$

The overall takt time for Oakview's ED would be:

Time: 1440 minutes (60 minutes x 24 hours)
Volume: 1575 patients in 15 days (60 + 135 + 255 + 390 + 480 + 255)
Volume for 1 day (average): 1575 / 15 = 105 patients per 24 hour period
Takt time: 1440 minutes / 105 patients = 13.7 or approximately 14 minutes

However, we noted that resources for this value stream must be allocated on a 4 hour increment due to the varying demand.

The following are the takt times for Oakview Hospital in 4 hour increments as indicated by the Distribution Report. The team was surprised to see that the takt time varied so much in each block of time. They knew that the ED was busier on the evening shift, but there was clearly a big difference between 0000 to 0400, and 1600 to 2000. "We need to change our staffing levels in ED," said one of the team members. But Sue quickly said, "Don't jump to solutions yet! We have a lot more Lean tools to consider before we make any changes."

Takt Times for ED

Hours	Available Time (minutes) (4 hours x 60 minutes)	Patient Volume (Average per 4 hours)	Takt Time (Time/Volume)
0000 - 0400	240	4	60
0400 - 0800	240	9	27
0800 - 1200	240	17	14
1200 - 1600	240	26	9
1600 - 2000	240	32	8
2000 - 0000	240	17	14

Takt time for customer demand must be balanced with the requirements of the other value stream demands to ensure people, equipment, and resources are scheduled appropriately.

Once takt time has been established, all efforts must be focused on meeting that demand. This is accomplished by the continued application of Lean tools, such as Leveling, that will be discussed in Chapter 4.

Takt time, even though it is a calculation, is not an exact science. The key is to find a reasonable time element to meet your demand. In healthcare, you will have many interruptions that require the services of a department or person; use takt time as a general guide or goal. Do not alienate process workers by using takt time as an edict. Keep the team informed as to the reason why takt time is calculated and then be flexible and reasonable to its application within the project.

Cycle Time

Cycle time is the amount of time required for a task or activity within a process to be completed. There are two types of cycle times: individual cycle time and total cycle time.

Individual cycle time is the rate of completion of an individual task or single operation of work. For example, entering patient data into the EMS/EMR database, transporting a patient to another area of the hospital, drawing blood, writing an order, dispensing a medication to a patient, calling in a prescription, etc. are a few examples of activities within a process.

Total cycle time is the rate of completion of a process or group of tasks that have a common element. This is calculated by adding up the individual cycle times for that process. For example, in ED, the Triage process would involve the following individual tasks: obtain history of patient, take vitals, determine level of pain, arrange for transport to room, notify physician, etc. each having separate cycle times. The total cycle time would be the summation of all those activities related to preparing the patient for the exam.

There are four steps in determining how to use cycle times for assisting in determining the number of staff required to support the takt time(s).

1. Obtain individual cycle times by adding all the steps (or individual tasks) for a process.

Cycle Time Table								
Staff - Unit Coordinator			**Staff - Nurse**			**Staff - Doctor**		
Step	**Description**	**Cycle Time**	**Step**	**Description**	**Cycle Time**	**Step**	**Description**	**Cycle Time**
1	Chart retrieval	3 min	1	Hx of patient	2 min	1	Review chart	2 min
2	Enter patient data	3 min	2	Reports to Dr.	3 min	2	Patient questions	2 min
3	Referral to specialist	10 min	3	Follow-up w/ patient	10 min	3	Exam	5 min
Total Time		**16 min**			**15 min**			**9 min**

2. Add the individual cycle times to obtain the total cycle time for the various steps.

	Unit Coord.	Nurse	Doctor	
Total Cycle Time =	**16 min** +	**15 min** +	**9 min** =	**40 minutes Total Cycle Time**

3. Calculate takt time. You calculate takt time by dividing the available work time for a day (minus meetings, breaks, etc.) by the total volume of work required for that day. (previous section).

Typical day for first shift in a facility:

0700 - 0710	Morning meeting - not available work time
0710 - 0930	Available work time **140 min**
0930 - 0940	Morning break - not available work time
0940 - 1100	Available work time **80 min**
1100 - 1200	Lunch - not available work time
1200 - 1400	Available work time **120 min**
1400 - 1410	Afternoon break - not available work time
1410 - 1440	Meetings (average this for the week) - not available work time
1440 - 1600	Available work time **80 min**

Total available work time is: 140 m + 80 m + 120 m + 80 m = 420 minutes per day
(m=minutes)

Let us say the volume of work is 30 patients per day.

$$\frac{\textbf{420 minutes per day} \text{ (Available Work Time/Day)}}{\textbf{30 patients per day} \text{ (Volume of Patients/Day)}} = \textbf{14 minute takt time}$$

4. Divide the total cycle time by the takt time to determine the total number of staff required for the tasks associated with that particular value stream.

Optimal number of staff required =

$$\frac{\textbf{40 minutes} \text{ (Total cycle time)}}{\textbf{14 minutes} \text{ (Takt time)}} = \textbf{2.86 staff} \text{ (or 3 staff members to meet the demand for that process)}$$

When determining the optimal number of staff needed:
- ◆ If decimal is greater than or equal to .5, round up
- ◆ If decimal is less than .5, round down (and kaizen in attempts to arrive at the lower number if at all possible)
- ◆ Remember to factor in any other functions performed by that staff member, as part of other value streams

Healthcare has a version of this already in existence. For example, on a med-surg floor, if the census is above the determined limit, the nurse/staff ratio is used and an extra staff member is called in.

Rules for developing the Cycle Time Table:

1. For each process step, determine the START and STOP points (from database retrieval, time stamps, observation methods, etc.).
2. Observe the process step at least 30 times and use average, if possible.
3. If an individual process step takes less than 15 seconds, bundle it with the next (or previous) process step.
4. Round up to nearest half-minute (30 seconds) or minute depending on the process.
5. Include wait time between the agreed-upon START and STOP points in all of the process steps (referred to as in-process delay or wait).

From the recently installed EMR system, Sue collected the following cycle times for Oakview's ED with 50 samples (rounded to the nearest 1/2 minute) for just one part of the entire ED Arrival to IP Bed value stream. Sue had thought from her previous Operational Excellence work that this area may be the focus for the team. This information will be used to populate or confirm the data on the current state value stream map, as well as used for further analysis when the team is assembled. Sue and Mary wanted to have as much data as possible for that first team meeting. Even though the worksheet is labeled as cycle time, there are in-process wait times included in the "total cycle time" number, which will be analyzed with additional Lean tools.

Note: Shaded processes are done in parallel with the 15 minute wait time in ED Clerk's step 3. For this case study we show that times are happening in a linear sequence (for simplification purposes only).

Note: This Cycle Time Table is the average (rounded up) for a sample size of 50.

Cycle Time Table for Oakview's Dispo-to-Admit ED Value Stream

Department ED

Data Collection Dates April 20 - 25

Type of Data Collection

- ✓ Historical (database retrieval)
- Direct Observation (real time)
- Voice of the Customer (survey)

Totals:

Physician	35.0	ED Clerk	18.5
Bed Coordinator	8.5	Registration	7.5
ED Clerk	19.0	ED Nurse	21.5
ED Tech	21.5	ED Nurse	3.5
Transporter	35.0		

TOTAL: 170 minutes (2 hours, 50 minutes)

Physician			**Registration**			**ED Tech/Nursing Asst**		
Step	Description	Cycle Time	Step	Description	Cycle Time	Step	Description	Cycle Time
1	Page PCP	15.0 min	1	Receive bed order from ED Clerk	.5 min	1	Perform clothing check	3.0 min
2	Discuss case with PCP	5.0 min	2	Change patient from ED to Inpt - Ecare (rm assg)	2.0 min	2	Call transporter/vitals	3.5 min
3	Write dispo/admit order	10.0 min	3	Print new wristband and IP face sheet	1.0 min	3	Wait for transporter, assist transporter	15.0 min
4	Perform medication reconciliation	5.0 min	4	Deliver wristband and IP face sheet to ED	4.0 min		Total	21.5 min
	Total	35.0 min		Total	7.5 min		**ED Nurse**	

ED Clerk			**ED Clerk**			1	Call IP Nurse Manager; patient leaving the ED	1.0 min
1	Note disp order in chart	.5 min	1	Receive wristband and IP face sheet from Adm	.5 min	2	Take vital signs	2.5 min
2	Call bed coordinator for available bed	1.0 min	2	Place face sheet in chart and record	.5 min		Total	3.5 min
3	Wait for available bed	15.0 min	3	Give wristband to nurse to place on patient	4.0 min		**Transporter**	
4	Process admit order in hospital IT system	2.0 min	4	Copy ED chart for IP chart	12.5 min	1	Gather chart, belongings, prepare pt for movement	6.0 min
	Total	18.5 min	5	Put IP chart copy in folder with pt belongings	1.5 min	2	Move patient to IP unit	18.0 min

Bed Coordinator				Total	19.0 min	3	Check in with Unit Clerk, sign pt log, hand chart	3.0 min
1	Receive request for bed from ED clerk	.5 min		**ED Nurse**		4	Move patient to room, place in bed	6.0 min
2	Check bed status for type of bed/room	2.0 min	1	Place IP wristband on pt	.5 min	5	Notify IP Nurse pt has arrived	2.0 min
3	Communicate with Ns Mgr and Hskp	3.0 min	2	Discuss admission with patient	5.0 min		Total	35.0 min
4	Confirm bed with IP unit/notify ED clerk	3.0 min	3	Complete Medication/ Allergy form	3.5 min			
	Total	8.5 min	4	Complete charting, record for IP unit	10.0 min			
PCP - Primary Care Physician			5	Call IP unit with report	2.5 min			
IP - Inpatient				Total	21.5 min			

Basics of Good Teams

New projects will require people meeting together on a regular basis that may have had very little experience working with others on a formal problem or issue. The individuals that have been working in their departments for many years may have been doing their jobs with little input from peers, managers, and/or an internal consultant (i.e., Lean-Sigma facilitator, Lean Sensei, etc.). Therefore, it is imperative that all those involved in the project learn to work together in a team atmosphere and have a positive experience if improvements are to be made and people's ideas respected. This effort does not come naturally. Everyone must understand team dynamics as well as their roles and responsibilities.

Ideas to Involve Others

Often a group or team will be comprised of people who may struggle with group (team) participation. This may occur for some of the following reasons:

- Previous ideas were shot down or not acknowledged
- Previous ideas were acknowledged as good, but not discussed any further
- Strong managerial control precluded input from the employees
- No standard method for reaching a consensus or decision-making
- Fear of public or group speaking
- People taking credit for the ideas of others
- Fear of job loss by improving the process(es)
- Highest ranking person in room takes over meetings and discussions
- Poor meeting facilitation

For success to occur, everyone must feel free to contribute. The use of Lean and Six Sigma tools will require adaptation and creativity - and change. People must understand the tools and have a desire to apply them in their area. The following are suggestions of how to involve everyone:

- Assign and rotate the functions of the facilitator, scribe, timekeeper, and any other functions among the team members, whenever practical
- Train and practice proper brainstorming techniques
- Constantly communicate that the Lean project is about improving processes, not eliminating people
- Acknowledge that improvements will involve change for everyone
- The team champion (executive sponsor) should visit the area frequently to acknowledge progress and lend verbal support

If for some reason an employee refuses to participate at the team meetings, attempt the following:

- Assign the hesitant participant to a more active role
- Have the manager or champion privately discuss the employee's concern(s)
- Have the manager or champion continue to coach the individual following the human resource policy

The Four Stages of Teams

Understanding the basics of team dynamics will enhance the entire process by recognizing some basic do's and don'ts about working in groups.

The four stages of team development which each team will go through are:

Stage 1 Forming or Getting Started
Stage 2 Storming or Going in Circles
Stage 3 Norming or Staying on Course
Stage 4 Performing or Full Speed Ahead

Stage 1 - Forming or Getting Started

The Forming stage of teaming involves reviewing the project, establishing team roles, determining meeting times, and ensuring the right members are on the team.

This is the stage where team members experience difficulties going from working as individuals to being a contributing team member. There is excitement, anticipation, and optimism. While there is also the pride a member may feel about being chosen for the team, the "flip-side" may be feelings of suspicion, fear, and anxiety of what is to come.

Additional points to consider at this initial stage are:

✦ Ensure roles are clearly defined and that a consensus (agreement) is achieved on all decisions
✦ Rotate team member roles (scribe, time-keeper, etc.)
✦ Conduct training activities on teaming or have team members attend a teaming workshop or seminar
✦ Establish team ground rules (i.e., turn cell phones/pages off or on vibrate, be on time, etc. - with each team creating their own set of ground rules)

The team leader can remain in control by conducting effective meetings, using proper communications, and respecting team members' ideas.

This stage of teaming is similar to a whitewater rafting trip where an experienced guide assists the team with specific duties, as well as calms fears about the unknown.

Stage 2 - Storming or Going in Circles

At this stage, the team members begin to realize the task is different and/or more difficult than they first imagined. Impatience about the lack of progress and/or inexperience on group dynamics has some team members wondering about the entire project. Also, the team may experience some of the following:

- ✦ Continuing to rely on their personal experience of team projects and resisting collaboration
- ✦ Arguing among members, even when they agree on the real issue
- ✦ Being defensive and competitive

This stage can be difficult for any team. Teams that do not understand and acknowledge the four stages - especially this stage - most likely will disband or continue to struggle in this stage without being able to move forward.

The following ideas may assist teams through this stage:

- ✦ Constantly acknowledge the four stages with the team
- ✦ Communicate to the team that disagreements are part of the teaming process
- ✦ Focus on the team's goals
- ✦ Acknowledge progress to date
- ✦ Always focus on the process, not people or their personalities
- ✦ Conduct effective meetings (next section)

If open resistance by one or two individuals occurs and creates an uncomfortable atmosphere for the team, a private meeting about this behavior with those individual(s) will need to be held. Individual team members may lose the initial burst of excitement and energy exhibited from the Forming stage. Acknowledge this to the team and slowly focus on what can be done, by whom, and when it can be finished.

In this part of the rafting trip experience, the raft is struggling down the river. Team members are learning as they go, but have a guide to help them along. People may need to change positions to better accommodate the team's mission (or prevent the raft from going in circles).

Stage 3 - Norming or Staying on Course

At this stage, team members accept the team concept. The team ground rules are being adhered to, communication is occurring without disruptions, and progress is being made toward the objective. At this stage, everyone feels that the team concept is working efficiently and effectively. Everyone is contributing in a positive way.

The team may also be doing some of the following:

+ Expressing criticism constructively
+ Attempting to achieve harmony by avoiding conflict
+ Confiding in each other
+ Exhibiting a sense of team bonding

Continued communications and acknowledgement of the team members' efforts should be done often, allowing progression to Performing (next stage) and preventing the team from falling back to the Storming stage, and therefore staying on course.

Stage 4 - Performing or Full Speed Ahead

By the time this stage has been reached, the team can begin to diagnose and solve problems with relative ease. This stage includes:

+ Making constructive self-changes
+ Achieving project milestones earlier than anticipated
+ Team members, in a supporting role, coaching and mentoring others
+ Team members requesting to help facilitate or contribute in some way in another improvement project

Everyone on the raft at this time is doing their roles as expected. As they go through the rapids, the team is confident - as well as excited for the next set of rapids. The rafting experience would be a positive recommendation to others.

Teaming can be a challenge the first time. Utilizing the VSM methodology will assist greatly in allowing the team to progress through all the stages of team development, minimizing the likelihood that some problem adversely affecting the project. Teams success with projects can be directly attributed to effective communications, within the team and to management. Team Charters, Meeting Information Forms, Status Reports, and Sunset Reports will assist in this communication process.

Team Charter

The **Team Charter** is a document detailing the team's mission and deliverables to ensure strategic alignment. Once the project has been identified, at least initially, the departmental manager (or process owner) should create a first draft of the Team Charter.

The Team Charter will then be reviewed, discussed, and a consensus reached at the first team meeting. The Team Charter has the following attributes:

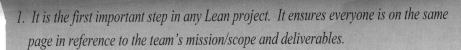

1. It is the first important step in any Lean project. It ensures everyone is on the same page in reference to the team's mission/scope and deliverables.

2. It is a living document and will change as conditions occur. It should be updated regularly and posted in a common area.

3. The Team Charter will list the deliverables appropriate to the project.

4. The Team Charter and its deliverables should be achievable and the team should have a consensus regarding them.

5. The team champion will ensure proper resources are committed. The champion usually does not attend all meetings, but is available to remove roadblocks, commit necessary resources, provide encouragement, and break down departmental barriers.

6. The team leader will be responsible for the day-to-day or week-to-week activities. The team leader will schedule the week activities, schedule meetings, and inform the champion of problems.

7. The champion should review the Team Charter and agree to it prior to any resources being committed.

8. The Team Charter duration should last no longer than six months.

There are many different types of Team Charters. Whichever type is used, ensure everyone is aligned on the team goals and how they are to be accomplished.

Two-and-a-half hours was scheduled for the first meeting (see next section on the Meeting Information Form). The following is the Team Charter for Oakview Hospital's Lean team.

Team Charter

Mission
The team will evaluate the Emergency Department process from "Dispo" to "Admit". This is from the time the physician determines that the patient needs to be admitted to the time the patient is placed in his/her inpatient bed and all hand-offs have been completed.

Outcomes
The team will create a streamlined process flow to achieve the following:
Reduce ED LOS for Dispo-to-Admit approx. 50% (from 170 mins to 90 mins)
Reduce ED LOS for Admit Patients by 25% (from 360 mins to 270 mins)
Improve ED (Patient) Satisfaction score by 50%

Deliverables
1. Create a current and future state value stream map of the ED patient experience.
2. Create and implement new standard work for the process of Dispo-to-Admit.
3. Create a Failure Prevention Analysis Worksheet to ensure mistake proofing of any process change.
4. Train all staff on new standards. Implement a 5S program throughout the ED.
5. Monitor changes (and adjust if necessary) to ensure changes are controlled and sustained over time.

Expected Scope/Approach/Activities
1. The scope of the team's authority and focus is: ED processes between physician order to admit and patient being placed into the bed. Changes to be approved during the event by the Process Owner, ED Manager, and Bed Placement Coordinator, with communication/training for other stakeholders as appropriate.
2. The approach will use the Value Stream Management methodology to achieve the deliverables.
3. In addition to the week-long focused Kaizen Event, the team will conduct preparatory meetings as needed to support the Event week, including contacting IT and facilities for expected support during the Event week.

Strategic Alignment Factors
- ED LOS for Admitted Patients
- Efficiency (decreased time in the ED places pt more quickly in less costly care on the inpatient unit)
- Growth (opening capacity and decreasing "Left Without Being Seen" for other patients)
- Clinical Effectiveness (care by the ED physician is focused on immediate conditions, while care by the admitting physician is focused on the patient's short and long term needs)

Team Process

Process Item	Frequency	Audience/Distribution
Stakeholder Check	• Daily, during, and 30-60-90 day post-Event	• Team members, face-to-face, for all stakeholders
Information Distribution	• Once, after first preparatory meetings • Daily, after each day of the Event • 30-60-90 day follow-up	• From team to stakeholders, after first preparatory meeting • From team to entire hospital staff
Team Meetings	• Three prep meetings in three weeks prior • Daily, during the Event, weekly follow-ups	• Team, Process Owner, Fac., Champion • Team, Process Owner, Facilitator
Status Reporting	• 30-60-90 Follow-up reports	• Team, Process Owner, Fac., Champion

Expected Results

Benefits (What results will be gained?)	Metrics (How will the results be measured?)
1. Reduced cycle time, Dispo-to-Admit by approx. 50% 2. Improved ED Patient Satisfaction by 50+%	1. Cycle time metrics collected weekly 2. Patient Satisfaction scores, weekly mean scores

Assumptions
- ED patient volumes will remain consistent
- ED staffing will support change

Risks
- ED staff will not follow new standards
- Some stakeholders will not support change

Internal Issues
- ED physicians not engaged after admit order written
- Disagreement among physicians who should write order
- Staffing concerns with nursing
- Nurse Planning may relieve staff on units due to low census

External Issues
- Joint Commission's new requirements on patient hand-offs and transportation between units

LAN Location/Revision #   **Facility Confidential**

The Mission statement from the Team Charter took a long time to discuss, because some of team members had different opinions about what was trying to be accomplished. For the Outcomes, they thought they could just plug in the target for ED Length of Stay (LOS) for Admit Patients of 4.5 hours and meet that number as the goal.

But, how long should the Dispo-to-Admit process take? After a spirited discussion, the team agreed to the following numbers:

	Current Total Cycle Time	Future Total Cycle Time
Door-to-Doc	45 minutes	30 minutes
Doc-to-Dispo	145 minutes	145 minutes
Dispo-to-Admit	**170 minutes**	**90 minutes (estimated)**
Total	360 minutes	265 minutes

The team decided to focus on the Dispo-to-Admit portion of the entire value stream (i.e., ED Arrival to Inpatient Bed), which included the patient being placed in the bed (Admit). They also agreed to the goal of reducing the 170 minutes of total cycle time to approximately 90 minutes.

One of the team members asked the reasonable question, "Why don't we start working on Door-to-Doc and reduce that to 15 minutes, rather than Dispo-to-Admit? There's a lot of pressure to get patients into the ED right away."

The facilitator asked a question in return, "What would happen if we were able to get patients into the ED more quickly, but hadn't worked on getting existing patients out? The result would be a pile-up in the ED. It is better to work from the back end - freeing up capacity, to make room for more patients coming in - and then work on the front end (Door-to-Doc) to streamline that process even more."

That concept made sense to the team, so they proceeded with a plan for improving the Dispo-to-Admit value stream.

The Deliverables were easier to establish, based on the standard expectations for Lean projects, and likewise, the Expected Scope/Approach/Activities were a little bit easier to develop.

The team added the Strategic Alignment Factors and Strategic Goals of the health system.

The Team Process section took a while to develop, as the team members debated how often to communicate, and who the audience would be. They decided that the second week in May would be the week they would hold the physical Kaizen Event, however, they knew that there would have to be a lot of work (and training) done prior to that time.

The discussion around the Expected Results was more heated, since some members passionately wanted to achieve a 50% reduction in the total ED Arrival to Inpatient Bed cycle time. However, a consensus was reached to focus the improvements on the Dispo-to-Admit portion of the entire value stream and work to attain a realistic 45 - 50% reduction in that measurement.

The conversation about Assumptions and Risks was also full of debate, with some team members saying there were so many risks that it would take a whole meeting to describe them! But after some delicate facilitating by Sue, the team decided to list two major risks.

Finally, for Internal and External Issues, the team likewise agreed to just list the major concerns and leave more detailed brainstorming for the project itself.

The discussions took longer than expected, however, at the end the team members agreed they had learned a lot from the process of developing the Team Charter and admitted that the project would most likely go forward more smoothly because they had done a good job with this important project management tool.

Meeting Information Form

*The **Meeting Information Form** provides the team with a structured approach to run an effective meeting, including detailed agendas and action items.* The Meeting Information Form ensures:

1. Everyone at the meeting is aware of the agenda, times, and topics
2. Action items are assigned and reviewed at each meeting
3. Project milestones are plotted to ensure Lean project completion
4. Management is aware of the meetings and topics to ensure continued alignment

The team leader or facilitator should fill out the Meeting Information Form and distribute it at least a week prior to the first meeting and 24 hours prior to subsequent meetings.

Margaret, as the process owner and team leader, took responsibility for sending the agenda electronically to the team members as well as to the stakeholders. The layout of the form made it easy to fill in. She created it as a template in Microsoft Word for easy access in creating new ones as needed. She also created a Distribution List for the project to save time in typing in the email addresses of the team members each time a meeting was to be scheduled. Margaret reserved the Conference room a week in advance for that first full team meeting to review the Team Charter, discuss the Goals for the project, introduce Lean concepts, and assign action items for the team to start observing the process. The following is the Meeting Information Form for Oakview Hospital's first team meeting.

Meeting Information Form

Logistics

Meeting Title:	ED Arrival to Inpatient Bed Team Kick-off
Date:	4/3
Time:	1300 - 1530
Place:	ED Conference Room
Purpose:	Review Team Charter and set goals for improvement project

Distribution

Participants	Roles
Bill, Anne, Sarah, John, Randy, and Dr. Ben	Core team members
Sue R.	Facilitator - Trainer
Margaret S.	Process Owner/ Team Leader
Mary H., Judy D.	Co-Champions

FYI Copies

Stakeholders	Roles
VPs, Execs	Support

Agenda

Time	Item	Who	Duration (minutes)
1300	Icebreaker, purpose of meeting, strategic direction, commitment from execs	J.A./M.H.	15
1315	Review Team Charter and Balanced Scorecard	M.H./M.S.	30
1345	Introduction to Lean, high level review of VSM	S.R.	60
1445	Introduction to healthcare waste (activity)	S.R./M.S.	30
1515	Determine tasks, schedule next meeting	S.R./M.S.	15
1530	Depart	All	

Action Items (to be completed by next meeting or sooner)

No.	Action Item	Who	Start Date	End Date	Status
1	Create VOC survey	S.S.	4/3	4/10	Open
2	Gather data for processes within ED	B.H.	4/3	4/10	Open
3	Gather benchmark data	J.L.	4/3	4/10	Open

LAN Location/Revision #	**Confidential**

Status Reports

Status Reports communicate the status of the project that was defined in the Team Charter, on a regular basis. They are completed by the team leader and forwarded to the team champion on a regular basis. For every area identified as an issue or problem, there needs to be a plan for resolution. This gives the champion confidence that the team has control of the project.

Sue completed the Status Report after the team's first meeting from the Action Items of the Meeting Information Form. Although there were no pressing concerns expressed at that time, Sue decided to capture some of the team's potential concerns to reflect that their opinions were valued and alert the co-champions to potential future issues.

The following is the Status Report from the first meeting.

Status Report

Team Name ED Arrival to Inpatient Bed Improvement Team

Date 4/3

Status

(Are you on schedule?)
Yes. The team had one meeting as planned to align theTeam Charter with the Balanced Scoreard and ED Goal Card. A brief overview of Lean, as well as a review of wastes in healthcare, was completed.
The team agreed to have weekly meetings to further analyze and plan for the improvements for the Dispo-to-Admit portion of the Level I value stream.
The second week in May was scheduled for the Kaizen Event week.
The detailed timeline for the tasks can be found at www.oakview.org/ED_DispoVSM_Timeline.

Accomplishments

Everyone was in attendance for the first meeting.

Concerns (Issues)

None at present. Future concerns may include how to train staff on new process; possible resistance by physicians; and, how to accelerate approvals for form changes.

Plans (How to Resolve Issues)

Stakeholders will be communicated to on regular basis per the team's mission and timetable.

LAN Location/Revision #1	**Facility Confidential**

The Sunset Report

Once the team has completed the project, a Sunset Report should be generated. *The Sunset Report is the document that contains a summary of what was learned from the project.* It is a form of knowledge management. It will explain: what went well, what tools were most useful, results, and what could have been improved. It is meant to be shared with others. The Leader normally completes the Sunset Report and places it on the Local Area Network as a reference and learning tool. A Sunset Report is similar to a Yokoten as described on page 230.

Team Charters, Meeting Information Forms, Status Reports, and Sunset Reports are valuable tools in providing the necessary communication for Lean healthcare to be a successful program within the organization.

Effective Meetings

For teams to be productive, the team member's time must be used wisely; this is accomplished through conducting effective meetings. Conducting effective meetings does not involve trial and error. Effective meetings are an efficient use of people's time when they are gathered together working to obtain a desired result. Meetings, like any process, can be studied and improved upon.

There are three keys to effective meetings:

1. Identify clear objectives for each meeting.
2. Create and adhere to rules and guidelines (i.e., standards).
3. Ensure everyone participates and is engaged.

Meetings can be one of the most powerful business tools or one of the least. Common complaints about meetings are that they:

+ Accomplish nothing
+ Are poorly organized
+ Have everyone with their own agenda
+ Last too long
+ Have people always arrive late
+ Have no one in control

However, people need to meet in order to benefit from the collective knowledge and experience of the group. While many decisions can be made by phone, email, or in an hallway discussion, there will be other times that people will need to meet and gain a consensus on an issue or problem that needs to be resolved. A more Lean way to conduct meetings with members that are distant is through video conferencing and/or document sharing and conference calls.

Effective meetings provide a forum to make necessary decisions and solve problems without wasting people's time. If meetings are effective, then something positive will be the result. People will arrive on time, participate, offer information and ideas, and have positive attitudes. However, if meetings are not effective, people will show up late, be less likely to participate, and their attention and ideas will be less productive. To achieve effective meetings, treat them as processes, create standard rules to follow, and then adhere to those rules.

Approach conducting an effective meeting as follows:

1. Agree on a clear objective and agenda for the meeting.
2. Choose the right people for the meeting and notify everyone in advance.
3. Clarify roles and responsibilities for the meeting (i.e., champion, leader, facilitator, technical representative, scribe, timekeeper, and team member).
4. Ensure everyone adheres to meeting etiquette (being on time, turning off cell phones/pagers, no text messaging during the meetings, etc.). (Also discussed under the Forming section of Teaming on page 84.)
5. Assign a scribe to take the meeting's minutes.
6. Assign a timekeeper to ensure the times allocated for each of the topics are adhered to
7. Evaluate the meetings and improve where needed.
8. Provide minutes to participants within 24 hours after the meeting.

Role Definitions of Team Members

The following are the definitions and activities of the various team member roles.

The **team champion** *is the person who has the authority to commit the necessary resources for the team.* The champion should "kick-off" the first meeting and then be updated regularly with Status Reports. Other duties of the team champion may include, but are not limited to: continually be involved and communicate often with the team leader, referee cross-functional resource requests by removing barriers to project success, assist to ensure the team is aligned with strategic goals, appoint the team leader, handle issues that the team leader cannot, and provide team guidance when the team is struggling.

The **team leader** *is responsible for the day-to-day or week-to-week running of the team.* Other duties of the team leader may include, but are not limited to: schedules and coordinates the meeting times (agenda, and location), has capacity to make change happen, has manager or supervisory authority, has complete buy-in to the project, suggests additional team members, understands team dynamics, and respects others.

The **facilitator** *ensures that everyone at the meetings stays on task and everyone contributes.* The facilitator should not have any vested interest in the project, one way or another - other than ensuring the meetings are effective. These duties include, but are not limited to: keeps discussion focused on topic, intervenes if multiple conversations are occurring, prevents one person from dominating, promotes interaction and participation, brings discussions to a close, and guides the group in accordance with the charter and agenda.

The **timekeeper** *is responsible for ensuring the scheduled times (start, stop, topics) are followed.* The timekeeper can manage the process and agenda. This frees everyone else to focus on contributing ideas. Other duties of the timekeeper may include, but are not limited to: monitors time with respect to the agenda, notifies team when it is behind schedule, updates the team on progress to time allocated, assists with determining appropriate time allocation for next meeting, and contributes as a team member.

The **scribe** is the person who records the notes of the meeting; and/or the person who captures the group's thoughts on flipcharts, blackboards, or the laptop that is being projected on the wall or screen, etc. The scribe is responsible to represent the ideas of the group, without imposing his/her own interpretation on them.

The **technical representative (tech rep)** - is the person from IT (or someone with advanced computer application skills) who provides insights into technology tools available and/or makes the team aware of upcoming technology that may impact the team's mission.

The **team member** - the most important part of the team - is responsible for keeping an open mind, being receptive to change, and contributing their ideas in a respectful manner.

Note: It is important that both the facilitator and scribe duties be not assigned to the same person. Many hospitals will have a continuous improvement specialist (Black Belt or Lean trainer) to act as the facilitator. The team leader and process owner can be the same person.

When teams meet, there should be ground rules (i.e, proper etiquette) that everyone follows. These may be initially created by the team leader and process owner prior to the first meeting and then reviewed and agreed upon by the team at the conclusion of the first meeting. These ground rules should be posted at the meeting location, distributed prior to the meeting, and/or reviewed at the beginning of each meeting session. Ground rules may include the following:

Attendance. Management should place a high priority on meeting attendance. There should be defined legitimate reasons for missing a meeting with a procedure to inform the team leader if a member cannot attend. The best way to ensure good attendance is to run effective meetings.

Timing. Meetings should begin and end on time. This avoids wasting time and makes it easier on everyone's schedule. Meetings are sometimes shorter when this rule is enforced. Each team should create specific ways to enforce this rule.

Participation. Every member can make a valuable contribution to the meeting. Emphasize the importance of speaking freely and listening attentively. If unequal participation is a problem, then the Team Facilitator can structure the meeting so that everyone participates through various types of structured and unstructured brainstorming techniques.

Basic Courtesies. Everyone, regardless of job description, should use basic conversational courtesies. Listen to what people have to say, do not interrupt, have only one conversation at a time, and respect others.

Breaks and interruptions. Decide when breaks for phone calls, text messaging, etc. are allowed, and when they are not.

Other ground rules (if appropriate). Decide on other ground rules that seem appropriate. For example, what kind of humor is acceptable? What kind of language? What is OK to talk about and what is not? Is it OK to receive and/or send text messages during the meeting?

Meetings, as stated previously, are a process like any other and should be evaluated on a regular basis. Use the following Effective Meeting Evaluation Worksheet with your team to continuously improve your meetings.

At the conclusion of the first meeting, the following Effective Meeting Evaluation Worksheet was completed by the team members to provide feedback to the team leader and facilitator. After analyzing the worksheets, it was determined that the meeting could improve by staying on track more and not diverting to other areas of the hospital that the team had concerns with.

Effective Meeting Evaluation Worksheet

Directions:
1. Spend only five minutes evaluating your meetings.
2. This form is most successful when everyone's responses are shared.
3. Focus on the weak spots, applaud the high ratings.

Rating System: 1 is the lowest score (Poor) and 5 is the highest (Excellent)

Poor — 1 2 3 4 5 — Excellent	Score
1. How well did we stay on the agenda?	4
2. Are we focusing on the right issues during the meeting?	3
3. How well did we look for problems in the process, rather than the person?	3
4. How well did we use our time?	2
5. How well did we discuss information? How clearly? How accurately?	4
6. How well did we all participate?	4
7. Was the meeting effective?	3
8. How was the pace, flow, and tone of the meeting? (Did we get bogged down or stuck?)	2
9. How well did we respond to each other's questions and comments?	4
10. In general, were all ideas explored to the extent possible given the time element?	4
TOTAL:	33
Please provide any other comments or suggestions for improvements.	

Value Stream Mapping

A **value stream map** is a visual representation of the material, work, and information flow, as well as the queue times between processes for a specific customer demand. The material or work can also be the patient. The map should represent all the main activities relative to the most downstream process (i.e., your customer demand or ocean, lake, or sea as described on page 35). Value stream maps are of two types: current and future state. Current state maps provide a visual representation of current work (or patient) flow. The future state map is a representation of the Lean tools applied to the current state map. It will serve as a visual road map displaying how to eliminate waste identified in the current state.

Do not use value stream mapping exclusively as a management tool. Ensure value stream maps are posted in common areas for increased awareness as improvements are made. Update them as necessary. Value stream maps should be posted next to the Team Charter along with any additional information relative to the Lean project.

It may be difficult to determine what exactly needs to be value stream mapped. Many organizations attempt to map all improvement projects on one map. When this occurs it can be difficult to "see" where waste lies. So, if the map does little in terms of identifying waste, then the mapping exercise was not a value-adding activity. The following guidelines can be used to determine if a value stream map should be created.

1. Does the Balanced Scorecard indicate certain areas that have never met the goal? (If just one or two months indicated a negative (not meeting goal) trend, then problem solving may be of more value with possibly analyzing a detailed timeline of those months, and then from that, determining the reasons for the negative trend.)
2. Is there a flow problem between processes?
3. Are there excessive delays between processes?
4. Is the competition forcing the organization to radically improve an area or consolidate services to remain in that business segment?
5. Are Balanced Scorecard measurements too broad for improvement activities to be understood and acted upon? (For example, if the Balanced Scorecard requires an increase in Growth as a goal, that could be further broken down in ER, Pediatrics, Surgical, etc., and then a value stream could be created for each one of those areas.)
6. Does the process work flow sequentially and is related to one customer base? (If there are many branches within a department or value stream being mapped, it is better to consider creating a different type of process map.)
7. Does overall productivity need to improve?

It is beneficial to do a current state value stream map if many of the questions listed above can be adequately answered with a Yes.

In the following illustration, notice that Radiology and Ortho would be a value stream while OB/GYN can be considered a separate value stream. The OB/GYN is separate because the patient would not have to go through the Physician Referral process.

	Patients/Monthly Avg.	Process A Physician Referral	Process B Admissions	Process C Prep	Process D Procedure
Radiology	30	X	X	X	X
Ortho	10	X	X	X	X
OB/GYN	20		X	X	X

The team decided to expand the information from the Distribution Report and Project Prioritization Worksheet to further understand departmental processes. They listed (while discussing) the following three parts of the ED value stream:

1. What has to happen BEFORE the patient comes to the ED?
2. What has to happen AFTER the patient leaves the ED?
3. What has to happen WHILE the patient is in the ED?
   a. Door-to-Doc
   b. Doc-to-Dispo
   c. Dispo-to-Admit (which includes patient to inpatient bed)
   d. Concurrent Processes

The team members were surprised by how many activities were related to a patient's ED visit!

The team listed as many upstream and downstream processes that impacted their value stream. This listing helped to bridge the three areas of ED (Door-to-Doc, Doc-to-Dispo, and Dispo-to-Admit) and provided more insight into the various processes and activities that may need to be considered throughout the scope of this project.

Brainstorming for pre-Value Stream Mapping

Balanced Scorecard metric to address: LOS for ED Arrival to Inpatient Bed

Upstream Processes/Activities:

Greeting
Registration
Old Chart from Medical Records
Forms generation
Supplies available
Housekeeping (clean rooms)
Stock med carts
Facilities maintenance
Point-of-care testing supplies
Computer/hardware maintenance
Staff training
Staffing and scheduling
Physician scheduling

Downstream Processes/Activities:

IP Nursing Units
ED - Chart to Medical Records
ED - Patient Coding and Billing
ED - Professional Coding and Billing

Value Stream Segments (for ease of understanding)

Door-to-Doc	Doc-to-Dispo	Dispo-to-Admit
-greeting	-orders written	-dispo written
-quick registration	-treatment given	-orders written/updated
-triage	-obtain results of tests	-med reconciliation
-ED bed assignment	-further orders written, tests	-prepare report to unit
-pt to ED bed	-diagnosis	-copy chart
-prep patient	-dispostion	-call transport
-nurse assessment		-pt to IP unit
-physician assessment		-pt in IP bed

Concurrent and Supporting Processes

ED bed control/assignment
Pharmacy
Laboratory
Radiology/Imaging
Dietary
Cardiovascular
Consults (Physician Groups)
Transport

The Current State Value Stream Map

Current state value stream maps *provide a visual representation of the way information and workflow is occurring presently.* It is recommended that a current state value stream map be drawn on a whiteboard or on a long sheet of white paper that can be hung on the wall. Post-it Notes can then represent various activities within a process. If a long sheet of paper is not available, then tape multiple flip-chart sheets on the wall and line them up horizontally. Number each flip-chart sheet to ensure they stay organized once the event is over.

Most current state value stream mapping exercises are done on paper that is posted on the wall. Yes, there may be waste involved if the team desires to subsequently recreate the map electronically. However, that type of waste is minimal compared to the engagement of the team members in creating a physical map that is displayed on the wall. Do not underestimate the importance of this!

If someone desires to create the map in Viseo, Microsoft Excel, or PowerPoint, etc. with the team, as it is being created (not recommended), then ensure the following occurs:

- ✦ The person is very proficient in using the software or otherwise team members will get frustrated watching someone learn-as-they-go
- ✦ The map is projected on a screen so everyone can see it
- ✦ Everything: LCD, projector, software, etc. is ready prior to the mapping exercise

The Chicken and the Egg Syndrome

Do you gather data prior to the mapping exercise? Or, do you create your map and then gather data? The answer to both of these questions is Yes. Most likely, you will have some data prior to creating the first pass of the current state value stream map, and then after reviewing it with the team, additional data will need to be collected and placed on the map. Either way, creating an accurate current state value stream map requires good data.

To have the first pass of a current state value stream map completely filled out (or populated) at the first team session would require:

1. Each process of the value stream map clearly identified and known
2. Activities listed under each process, accurate cycle times through reports, observations, and/or historical analysis (cycle time is the time elapsed from the beginning of a work process or request until it is completed)
3. Overall start and stop times for each process are obtained from an appropriate sample size to establish overall lead time and queue/delay time between processes

It will not be likely that a current state value stream map will be totally completed and accurately populated prior to meeting with the team for the first time, however, certain parts of it can be completed and serve as a strawman for the initial team meeting.

See the section on Data Collection Techniques for further understanding on how data can be collected.

You would gather additional data after a value stream mapping exercise if:

1. The processes were not clearly known from the information contained in the Team Charter
2. The various process activities and their cycle times have never been obtained
3. The value stream has not been clearly identified or was too broad
4. No one had enough reliable data about the processes (which is very likely)

Either way, accurate, reliable, or the most current data should be conveyed on the map. Be careful to not place estimates of the cycle times and queue times on a value stream map. This would compromise the integrity of the improvements obtained once the future state map had been implemented.

Value stream mapping begins with creating the current state and proceeds according to the following steps:

1. Use the following icons to draw a "shell" of the current state, listing the main processes, customers, and suppliers (internal and external). Consider creating additional icons that may be appropriate to your value stream (e.g., creating a laptop icon to demonstrate interactivity with the EMR/EMS system).

   Dedicated Process Box - the main process, department, or area where value-added and/or non value-added work occurs (admissions, registration, Triage, X-ray, Radiology, Orthopedics, Billing, Transport, etc.)

   Shared Process Box - where multiple value streams all inter-relate (mail rooms, human resources, billing/coding, admissions, etc.)

   Attribute Area - characteristics of the process (cycle times of individual tasks, number of people, internal defects, delay time (denoted by shaded area with time)

   Customer or Supplier - the upstream and downstream customer or supplier, with its respective attributes

   Truck Shipment - denotes the physical arrival or departure of work related to the value stream (e.g., transporting linen, supplies, etc.)

   Helicopter Use - denotes the physical arrival or departure of work related to the value stream (e.g., organs, patients, etc.)

W   Queue (Wait) Time - the amount of time, work, people, or information that resides between two processes

Database Interaction - computer interaction (EMR/EMS, Email, WEB, etc.)

Manual Information Flow - physical conveyance of work or patients between two processes within the value stream (e.g., hand carrying work to another area, transporting patient, etc.)

Electronic Information Flow - the electronic signal that communicates information from database to process or from database to database

Mail - the arrival or sending of metered mail

Folder - a single unit of work (i.e., chart, order, lab, etc.)

Folders - multiple units of work grouped together and moved through a common process

X   Exceptions or disruptions - any major obstacle that prevents flow from occurring throughout the value stream

Go-See Scheduling - the physical viewing and collecting of information on the processes to determine work loads (e.g., charge nurse assessing staff work loads)

Push - the movement of the patient, work, or information downstream regardless of the need

Staff - the person(s) assigned to the particular process

2. Visit the areas, beginning with the most downstream process, and collect the attributes (i.e., cycle times, defects, etc.) related to the value stream and determine if data can be gathered during this time. As discussed earlier, data collection for the value stream can take many forms. Gather actual data, use a stopwatch (if practical), and clearly communicate to everyone in the area what you are doing and why.

3. Determine the amount of time between processes. This is the main determinant of the separation of process boxes on a value stream map. Mapping this queue time can be done in either of two methods as shown in the following example.

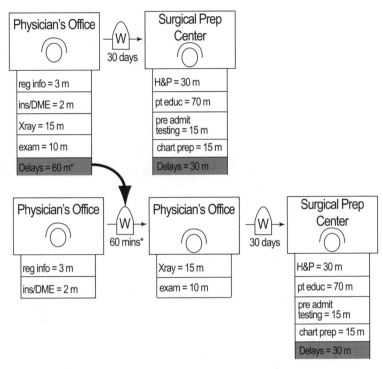

*Delays more than 60 minutes are separated.

You can determine that if delays are occurring with a process more than a certain percentage (say 10% of the overall lead time), then that may warrant a separation of those processes on a value stream map. (Later, additional tools will be used to further analyze these delays within the process.)

Whichever method is utilized to visually show the delays, ensure it is consistent for the entire value stream map and denote it as such on the map.

4. Determine the quantity of work that arrives at each process (i.e., # of patients, nursing hours, admits, interruptions, etc.). The Distribution Report can be helpful here.

5. Determine what is done with the work after the process has been completed. What is the next process? Does anything special need to be done prior to the work arriving at the next process?

6. List all the process attributes on the current state map. If there are other departmental or process attributes (i.e., cycle time of the activity, # patients seen, # beds available, errors/defects/mistakes, etc.) specific to the process, list those as appropriate.

7. Draw all forms of communication, electronic and/or manual.

8. Total the process cycle times within the process box. This is typically the value-added time which may include some of the non value-added time due to a poor process (which can be later analyzed for waste). If delays are listed within the process attributes, then it would be acceptable to include those delays within the total process cycle time. Additional Lean tools will be used to separate and eliminate those wastes; however, many times the larger waste of time (i.e., delay) will be between the processes. There is no right and wrong method to list delays, just be consistent in your approach when mapping.

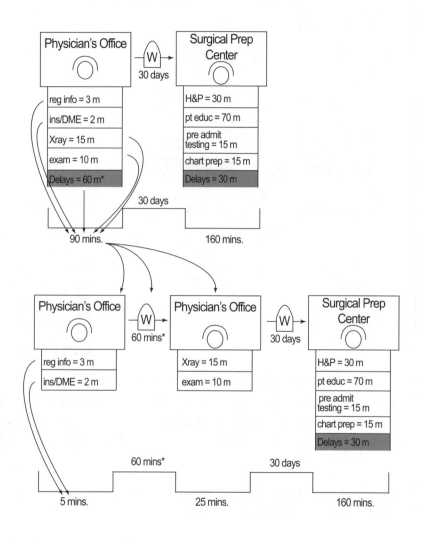

*Delays 60 minutes or more are separated.

Note: The Total Joint Replacement (Knee) Current and Future State Value Stream Maps for Surgical Services are detailed in the Appendix.

9. Compile a step graph at the bottom of the value stream map displaying the total cycle time for each process, including the queue/wait/delay times between processes.

10. The map should convey the total lead time and total queue time, along with any other key metrics that the team has found to be significant.

After Sue reviewed the basic symbols comprised of a value stream map, the team used the Cycle Time Table Worksheet, Distribution Report, Brainstorming for pre-Value Stream Mapping Worksheet (and other information) and created their first pass of their Current State Value Stream Map.

The overall value stream (referred to as Level I) was separated into the three separate value streams of Door-to-Doc, Doc-to-Dispo, and Dispo-to-Admit (each referred to as Level II). The team decided to work on the Dispo-to-Admit portion; however, they knew that many of the improvements they would implement would impact the Door-to-Doc and Doc-to-Dispo as well. The Dispo-to-Admit includes all activities up through the patient arriving in the patient bed (or unit).

Note: This map also displays the Billing and Coding communications to bring attention to its importance that may provide additional opportunities for improvement.

Oakview Hospital's ED Arrival to Inpatient Bed Current State Value Stream Map

* This information is not included in the total lead time for this value stream.

The team decided to do another level of process analysis via a value stream map (which can be referred to as a Level II value stream map) for the Dispo-to-Admit portion of the value stream. The data from the the Cycle Time Table Worksheet would be used. The following is the Dispo-to-Admit Current State Value Stream Map (Level II).

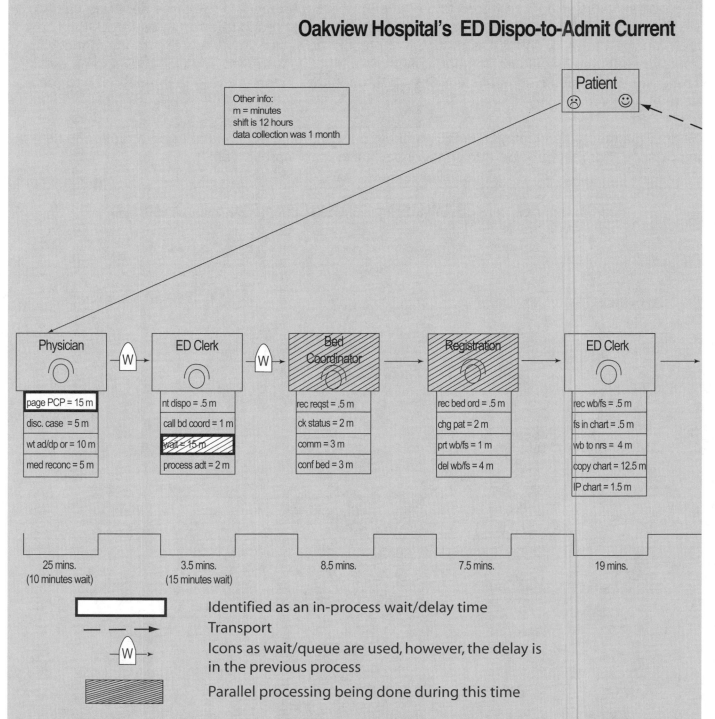

Oakview Hospital's ED Dispo-to-Admit Current

Other info:
m = minutes
shift is 12 hours
data collection was 1 month

Patient

Physician		ED Clerk		Bed Coordinator		Registration		ED Clerk
page PCP = 15 m		nt dispo = .5 m		rec reqst = .5 m		rec bed ord = .5 m		rec wb/fs = .5 m
disc. case = 5 m		call bd coord = 1 m		ck status = 2 m		chg pat = 2 m		fs in chart = .5 m
wt ad/dp or = 10 m		wait = 15 m		comm = 3 m		prt wb/fs = 1 m		wb to nrs = 4 m
med reconc = 5 m		process adt = 2 m		conf bed = 3 m		del wb/fs = 4 m		copy chart = 12.5 m
								IP chart = 1.5 m

| 25 mins. | 3.5 mins. | 8.5 mins. | 7.5 mins. | 19 mins. |
| (10 minutes wait) | (15 minutes wait) | | | |

Identified as an in-process wait/delay time

Transport

W Icons as wait/queue are used, however, the delay is in the previous process

Parallel processing being done during this time

Note: There is 40 minutes of obvious waste from this Level II value stream map identified by 10 minutes of wait time to Page PCP (5 minutes are value-added), ED Clerk's 15 minutes of Wait for Available Bed, and ED Tech/Nursing Asst's 15 minutes Wait for Transporter. Parallel processing is identified by the diagonal lines within the process boxes.

State Value Stream Map (Level II)

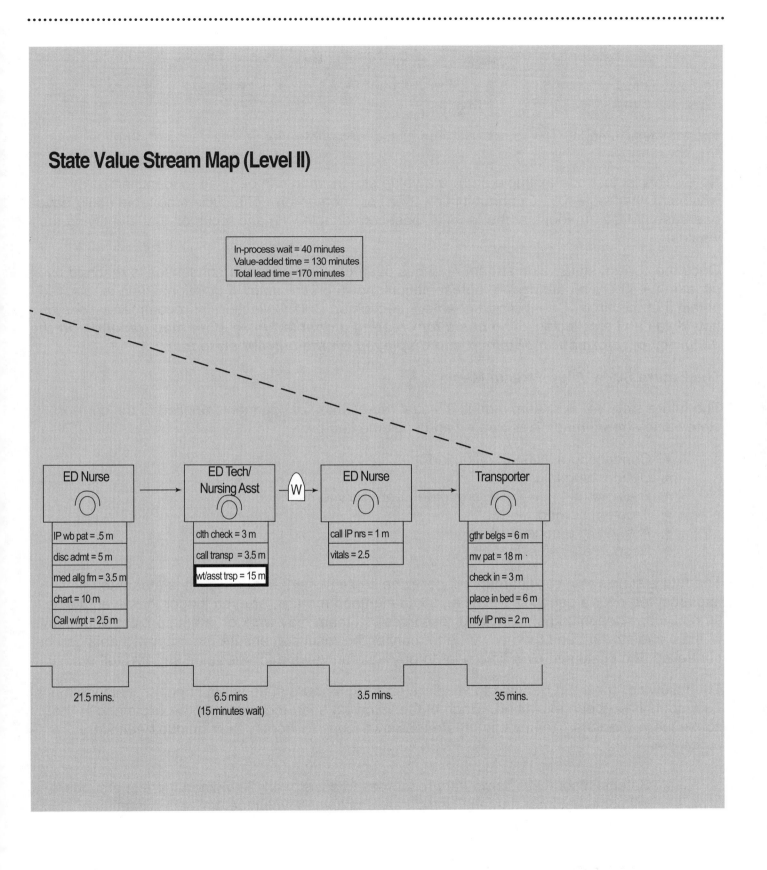

In-process wait = 40 minutes
Value-added time = 130 minutes
Total lead time =170 minutes

ED Nurse	ED Tech/ Nursing Asst		ED Nurse	Transporter
IP wb pat = .5 m	clth check = 3 m	W	call IP nrs = 1 m	gthr belgs = 6 m
disc admt = 5 m	call transp = 3.5 m		vitals = 2.5	mv pat = 18 m
med allg fm = 3.5 m	wt/asst trsp = 15 m			check in = 3 m
chart = 10 m				place in bed = 6 m
Call w/rpt = 2.5 m				ntfy IP nrs = 2 m

21.5 mins.

6.5 mins
(15 minutes wait)

3.5 mins.

35 mins.

The total wait time (in-process delays) time is: 10 mins. + 15 mins. + 15 mins. = 40 mins.

The cycle time is: 25 mins. + 3.5 mins. + 8.5 mins. + 7.5 mins. + 19 mins. + 21.5 mins. + 6.5 mins. + 3.5 mins. + 35 mins. = 130 mins.

The total lead time is: The total cycle time of 130 mins. + the total queue time of 40 mins. = 170 mins.

Note: This is just one example on how a value stream map can be used to identified delay wastes. Other tools (i.e., Opportunity flowchart) or another form of a cycle time table could have been used. Use the tool that the team is most comfortable with and focus on just identifying the wastes!

Once the current state value stream map has been created, ensure a consensus is reached by all team members regarding the representation shown on the map. If additional data is required, obtain it at this time. See the next chapter's section on Data Collection for recommendations on how data can be collected. **_The basis for creating a doable future state map depends on the accuracy of information obtained and displayed on the current state map._**

The Future State Value Stream Map

The future state value stream map is a visual representation Lean tools applied to the current state value stream map. It is created and implemented by:

- ✦ Conducting a Waste Walk (Audit)
- ✦ Determining takt time
- ✦ Brainstorming on the appropriate Lean tools to use
- ✦ Problem solving
- ✦ Arriving at a consensus
- ✦ Resource availability

The future state value stream map will never be implemented all at once. It is meant to be implemented over a period of time (i.e., six to eighteen months, or even longer for Level I value stream maps depending on allocated resources). A team may work on a beta project (a portion of the value stream) and then continue to monitor the results to ensure the improvements can be controlled and sustained over time prior to any enterprise-wide (or full value stream) roll-out.

The following icons can be used to visualize (create) a future state value stream map once the Lean tools have been explained. Each of the following Lean tool icons will be explained in the subsequent chapters. Teams can create their own icons to identify their unique healthcare processes.

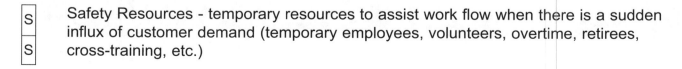 Safety Resources - temporary resources to assist work flow when there is a sudden influx of customer demand (temporary employees, volunteers, overtime, retirees, cross-training, etc.)

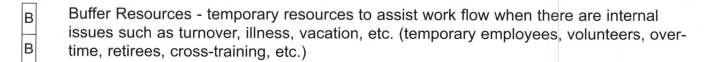 Buffer Resources - temporary resources to assist work flow when there are internal issues such as turnover, illness, vacation, etc. (temporary employees, volunteers, overtime, retirees, cross-training, etc.)

Cart - a device used to distribute work units or supplies throughout the value stream (crash cart, surgical prep cart, etc.)

Kanban - work unit(s) or information packets for delivery to a process

Supermarket - a physical location located between two processes to hold work until it is required downstream

U-Shaped Work Area - the arrangement of desks, fax machines, copiers, gurneys, IV poles, laptops, etc. to accommodate efficient work flow

Pull - the representation of work (i.e., patient chart, labs, consults, etc.) being requested from a downstream process

Pitch Board - the physical device used to hold work based only on volume

FIFO - a physical location located between processes to hold work (or patients) sequentially for the downstream process

Heijunka Box - a physical device used to hold work based on volume and variety

Runner's Route - the route the runner will use to deliver and pick up work (kanbans, patients, etc.) throughout the day

Production Board - the physical device where daily goals are made visual

Kaizen Event (improvement activity) - a focused effort in the application of the Lean tools to a specific area of the value stream

The overall goal of creating a current and future state value stream map is to clearly identify where waste lies, create a shared need for improvement, and determine which Lean tools can be used for waste elimination. The activities in creating a current state establishes a common understanding on the importance of accurate process measures. Future state maps will require numerous iterations as progress is made as team members learn from their Lean implementation experiences. The future state map, similar to the Team Charter, is a living document, and will reflect all changes as they occur or are projected to occur. Before developing a future state map using the Waste Walk and Lean tools, it has proven useful for the team to draw an ideal future state map with no existing limitations of the current facility. This is usually a radical and simplified value stream with no waste. From this, the team usually can obtain several ideas which they can include in their future sate map over the next 6-18 months.

The future state map for Oakview will be presented at the end of the Treat phase, Chapter 4.

The value stream map is a great tool to use if processes are sequential and there are flow issues (i.e., delays) that need to be addressed. However, there may be times when there are just too many activities (i.e., decisions on where information or work flows) to easily present all those on a value stream map. If that is the case, then a type of process map may be a good tool to use.

Flowcharts (or Process Maps)

A **flowchart** (or process map) is a visual representation of a series of operations (tasks, activities) consisting of people, work duties, and transactions that occur in the delivery of a product or service. Note: In this book, process maps and flowcharts are used interchangeably.

When creating a flowchart, the project team should tackle the activity as if it were doing an investigation: find out exactly what is occurring, and what is and is not happening in the process. Flowcharts use standard symbols to represent a type of operation, process, and/or set of tasks to be performed. The use of standardized symbols provides a common language for the project team to visualize problems and also allows for the process to be easier to read and understand, thus making it a viable source to see areas of waste, process variation, and/or redundancy.

Flowcharts

Creating a flowchart or process map allows for a visual representation of a sequence of activities or tasks consisting of people, work duties, and transactions that occur for the delivery of a product or service. This will assist the team to gain a consensus of exactly what is happening in the process. The following is a review of value stream and process mapping.

Value Stream Mapping	Process Mapping
✔ Makes the waste and source visible	✔ Makes waste visible, can show source by identifying function
✔ New icons	✔ Familiar flowchart
✔ Fairly new tool	✔ Commonly used to analyze business processes
✔ Requires repeatable sequential processes	✔ Can be done with a repetitive or non-repetitive process
✔ Customer focused driven	✔ Task/activity driven
✔ How value is created	✔ How the work flows
✔ Highlights delays between processes	✔ Highlights extraneous steps wtihin a process

There are five types of flowcharts: basic, deployment, opportunity, spaghetti diagram and process.

1. **Basic flowcharts (macro level)** *identify all the major steps in a process - usually no more than six steps.* They are mostly used for the 30,000 foot view for management review.

2. **Deployment flowcharts** *map out the process in terms of who is doing the steps, and is conveyed in the form of a matrix, showing the various participants and the flow of steps among these participants.* These flowcharts are helpful if the process being mapped crosses departmental boundaries.

3. **Opportunity flowcharts** *list the various activities that comprise the process and list differences between value-added and non value-added activities.*

4. **Spaghetti diagram flowcharts** *use a continuous line to trace the path of a part, document, person, or service that is being provided through all its phases.* Spaghetti diagrams expose inefficient layouts and large distances traveled between steps. These diagrams should also display electronic information flow (e-mails, spreadsheets, documents, etc.).

5. **Process flowcharts (micro level)** *examine the process in detail and indicates all the steps or activities that would include the decision points, waiting periods, tasks that frequently must be redone (rework), and any feedback loops.* This is the ground level listing of the tasks and activities.

The following flowchart symbols can be used to map your current process flow. Just as with creating a value stream map with a team, ensure the team can view it as it is being created.

Ovals are used to represent the beginning and ending points of the process.

Rectangles are used to describe an action taken or a task completed.

Diamonds contain questions that require a "Yes" or "No" decision and indicate appropriate process flow.

A Document is used to represent a paper document produced during the process.

Multi-Page Documents are used to represent a report or an output with multiple pages.

A modified rectangle represents a standard to follow (i.e., protocol, standard of service, standard operating procedure, governmental regulation, etc.).

—————▶ An arrow represents the direction of the process flow.

A queue symbol represents a delay in the process.

A circle is used to show that the flow continues on a different page or to another process.

Note: This is the standard set of flowchart icons. The team can create new ones if that would help to improve the visualization of the process flow.

The following are examples of each type of flowchart for a medical office visit, something we are all familiar with, as well as the basic steps to follow. *The last flowchart will denote the Oakview Hospital example.*

Basic flowchart (macro level)

Approach creating this flowchart as follows:

1. Define the process boundaries with the beginning and ending points of the process.
2. Create no more than six boxes denoting what is occurring between the start and end points.
3. Review the flowchart with management to ensure everyone is on the same page with this macro view of the process, or work flow.
4. Continue with more detailed flowcharting or value stream mapping (if appropriate) and follow the VSM methodology.

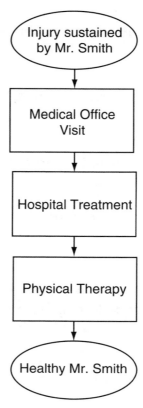

Deployment flowchart

Approach creating this flowchart as follows:

1. Identify the right people needed to develop the flowchart.
2. Define the process boundaries with the beginning and ending points of the process.
3. List the major steps (or time element) of the process on the left side of the sheet.
4. List the responsible department (or process worker) across the top, each in a separate column.
5. List all the steps in their appropriate column and ensure they are connected by arrows.
6. Circulate the flowchart to other people within the process for input and/or clarification (if appropriate).
7. Identify areas for improvement.
8. Create the new flowchart and continue with the VSM methodology.

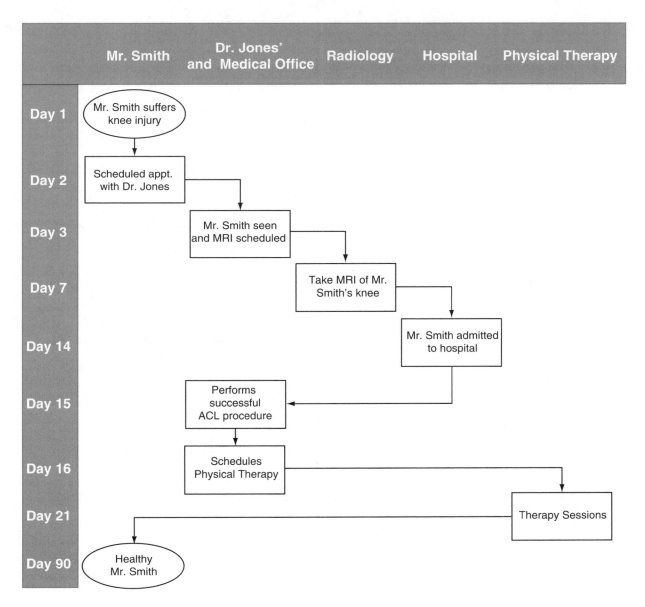

Opportunity flowchart

Approach creating this flowchart as follows:

1. Create a process flowchart (micro level).
2. Create separate columns on a flip chart or whiteboard. Label one Value-Added and the other one Non Value-Added (or Cost-Added Only).
3. List each step from the process flowchart in either column and ensure they are connected by arrows. Expand the steps to show specific areas of concern, if needed.
4. Identify areas for improvement.
5. Create the new flowchart and continue with the VSM methodology.

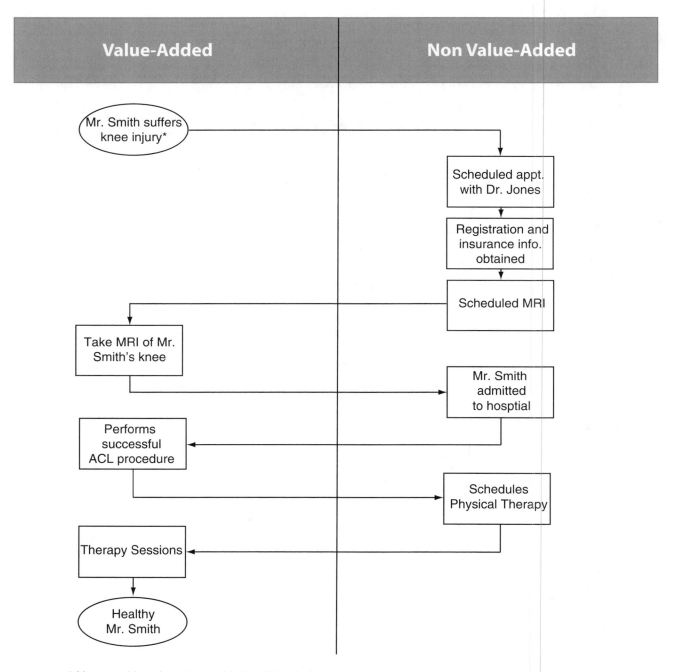

* Not considered a value-added activity, but listed here for informational purposes only.

Spaghetti diagram flowchart

Approach creating this flowchart as follows:

1. Define the beginning and ending of the process.
2. Obtain an engineering drawing or create a scale representation of the physical layout of the process.
3. List each step of the process on the flowchart (or on a separate piece of paper).
4. Label and draw each of the steps (3) sequentially as how the process flows. Connect each step with an arrow line denoting the flow.
5. Gain a consensus if the process is inefficient (i.e., too many touches, too many hand-offs, too much travel, etc.).
6. Identify areas for improvement.
7. Create the new flowchart and continue with the VSM methodology.

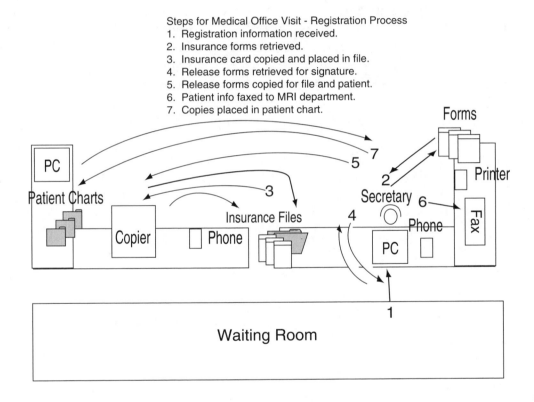

Steps for Medical Office Visit - Registration Process
1. Registration information received.
2. Insurance forms retrieved.
3. Insurance card copied and placed in file.
4. Release forms retrieved for signature.
5. Release forms copied for file and patient.
6. Patient info faxed to MRI department.
7. Copies placed in patient chart.

Process flowchart (micro level)

Approach creating this flowchart as follows:

1. Identify the right people needed to develop the flowchart. This may require people from outside the project team for their expertise and knowledge.
2. Define the process boundaries with the beginning and ending points of the process.
3. Define the level of detail required.
4. Determine conditions and boundaries for the process flow.
5. List all the steps contained within the process flow. The project team may need to walk the process.
6. Circulate the flowchart to other people within the process for input and/or clarification.
7. Identify areas for improvement.
8. Create the new flowchart and continue with the VSM methodology.

Among the many process maps (flowcharts) that the team developed, was the process of getting the patient admitted as an inpatient, once the patient room had been identified. They originally thought that this was a simple process - the order prints in Admitting, the clerk makes the face sheet and wristband, and then brings it over to ED. They were surprised to find how many steps were involved and that there could be delays between many parts of this process. The process flowchart tool provided the team with a consensus of the process activity. The additional tools of the Fishbone Diagram and 5 Why Analysis (next chapter) will guide the team to specific opportunities for improvement. The following is the Registration process flowchart at the micro (detailed activity) level.

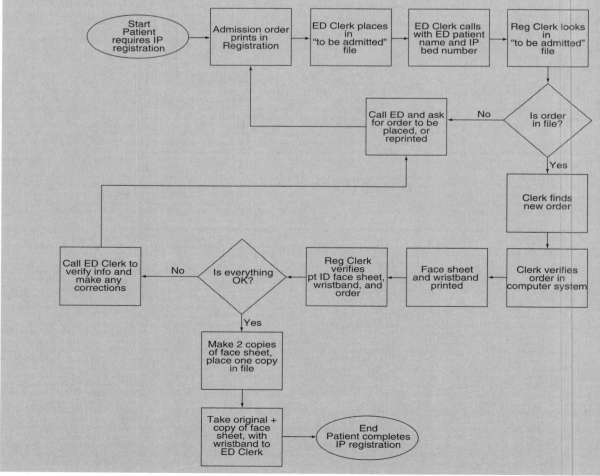

Readiness Guide for Assess

The Readiness Guide for Assess should be reviewed with the team to ensure all appropriate tools have been used. The team should spend approximately 10 minutes to reach a consensus on each of the items. This is also a good indication on how well the team understood the various tools contained in this chapter. At least fifty percent of the questions should be answered with a Yes before proceeding to the next chapter (or phase).

Readiness Guide for the Assess Phase

If you answer No to more than half of these, then consider using additional tools in the Assess phase.

1. Does everyone understand the business case (need) for improvement? ☐ Yes ☐ No

2. Does everyone understand Lean? ☐ Yes ☐ No

3. Does everyone understand kaizen? ☐ Yes ☐ No

4. Has management attended any of the meetings? ☐ Yes ☐ No

5. Has everyone in the department been made aware of the project? ☐ Yes ☐ No

6. Has a Balanced Scorecard been reviewed to determine project? ☐ Yes ☐ No

7. Has a Project Prioritization Worksheet been completed? ☐ Yes ☐ No

8. Has a Team Charter been created? ☐ Yes ☐ No

9. Has the Team Charter been udpated (if appropriate)? ☐ Yes ☐ No

10. Are Status Reports being used to communicate to the champion? ☐ Yes ☐ No

11. Is the process owner part of the team? ☐ Yes ☐ No

12. Is the team aware of the four stages of team development? ☐ Yes ☐ No

13. Are meetings run effectively? ☐ Yes ☐ No

14. Are Effective Meeting Evaluation Forms being used? ☐ Yes ☐ No

15. Has a value stream (or process) map been created? ☐ Yes ☐ No

16. Has the value stream (or process) map been posted? ☐ Yes ☐ No

17. Has a Goal Card been created? ☐ Yes ☐ No

18. Has a Goal Card been posted? ☐ Yes ☐ No

19. Have appropriate measurements been reviewed? ☐ Yes ☐ No

20. Are Idea Kaizens being captured? ☐ Yes ☐ No

Chapter 3: Diagnosis

Topics Include:

✦ **Waste Overview**
✦ **The Elevator Speech**
✦ **How to Conduct a Waste Walk**
✦ **Waste Audit Applied to Oakview's Current State Value Stream Map**
✦ **Data Collection**
✦ **Brainstorming, Cause and Effect Diagram, and 5 Why Analysis**
✦ **Financial Analysis**
✦ **Readiness Guide for Diagnosis**

Each of these topics throughout the next three chapters will be thoroughly explained, as well as referenced to their application in the Oak Valley Health System (Oakview Hospital) case study. This should provide you with enough in-depth knowledge to apply these Lean tools or concepts to your healthcare process.

Note: If the Diagnosis phase is not done correctly, it will not provide the proper Lean foundation for sustainable improvements.

Waste Overview

The healthcare industry is very competitive, not only in their local geographical areas, but also from competition abroad. This situation will not resolve itself and has launched healthcare services into the global market. One of the basic methods to compete in this global market is educating the staff to fully understand the concept of waste and its associated costs. Waste is defined as anything that adds cost or time to a product or service without adding value to the customer (or patient). Keep in mind that the customer can also be the physician or other departments.

The purpose of Lean practices is to identify, analyze, and eliminate all sources of process inefficiencies. Lean is not meant to eliminate people, but to use them wisely and to make people more valuable to the organization. With that in mind, work elements or job functions may need to be reviewed and modified to accommodate this waste-free environment.

Any time a process exists, there is the potential for waste or non value-added activities. Healthcare, like all other industries, is comprised of many processes.

HealthMEDX, a provider of information system solutions for the extended care market, reported the following:

"For every dollar spent on healthcare, over 75 cents is spent on the non-patient care activities of communicating, scheduling, coordinating, supervising, and documenting care."

In an article in Industry Week, a nurse medical researcher stated:

"The national numbers for waste in healthcare are between 30% and 40%, but the reality of what we've observed doing minute-by-minute observation over the last three years is closer to 60%. That's a waste of time, waste of money, and a waste of material resources. The waste is not limited to administrative costs, which most research on healthcare spending has documented. It's everywhere: patient care and non-patient care alike."

Lean eliminates waste or non value-added activities. Waste is defined through the eyes of the customer. Non value-added activities do not add value to the final product or service and customers are not willing to pay for. On the other hand, value added activities are what the customer is willing and should pay for. For example, a patient does not want to pay for a second surgical tray if only one instrument was used from it. All non value-added activities may not be waste, careful consideration as to their overall value must be considered.

A typical process is comprised of both value-added activities as well as non value-added activities (or some of the seven wastes).

Eliminating waste will accomplish the following:

+ Improve patient care and safety
+ Improve productivity and process efficiency
+ Improve quality (reduce the opportunity for errors or mistakes)
+ Reduce cost to the facility
+ Reduce wait (queue) time between processes
+ Make the facility more competitive
+ Encourage teamwork and staff involvement

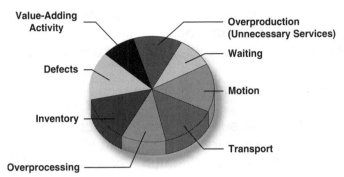

To fully grasp the power of Lean, you first need to be able to understand and identify waste. Waste is a symptom and Lean tools and concepts are used to find and eliminate its root cause(s). The following seven wastes are explained in detail along with questions to assist in their identification and elimination.

1. The Waste of Overproduction (Unnecessary Services)

This waste is producing work or providing a service prior to it being required or requested; this is the greatest of all wastes. If you overproduce some type of work or service, it creates many of the other wastes. For example, dietary may send extra meal trays when a patient has been discharged or moved to another floor or unit, creating wastes such as excessive processing, transport, motion, overproduction, etc.

Examples of overproduction wastes are:

+ Treatment (meds, dressing changes, etc.) given early to suit staff schedule
+ Testing ahead of time to suit lab schedule
+ Treatments done not on scheduled times but instead at times to accommodate hospital staff and/or equipment capacity
+ Making extra copies of charts, reports, labs, etc.
+ Printing, emailing, sending, or faxing the same document multiple times
+ Entering repetitive information on any type of documents or forms

To eliminate this type of waste:

+ Establish continuous work flow in terms of product or service needed at the appropriate time to the downstream customer
+ Ensure information is only entered into one common database for authorized users (EMR/EMS initiatives)
+ Create checklists to ensure all necessary information is attained
+ Create visual controls to prevent early processing of information or services
+ Ensure email distribution lists, reports, etc. are sent to only necessary staff
+ Provide continuous improvement directions to staff when time is available

2. The Waste of Waiting

Waiting for anything, be it people, equipment, signatures, supplies, or information, is waste. This waste of waiting is "low hanging fruit." It is easy to identify and "ripe for the taking." We often do not think of paper sitting in an "In-basket" as waste. However, when looking for an item, how many times do we search through the In-basket to find it? This is identified as a time waster. How many times do you actually touch something before you complete the task? The "finish, file, or throw it away" system can help with eliminating this waste.

Examples of waiting wastes are:

- Delays for bed assignments
- Waiting for admissions to ER
- Excessive signatures or steps to obtain approvals
- Delays for lab test results
- Delays in receiving information or patients
- Cross-departmental resource commitments
- Patient back-ups due to equipment not working properly or not available

To eliminate this type of waste:

- Review and standardize signature and approval requirements.
- Cross-train staff to accommodate changes in service demands.
- Balance work loads throughout the day and ensure staff members are working optimally.
- Identify and eliminate bottlenecks.
- Ensure equipment and supplies (IV poles, wheelchairs, gurneys, meds, etc.) are located in close proximity of their required use.
- Ensure work items are labeled and at point-of-use (as appropriate).

3. The Waste of Motion (excess)

Any excess movement of people, equipment, paper information, or electronic exchanges (emails, etc.) that does not add value is waste. This waste can be created by poor physical layout or design, which can be responsible for more walking, reaching, or bending than necessary.

Examples of motion wastes are:

- ✦ Searching for patients
- ✦ Searching for charts and/or doctor's orders
- ✦ Searching for medications, wheelchairs, or other needed equipment
- ✦ Hand-carrying paperwork to another process
- ✦ Searching for poorly located supplies
- ✦ Obtaining equipment that is not centrally located

To eliminate this type of waste:

- ✦ Ensure supply areas are well organized utilizing color codes and labels for quick access.
- ✦ Arrange Desktop PC files for easy retrieval (establish file naming conventions for the department).
- ✦ Establish standards of communication ensuring doctor's orders and charts are easily accessible for authorized staff.
- ✦ Relocate staff, equipment, etc. to closest area that requires service.

Mini Case Study for Motion Waste

The Clean and Dirty Utility rooms were located side-by-side in an internal hallway. Each room only had one door, on the side farthest away from the patient areas. The ED team asked Facilities whether the doors could be moved or additional doors could be added on the other side of the rooms. Facilities determined that the walls were not load-bearing walls, and said that adding another door would be less expensive than moving the door to a new location and closing the former doorway. Having two doors for each room caused some concern about the space inside these utility rooms, so the team did a 5S on both rooms. With the space freed up, they were able to remove one set of shelves in the dirty utility room, and replace a large refrigerator in the clean utility room with a smaller counter-top refrigerator. When room for the two new doors was made, Facilities added the new doorways over the course of a few days.
With about 20 feet of "motion waste" removed, ED staff now had access to the rooms in a more efficient manner.

---

4. The Waste of Transport (or excess Conveyance)

Transporting materials, information, and/or patients further than necessary is waste. Also, excess time and energy spent locating, filing, stacking or moving charts, labs, etc. can be waste. It is this excess movement of work (or patients) that does not add value.

Examples of transport wastes are:

✦ Transporting the surgical patient from outpatient area to preop area prior to surgery
✦ Placing a gurney in the hall and constantly having to move it
✦ Moving samples, specimens, or equipment too early or late, and/or to the wrong location

To eliminate this type of waste:

✦ Ensure the distance to move something is minimized.
✦ Establish standard times for patients to arrive prior to procedures (maybe within a 5 minute window, but not 15 minutes prior or 1 minute late).
✦ Create standard locations for supplies and equipment.
✦ Create visual controls and communicate standards for use of supplies and equipment.

5. The Waste of Overprocessing

Putting more work or effort into things that a patient, physician, healthcare provider, etc. does not want or ask for is waste. Overprocessing does not add value and the customer will not want to pay for it.

Examples of overprocessing wastes are:

✦ Ordering more diagnostic tests than the diagnosis warrants (i.e., ordering a Chem 24 when a Chem 6 will suffice, or replacing a heparin lock before policy dictates it to be changed)
✦ Requesting and processing information that will never be used
✦ Entering repetitive information

To eliminate this type of waste:

✦ Review all steps within a process and eliminate non value-added activities.
✦ Standardize work procedures to best practice.
✦ Eliminate redundant information required on forms by consolidating forms (or information required).

6. The Waste of Inventory

Excess stock, work piles, and supplies are waste; they all take up space.

Note: Time is considered excess inventory if it is not used efficiently.

Examples of inventory wastes are:

- ✦ Duplicate medications and supplies in excess of normal usage
- ✦ Extra or outdated manuals, newsletters, or magazines
- ✦ Excessive office supplies
- ✦ Obsolete charts, files, and equipment
- ✦ Insufficient cross-training of staff
- ✦ Redundant materials/supply locations within the same department
- ✦ Patients in a waiting room

To eliminate this type of waste:

- ✦ Produce or provide only the necessary information, supply, or service to satisfy the downstream customer.
- ✦ Standardize minimum and maximum levels for supplies and keep organized.
- ✦ Audit the supply replenishment system to ensure correct levels of supplies are always on hand and available.
- ✦ Ensure work (charts, lab requests, patients, etc.) arrive at the next process on time

7. The Waste of Defects (or mistakes)

This category of waste refers to all processing required to correct a defect or mistake. Defects (either internal or external) result in additional processes (and possible services) that will add no value to the product or service. The idea is that it takes a shorter time to do the process or activity correctly the first time than it does to do it over again and correct the problem. Whether a staff member is administering care, updating a patient's chart, or entering codes for the insurance company, each time they are interrupted by someone for any reason, an opportunity for error is created.

Examples of defect wastes are:

- ✦ Retesting (i.e., performing a second 24-hour urine test because a staff member obtained the first specimen incorrectly)
- ✦ Medication errors
- ✦ Wrong patient information
- ✦ Wrong procedure
- ✦ Missing information

To eliminate this type of waste:

- ✦ Create visual controls to ensure work standards are met.
- ✦ Create work standards that meet best practice.
- ✦ Ensure preventive maintenance schedules are adhered to for all equipment.
- ✦ Ensure cross-training is conducted to accommodate increases in demand.

(8.) The Waste of Unused Creativity

You will also find an eighth waste - unused creativity. This waste does not utilize the available talents and skills of staff to their fullest.

Examples of unused creativity wastes are:

+ No defined performance management system
+ Little or no cross-training

To eliminate this type of waste:

+ Develop a performance management system for employee development.
+ Create training and development plans for each employee.

Consider the following questions:

1. "How can I start to communicate about these wastes throughout the department or facility?" (What are the quick and obvious wastes that can be easily addressed?)
2. "What are the low-hanging fruit?"
3. "What can be done immediately to improve patient, provider, and staff satisfaction?"

These types of question should stimulate similar questions and allow for open communications regarding waste.

Once the concept of waste is understood, it becomes easier to diagnose its presence, apply treatment, and improve its condition through the use of Lean practices and principles. This can be accomplished by conducting a Waste Walk with the team and then conveying the information obtained to the current state value stream map. Prior to conducting a Waste Walk the team should create a standard message that can explained to the employees when the team member visits the area.

The Elevator Speech

*An **elevator speech** is a brief, comprehensive verbal overview on the purpose and related-activities regarding a product, service, or project.* The name reflects the fact that an elevator pitch can be delivered in the time span of an elevator ride (say, thirty seconds or 100-150 words). It was derived from the way important decisions were made on the floor of the United States's House of Representatives and Senate. These conversations were made "within the span of an elevator ride" as a staff aide whispered into a Congressman's or Senator's ear while they headed down to the floor to cast their vote. A good elevator speech accomplishes the following:

+ Conveys what the service, problem, or activity is
+ Informs the need in terms of the audience (to whom the speech is for)
+ What will be done
+ Requests what is needed from the person or how they can assist the team

An elevator speech is not just for top level management. It is used anytime that a common message must be sent across different groups and people. For example, in a Kaizen Event, when teams conduct their Waste Walk, they should have prepared an elevator speech as to why they are there and what they are doing.

At Oakview Hospital, the team created the following elevator speech prior to their Waste Walk.

"This project is about getting our patients into the right level of care as soon as possible. It's important because the ED is a place for short-term, immediate-need care only. When we're successful, we'll see patients admitted to a hospital bed within 90 minutes after the dispo has been written. We're looking for your help with ideas and suggestions to cut down on wasted effort and delays in getting our patients admitted right away."

The team found that working on the elevator speech generated a lot of discussion about what the project was "really" about, and what success would look like. In fact, developing the speech turned out to be a team-building exercise, as well.

Whatever form your elevator speech takes, ensure it is a standard statement, short, concise, and to-the-point.

How to Conduct a Waste Walk

A **Waste Walk** is activity when of project team members visiting the process area that is being considered for improvement, asking questions, and then identifying the wastes on the current state value stream map. Many of the team members will be very familiar with the project area as it is their actual work area. Conducting this Waste Walk, the team members, along with their Lean training, will be viewing their areas with a fresh perspective as they look at the overall processes and flow.

The Waste Walk accomplishes the following:

- ✦ Ensures everyone is aligned to the physical location of the processes being analyzed
- ✦ Ensures process workers are engaged in the Kaizen Event
- ✦ Allows for all process workers to provide input
- ✦ Allows for open communications about the team's project
- ✦ Allows for discussions about the process to clear up any questions

To conduct a Waste Walk consider the following:

1. Communicate to the employees working in the prospective areas/processes/departments when you will be bringing the group through and explain your purpose using the elevator speech.
2. Assign one person in each group to take notes. Use the following Waste Audit as a guide.
3. Ensure the team has thought of questions to ask, including: What are some of your issues affecting your work? What could be improved? Do you help out when things get busy? If not, why? Do you know when you are behind schedule? Do you know when the work you provide is needed downstream (to the next process)?
4. Do not cause any disruption to inpatient care and/or delivery of services. (e.g., If a Waste Walk is to be conducted through ED, if possible, schedule a walk during their least busy time as well as one during their busy time.)
5. If the group is larger than 5, break into smaller groups.
6. Start with the most downstream process and work upstream.
7. Thank the person(s) (and departmental manager/supervisor) for their time.

The following information is referred to as a Waste Audit. It is a summary of wastes used to analyze the processes, before, during, and after the Waste Walk.

The Waste Audit

Waste Category	Definition	Examples in Healthcare
Overproduction (Unnecessary Services)	This category of waste describes when information (paper based or electronic) is duplicated or more service is provided to the customer than what they requested. This is the greatest of all the wastes because it diminishes capacity and leads to the creation of additional wastes.	Pills given early to suit staff schedule Testing ahead of time to suit lab schedule Treatments done not on schedule to balance hospital staff and/or equipment workload Making extra copies Printing, emailing, sending, or faxing the same document multiple times Entering repetitive information on documents or forms
Mistakes (Defects)	Anytime someone acts against a standard, there are wasteful consequences. Many of the checks, cross-checks, and customer complaints are due to mistakes. This category of waste refers to all time spent redoing, correcting, or reworking a process. The work should have been performed correctly the first time. Waste results in the expenditure of additional time, materials, energy, equipment, and labor.	Medication errors Wrong patient information Wrong procedure Missing information Retesting (i.e., performing a second 24-hour urine test because a staff member obtained the first specimen incorrectly)
Waiting (Delays)	Delay waste is further categorized into waiting time waste and equipment failure waste. Waiting for anything such as (people, paper, equipment, or information) is waste. Waiting means that there is idle time causing work to stop. It means that people and processes are idle. Time spent waiting because of equipment downtime, ineffectiveness, or slowness is also waste. This includes complete breakdowns, as well as slowdowns, due to poor maintenance, scheduling, software updates, etc.	Delays for bed assignments Waiting for admissions to ER Excessive signatures or approvals Delays for lab test results Delays in receiving information or patients Cross-departmental resource commitments Patient back-up due to equipment not working properly
Excess Motion	Any excess movement of people, equipment, paper information, or electronic exchanges (i.e., emails, text messags, etc.) that does not add value is waste.	Searching for patients Searching for charts and/or doctor's orders Searching for medications, wheelchairs, or other needed equipment Hand-carrying paperwork to another process Searching for poorly located supplies Obtaining equipment that is not centrally located

The Waste Audit

To Detect This Waste Ask	Questions for Your Target Area
Is the service or work to be performed a repeat? Is this form a duplicate of some other form? Can the information on this form be used for other similar processes? Are the right people communicated to at the right time to receive all relevant information? Is there a preparing of charts, laundry carts, etc. ahead of time that are not utilized?	
Is a task routinely being done that is not part of a procedure? Is there extra paperwork? Can information be consolidated for ease of use? Are there reasons why there may be incorrect information? Does paperwork need to be resubmitted? Are there clear procedures for doing the work? Is the equipment properly maintained?	
Does all equipment have a maintenance schedule? Is the equipment maintenance record up-to-date? Are there delays in the delivery of equipment, information/data to a location or process? Are there issues with punctuality with employees? Is there a bottleneck or delay in the process due to obtaining information, supplies, equipment, etc.? Are there too many approvals?	
Can walking be reduced by repositioning equipment, people, and/or supplies? Can point-of-use information be utilized? Are all current and new employees trained to best standard procedures? How does the current layout impede the process flow?	

The Waste Audit

Waste Category	Definition	Examples in Healthcare
Overprocessing	Putting work or effort into things that a customer (internal or external) does not want or ask for is waste. Overprocessing wastes energy and time, and does not add value for the customer.	Ordering more diagnostic tests than the diagnosis warrants (i.e., ordering a Chem 24 when a Chem 6 will suffice or replacing a heparin lock before policy dictates it to be changed) Completing excessive paperwork Entering repetitive information
Excess Inventory	Excessive stock (i.e., duplicate supplies, manuals, periodicals, etc.) of anything is waste. Excessive supplies take up needed space and are a waste. Patients, who are waiting, can be considered inventory. Time can also be considered inventory.	Duplicate medications and supplies in excess of normal usage Extra or outdated manuals, newsletters, or magazines Excessive office supplies Obsolete charts, files, and equipment Obsolete office equipment Insufficient cross-training of staff
Excess Transport	Transport is an important element in providing a service to the customers. Many times information (paper or electronic), as well as those that must provide a service to a customer, must be moved more than once. Any unnecessary transportation of information or people is a waste.	Transporting the surgery patient from outpatient area to preop area prior to surgery Placing a gurney in the hall and constantly having to move it Moving samples, specimens, or equipment early or late and/or to the wrong location
Unused Creativity	Many times this will be considered an eighth waste. This is the waste that does not utilize people's skills to their fullest.	Not having self contributing ideas for improvements Not being cross-trained No performance management system No employee training and development plan

The Waste Audit

To Detect This Waste Ask	Questions for Your Target Area
Has this paperwork been done before? Is this a repeat of information already processed? Are there redundant phone calls and emails? Is there more information available than what needs to be processed?	
Are there out-of-date manuals, books, regulations, standards in the area? Are there supply boxes sitting on the floor? Is there extra equipment laying around? Are you overstocked in the target area? Are you using the hall for storage space? Does staff often complain about a lack of storage? Do you frequently see patients waiting in groups?	
Is data or are patients moved to temporary locations? Do you spend a lot of time searching for supplies, charts, orders, labs, etc. Do you spend time walking to a fax, copier, or to deliver information? Do you hand deliver documents, etc. that could be electronically delivered?	
Are employees cross-trained? Are employees encouraged to suggest improvements? Are employees encouraged to implement improvements? Are processes designed that build in underutilization of staff?	

Once the Waste Walk has been completed and the information is fresh in everyone's mind, it is time to relate the wastes to the current state value stream map. This is accomplished in the following ways:

1. Distribute different color Post-it Notes to each group (if the team was divided into two groups to conduct the Waste Walk). It is suggested that groups be no larger than 5.

2. Allow 15 minutes for each person to write the various wastes that were identified on the Waste Walk onto the Post-it Notes.

3. Direct each group (individual) to place their Post-it Note on the area of the value stream map where they believe the waste is occurring. If this map was created via a laptop and LCD projection unit, project the map on a whiteboard so the physical placement of the Post-it Notes can be done on the image.

Keep in mind that the wastes may be listed as process steps or specific activities instead of the exact name of the 7-8 wastes. If that is the case then the facilitator should attempt to relate those items listed to the actual waste to ensure that everyone understands the overall concept of waste.

Waste Audit Applied to Oakview's Current State Value Stream Map

The following is the result of the Oakview Hospital's Waste Walk as conveyed on their current state value stream map. Since the team was familiar with the entire ED process, they decided to use the overall ED Arrival to Inpatient Bed Current State Value Stream Map and not just the Dispo-to-Admit Current State Value Stream Map to identify wastes. They thought if additional ideas were generated for the other value streams, then that information could be used for additional Operational Excellence projects.

Oakview Hospital's ED Arrival to Inpatient Bed Current State Value Stream Map

If two or more teams did separate Waste Walks, then they would probably identify the same wastes on the map. This is OK. Allow all wastes from all groups (and individuals) to be displayed. Review with the group the various wastes identified on the value stream map. At this time, allow the group another 15 minutes, using a different color Post-it Note, but this time be specific as to the process activity that is occurring that may be causing that waste.

The following is the updated result of the Oakview Hospital's Waste Audit on the value stream map with ideas on the potential reasons of why the wastes are occurring. This will further assist the team in determining any additional data that may need to be collected.

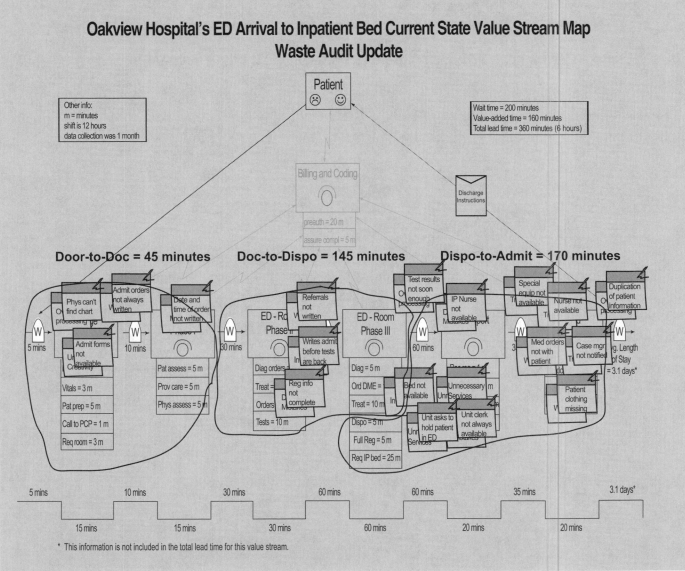

Do not be concerned about the process activities that are listed, in that, they directly correspond to the exact definition of a particular waste. The Waste Walk and the listings of the wastes to the value stream map processes/activities/tasks are meant to bridge the Waste Walk (and Audit) to the current state value stream map.

Note: You can conduct this as a two-step approach, or you can combine both steps into one and use the Post-it Notes to identify the activities that appear to be waste.

Data Collection

Data collection is probably one of the most important functions of a team. It is confusing, at times, to the team members as they struggle with questions such as:

1. What data do I collect? From which processes in the value stream?
2. How much data do I collect? What is the sample size? What is the total population of the sample size?
3. Who will collect the data? Can we rely on a report generated from the system? Is it accurate or not?
4. Will the data be easy to collect? Do we need to do observations of an area or process to obtain actual numbers? If so, how many hours, days do we observe the process?
5. If data is not accessible and cannot be observed, can I rely on the process worker to provide accurate data?

Before those questions are answered, let us cover a few aspects of data collection (and display).

There is a fine line between collecting too much data and falling into the "analysis by paralysis" trap and not collecting enough data to base long term solutions and/or enterprise-wide improvements upon.

Data collection and its subsequent analysis allows for "data" or "numbers" to provide meaningful information for the Lean project. This collection of data is a crucial part of the Lean transformation. The highest quality data must be attained through proper planning on how to gather the data to ensure stability and reliability in the collection process. Failure to properly gather data will compromise the project as well as create wasted time as staff generate additional efforts to gather the necessary data.

Steps to Good Data Collection

Use the following steps as a guide when you plan to collect data. The four steps ensure that the most accurate data will be collected using a reliable methodology.

1. Plan for data collection. This is where you would specify the goals and objectives for the data to be collected. This would include providing an overview of the process or processes and the reasoning behind the data collection (e.g., need to populate the value stream map to be able to establish a benchmark). Determine what data is to be gathered and how, the amount (time, duration) of data to be gathered, and at which processes that this data will be collected. The area/department/process/person should be notified well in advance if the observation method is to be used.

2. Standardize how cycle times are measured. It may be a challenge to obtain exact cycle times for some of the activities within a process, but do not let that stop you - be as accurate as you can and improve from there.

3. Collect the data. This is a collection of data as defined by the parameters in (1 and 2).

4. Analyze and present the data. This is where you determine the data's repeatability, accuracy, and stability. For example, if an area was observed and the data was skewed (distorted or biased in some way) then another observation may be necessary. The team must reach consensus on the data that was collected as to its accuracy and reliability. This is not to say that the empirical data collected should give-way to the opinions of the team, however, the data or method in which the data was collected, should be reasonable as to what team member's experience has been. When there is a thought like, "that can't be right" from team members regarding data collected, discuss it with the team and proceed back to (1). Also, present as much of the data in graphical form, i.e., bar chart or table, when appropriate.

Note: At the first team meeting, the facilitator should be careful not to present too much historical data (i.e., trends, mediums, modes, frequency, variances, etc.). Team members can be overwhelmed if they are overburdened with numbers at an early stage. If historical data is available, then a few overall numbers may be used. Too many Six Sigma projects have failed because Black Belts were too aggressive in presenting data. As good and accurate as this data may be, it is still about getting the process worker involved. Work with the team at that first meeting to reach a consensus on which data will be most useful. Determine which type of data collection technique is appropriate for your project.

Types of Data Collection

Observation

Observation is a way to collect information about a process by watching and documenting on how people do their jobs. There are two methods of collecting data: Participant observation - where the team member takes part in the situation he or she observes; and non-participant observation - where the team member watches the situation but does not participate.

Observation should be used when:

✦ Direct information is required and historical data is too broad or does not relate to the specifics of the project
✦ Historical data cannot be obtained
✦ There is a discrepancy between historical data and the experiences of the team
✦ The team requires better understanding of the process
✦ Cycle times are not known
✦ The process is not clearly known
✦ Interruptions impact the process and cycle times and have never been documented

When deciding on what and who to observe (the busiest time of the day/week, the person who does that process the best, the person that has had trouble with the process, or a new person) ensure you have enough data to be able to make an inference about the total population.

For the observation method to be useful and credible, the observations need to be accurately recorded. The following tools can be used with either the participant or non-participant observation method.

An *Observation Guide* is a printed or web-based form that provides space for recoding information about the process being analyzed. The more structured the guide, the easier it will be to total the results and *less likely* for variation in the data collected. A form with specific activities listed would be provided and it would be up to the process worker and/or person observing to fill out the required information (i.e., activity or step, cycle times, interruptions, etc.).

Based on wastes observed during the Waste Walk, the team developed an ED/Inpt - Delay Worksheet to capture more information about the potential reasons for long delays in the Dispo-to-Admit value stream. The team asked the staff to complete the delay worksheets for one week. Delays were simply defined as taking longer than expected, given their own experiences in the ED. The team was focused more on the staff's perceptions of the delays. From the initial communications, they believed they would get a good number of responses. Delays have always been an issue within the ED.

The Lean team conducted quick staff meetings (5 minutes or less) at the beginning of each shift to orient the staff to the worksheet. The team placed a basket on the ED clerk's desk labeled "Study Sheets" (so the patients would not think there were delays being measured!). Each day, the sheets were collected and collated onto a summary sheet (next page).

The team thought the doctors might not want to assist in this, however, they indicated that they would be glad to help in collecting the data. They said that if the forms were placed in the front of the chart for easy access, then that would remind them to fill out the form.

The following is an example of an Observation Guide used by the Oakview Hospital Lean team.

ED/Inpt - Delay Worksheet

Instructions:
1. *Triage Nurses*, please begin this form by writing the patient name and adding it as the last page of the chart.
2. *Nurses, Physicians, HUCs, Techs, and anyone else helping with patient care*, please note the delays on this form.
3. If there has been a delay, *as defined from your ED experience* at Oakview for a patient, please place an "X" in the appropriate box. More than one reason for delay can be selected. Please add comments as needed to explain the delay, and indicate on each line, in your best estimation, the length of the delay.
4. *Health Unit Clerk*, please remove this form when breaking the chart down. Place it in the designated area by the end of your shift for pick-up by the Lean team member.

Patient Name: _____

Admitting Order Delays:
Delay in finding admitting form: _____
Delay in finding chart: _____
Delay in giving chart to clerk: _____
Patient needs extended conversation: _____

Doctor wants to write dispo, doesn't have all lab/radiology results: _____
Doctor wants to write dispo, patient hasn't received meds yet: _____
Delay in writing admitting orders: _____
Delay in writing prescriptions: _____
Delay in writing referrals: _____

Prep for Admitting Delays:
Waiting for available bed: _____
Special equipment not available: _____
Delay in writing report to unit: _____
Other: _____

Inpatient nurse not available to take report: _____
Search for belongings: _____
Delay in copying chart: _____

Patient to Unit Delays:
Transporter not available: _____
Other: _____

Other Delays:
Problem finding chart: _____
Waiting for consults: _____
Waiting for bed: _____

Other (please specify):
_____
_____
_____

If you have any questions, please contact Sue at x2244. Thank you for your time.

By the end of the week, the team had completed the forms for 100 patients. The following is a summary for 19 of the collected forms (which later will be displayed in the Pareto Chart on page 143). The data on the 81 remaining forms conveyed very similar trends for all the categories.

ED/Inpt Delay Worksheet Summary

Patient ID	Delay in finding admitting form	Delay in finding chart	Delay in giving chart to clerk	Patient needs extended conv.	Dr. waiting on lab/radiology results	Dr. waiting, patient has not rec'd meds	Delay in writing admitting orders	Delay in writing prescriptions	Delay in writing referrals	Wait for available bed	Special equipment not available	Delay in writing report to unit	IP nurse not available for report	Search for pt belongings	Delay in copying chart	Transporter not available	Unit asks ED to hold pt	IP clerk not available on unit	IP nurse not available on unit	Problem finding chart	Waiting for consults	Waiting for bed	Other ___ (specify)	Other ___ (specify)	Other ___ (specify)
	Admitting Orders									**Prep for Admit**						**Pt to Unit**				**Other**					
1567	✓	✓				✓				✓	✓	✓		✓		✓	✓					✓			
2239	✓			✓							✓		✓		✓					✓					
9433					✓		✓																		
4239	✓		✓	✓		✓		✓	✓	✓	✓								✓						
1555	✓		✓		✓							✓	✓												
1196						✓	✓					✓			✓										
6767					✓					✓					✓						✓				
0688			✓				✓			✓					✓		✓		✓						
2299	✓				✓				✓						✓										
1810			✓			✓			✓	✓				✓	✓	✓	✓	✓							
3116												✓													
1237						✓							✓								✓				
1313	✓	✓				✓	✓		✓	✓						✓									
4114	✓								✓								✓		✓						
1543					✓							✓	✓		✓	✓			✓						
1629			✓			✓				✓						✓									
8117	✓					✓		✓	✓										✓			✓			
1818					✓									✓											
9190									✓							✓	✓	✓							
2020						✓			✓			✓				✓				✓					
Totals	8	2	5	2	6	9	4	2	8	7	3	6	4	4	7	7	5	2	5	2	2	2			

Note: In the Standard Work section of this book, other tools will be used to further ana-lyze process data.

The number of observations should be more than 1 and can be less than 30. The larger the sample size (n=X), the more accurate the overall data will be. If you do a sample size of n = 12 prior to Lean, then also do the same sample size (n = 12) after the Lean project. If you have months worth of data, then take a good representation of that and use for pre-Kaizen Event analysis.

After data has been collected, it is recommended that it be compiled into a type of pie, bar, con-trol, run, or pareto chart. (See the Data Display section later in this chapter.)

Another type of Observation Guide is referred to as a Document Tagging Worksheet.

*The **Document Tagging Worksheet** is a form to capture the work elements and steps accurate-ly, as a chart, patient, or document moves throughout an entire process or value stream.*

Document tagging:

- ✦ Continues to create awareness of how time is being used within a process
- ✦ Involves everyone connected to the process
- ✦ Promotes an accurate analysis of the process based on actual times
- ✦ Provides (or validates) data for the value stream map

The Document Tagging Worksheet is used when the activity steps are fairly well-defined. This worksheet is typically attached to a chart, work document, etc. to capture the entire process flow of work, along with who touches it, when, and for how long.

Use the following steps as a guideline when creating and using a Document Tagging Worksheet.

1. Determine the process(es) or value stream on which data will be collected.

2. Create the Document Tagging Worksheet in Microsoft Word or Excel and label the vari-ous columns.

3. Communicate to the group what information is required on the form. Ensure the tasks are described as a verb-noun combination (e.g., review doctor's orders, verbally pre-pare the patient, prepare arm, draw blood, etc.).

4. Distribute the form to the most upstream process in the value stream. This will be where the work or patient originates. This is like placing an "alert" or tag on a docu-ment (e.g., patient chart) and following it through the various processes until it reaches the most downstream process.

5. Collect all of the data. Complete 10-15 different worksheets for the process or value stream, and then average. Determine a good sample size and account for trends. The staff is required to document the following columns:

> Step - this should be sequential
> Name/Dept
> Date
> Time In
> Date
> Time Out
> Task/Activity

6. Utilize data to establish the cycle times for the process(es). Once the document has reached the final process, the following information should be analyzed:

> Delay/Wait Time: Subtract In Time from the Out Time of the previous step
> Cycle Time: Subtract the beginning time of the step from the end time of the step
> Elapsed Time: Add Delay/Wait Time to Cycle Time, plus Elapsed Time from previous step
> Value-Added Time: The time required to physically (or electronically) transform the service into value for the patient or customer (other healthcare provider or department). It is the cycle time minus any delay or wait time for that step. If the entire step is considered waste, then it should be included as non value-added time.
> Non Value-Added Time: Add the Delay/Wait Time to any cycle time that does not add value (i.e., additional wait time, cycle time that adds no value, etc.)

7. Update the current state value stream map (or process map).

The purpose of document tagging is NOT to capture all of the steps in the workflow, but to track how a particular item is moved through the process (specific areas of the value stream that times cannot be determined with accuracy). For example, perform document tagging on just the chart - how often is it touched, moved, reviewed, or annotated during the patient stay. Or, perform on lab results - from the time they print in the ED, through placement in the chart and/or transfer to physician's or nurse's attention, what is the flow? Or, from the patient's perspective - what happens directly with the patient? In this way, the team can gain valuable perspective on how the parts of the process flow so that improvement ideas can be developed.

Note that this is a different way to capture data than that described on page 82 for the Cycle Time Table. Here we are focusing on ONE ELEMENT as it flows through the process, rather than all of the activities related to that process. Remember, you will most likely not account for every single second or minute on the processes (or value stream). Do not let that deter your drive to gather this data. Be satisfied with 80% and move on!

The team decided to perform document tagging on the chart information, from the time the disposition was entered by the physician to the time the patient left the ED (from the middle part of ED Room Phase III (Dr. writes Dispo/Admit order) to IP Bed Request process as displayed by the current state value stream map) (page 103). They agreed to track both the original chart and, after it was copied for inpatient admission, the copy as well. The team developed their Document Tagging Worksheet and agreed to track 10 charts during the following week. The smallest increment of time to be used was 1 minute.

The following is the first chart that was studied using the Document Tagging Worksheet.

Document Tagging Worksheet

Value Stream Dispo-to-Admit   **Start Date In** 4/10

Process ED Dispo to Chart Prep   **Start Date Out** 4/10

Step	Name/Dept.	In Date	In Time	Out Date	Out Time	Task/Activity	Delay/Wait Time from Previous Step	Cycle Time	Elapsed Time	Value-Added Time	Non Value-Added Time
1	Doctor	4/10	0823	4/10	0833	Write Dispo/Admit Order	0	10	10	10	0
2	Doctor	4/10	0833	4/10	0838	Perform medication reconciliation	0	5	15	5	0
3	Doctor	4/10	0840	4/10	0841	Not Dispo (Admit) Order in chart	2	1	18	0	3
4	ED Clerk	4/10	0857	4/10	0859	Process Admit Order in IT system	16	2	36	0	18
5	ED Clerk	4/10	0907	4/10	0908	Place face sheet in chart	8	1	45	0	9
6	ED Clerk	4/10	0912	4/10	0925	Copy ED chart for IP chart	4	13	62	0	17
7	ED Nurse	4/10	0932	4/10	0936	Complete Med/Allergy form	7	4	73	4	7
8	ED Nurse	4/10	0936	4/10	0946	Complete charting record for IP unit	0	10	83	10	0
9	ED Nurse	4/10	0946	4/10	0949	Refer to chart when IP unit is called	0	3	86	3	0
10	ED Tech	4/10	0952	4/10	0955	Complete clothing check form in chart	3	3	92	0	6
11	ED Tech	4/10	0957	4/10	0958	Note vital signs in chart	2	1	95	1	2
12	ED Tech	4/10	1001	4/10	1004	Call transporter, note in chart	3	3	101	0	6
13	ED Nurse	4/10	1007	4/10	1010	Note last vital signs	3	3	107	3	3
14	ED Clerk	4/10	1012	4/10	1014	Place chart, face sheet, wst band, und. matt.	2	2	111	0	4
15	ED Nurse	4/10	1019	4/10	1020	Note call to IP Ns. Mgr. when patient leaves	5	1	117	0	6
16	Transporter	4/10	1023	4/10	1024	Check chart is ready to travel w/ patient	3	1	121	0	4
						TOTALS	58	63	121	36	85

Notes:
Delay/Wait Time is calculated by subtracting the In Time from the Out Time of the previous step.
Cycle Time is calculated by subtracting the beginning time of the step from the end time of the step.
Elapsed Time is the Delay/Wait Time plus the Cycle Time accumulated from each step (running total).
Value-Added Time is the time required to physically (or electronically) transform the service into value for the patient or customer (other healthcare provider or department). It typically is the cycle time minus any delay or wait time for that step.
Non Value-Added Time is calculated by adding the Delay/Wait Time plus any Cycle Time that does not add value to the patient (or customer).

Analysis:
Total chart activity time, from Dispo written to patient leaving, was 121 minutes or 2 hours, 1 minute (from 0823 to 1024). Note: this is less than the 170 minutes total lead time for the Dispo-to-Admit value stream because the Document Tagging ends when the patient leaves the ED.
The value-added time was 36 minutes.
Therefore, the chart was being used approximately 30% of the time, with the other 70% of the time being inactive.
This demonstrated the amount of information that must be ready prior to the patient being transferred to the inpatient bed from the ED. More importantly, it validated much of the information from the Cycle Time Table and other data collection tools used to create the current state value stream map. It also provided additional insight (and possible solutions) to the delays that were occurring.
This information was used to provide more detail to the current state value stream map. *It will not match exactly the Cycle Time Table because the focus of this data was the chart information process.*

Historical Data (or using current data available)

Data can be collected by creating various reports from EMR/EMS databases or from other vendor electronic information systems. Usually, there is a large amount of data available from these systems, although it may not necessarily have been analyzed. The advantage of using existing data is that its collection is fairly inexpensive. However, it is sometimes difficult to gain access to the specific information in the right format required; therefore, IT may need to be involved to help create the report needed.

The **Voice of the Customer (VOC)** *survey captures (via direct discussions, interviews, surveys, focus groups, observations, reports, logs, web questionnaires, etc.) customer (internal or external) requirements and uses that data to provide the best-in-class service.* The Voice of the Customer (VOC) is another method to gather process data. It should be used when there are doubts to what type of data is useful and/or if there is some indifference among the team to what is the perceived value from the customer perspective. It is recommended this survey be conducted early in the project. The information can then be used for consideration when brainstorming for improvement ideas.

There is no one single voice of the customer. Customer voices are diverse and are subjective to what they perceive as value. The Voice of the Customer survey should be created by determining those critical "touch points" that define the quality of the service as defined from the customer. *A **touch point** is the direct and/or critical contact between a service provider and the customer.* For example, it may be the first contact that a Triage nurse has with the patient in those first few minutes of an ER visit, versus subsequent administrative support in obtaining insurance information. It is recommended that, if at all possible, the survey be reviewed by the target audience (customers) before it is used. This will ensure a higher confidence on the data that is obtained.

Additional points to consider when creating a Voice of the Customer survey:

- ✦ Analyze *current* customer satisfaction levels
- ✦ Ensure a cross-functional (or multi-disciplinary) team has input
- ✦ Determine competitor's strengths and weaknesses, if appropriate
- ✦ Use quantitative (e.g., complaint logs, etc) and qualitative (e.g., mini-surveys, etc.) data

Use the information obtained from the Voice of the Customer survey as one of your determinates in creating your Lean future state.

The team knew they needed to obtain the "Voice of the Customer" to understand how the patients viewed their stay. Focusing on the time it took to get the patient from the ED to the hospital bed, they devised a VOC survey and arranged for it to be given to the patient, or a family member, the morning after admission. The team decided to collect a minimum of 30 forms so the responses could be averaged. The team felt that 30 was a reasonable number; if more were collected, that would be great.

The team discussed the issue of patient perception compared to actual elapsed time. It was probable that the perception of passing time for an ED patient might not be accurate, but the team decided that addressing perception would be an important part of the solution when reducing the actual cycle time.

The team expanded the VOC to include areas outside the specific Dispo-to-Admit value stream to further understand the entire ED value stream. The following is the VOC survey for Oakview Hospital.

Voice of the Customer (VOC) ED/Inpt Survey

In an effort to improve our Emergency Room services we are requesting you fill out this survey. Focus your attention to the timeframe between being notified of being admitted to the time of bed placement.

PLEASE SEND THIS WITH YOUR DINNER MENU SELECTION TODAY!

Name:_____ Date:_____

1. Of the following options, what is most important to providing you with the best ER experience possible?
   Rank 1 - 5 in order of importance with 1 being the most important and 5 the least important.

   _____ **Skill of physicians/nurses**   _____ **Cleanliness**

   _____ **Attitude of staff**   _____ **Timeliness/waiting**

   _____ **Keeping me informed of care plan**   _____ **Keeping me informed of delays**

2. Please estimate the time and service levels you experienced from the time you received the information you were to be admitted to the time you were in the hospital bed.

	How long? Note minutes or hours.	Was this acceptable?	If No, how long would have been acceptable? Note minutes or hours.
From the time you were told that you would probably be admitted, to the time you were told that you were definitely going to be admitted?		Yes No	
From the time you were told that you were going to be admitted, until you (or your family) were told what room number you were going to?		Yes No	
From the time you knew what unit and/or room number you would be going to, until the time you left the ED?		Yes No	
From the time you left the ED, until the time you were comfortably positioned in your inpatient bed?		Yes No	

3. Would you choose one hospital for ER care over another if you knew that a doctor would see you within 30 minutes? Cirlce one.

   Yes   No

4. Is there anything else that you would like us to know, either good or bad, about your ER visit?

Thank you very much for your time in completing this survey. This information will be very helpful in improving the service we provide to you (and your family).

Please return all forms to Sue Richards (Lean-Sigma Lead, Building 1, 4th Floor).

The following is a comparison using the various methods to collect data (not all-inclusive).

Technique	Advantages	Disadvantages
Historical Data Collection (EMR report, vendor electronic information report)	Inexpensive Data available Can identify trends over time Very efficient use of people's time Sample size good	Data may not be in correct format May require IT support Must be proficient with Excel or information system program to properly organize data
Observation Data Collection (Document Tagging Worksheet, Observation Guide, VOC Survey)	Provides process level activity information Permits collection of events that may impact area being analyzed Sample size limiting Involves process workers (if participant observation method used) Involves customers (VOC)	Provides process level activity information Permits collection of events that may impact area being analyzed Sample size limiting Presence of someone collecting data may influence information Time consuming for the team (if non-participant observation method used) Data has to be organized

Data Display

Once data has been collected there are many forms in which to display the data. The following guidelines should be used when presenting data:

1. Determine who the data is for and what the purpose of it is.
2. Write the message that needs to be conveyed in 1-2 sentences.
3. Use the right type of graph (line, bar, pie, pareto, scatter, histogram, table, etc.) using key words from (2).
4. Use a display method that *will express* the data and *not impress* (keep the graphs simple and on point).

The following is how some of the data collected by the team was displayed.

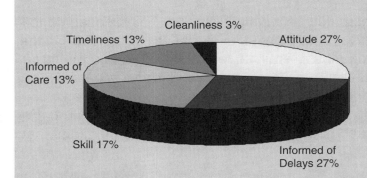

Timeliness 13%
Cleanliness 3%
Attitude 27%
Informed of Care 13%
Skill 17%
Informed of Delays 27%

A Pie Chart is a circular chart divided into sectors, illustrating relative magnitudes, frequencies, or percents.

The Pie Chart on the left conveys the data from the Voice of the Customer (VOC) ED/Inpt Survey (question 1) which validated the team's focus regarding reducing the delay time.

The Pareto Chart is a type of bar chart used in problem identification. It lists the issues in descending order of importance. These charts are used to prioritize and break down complex problems into smaller sections. They also help to identify multiple root causes by looking at the highest percentage of involvement. When the major categories are identified and dealt with, the other categories are often resolved.

The Pareto Chart on the right is displaying the data for those 19 patients from the ED/Inpt Delay Worksheet Summary.

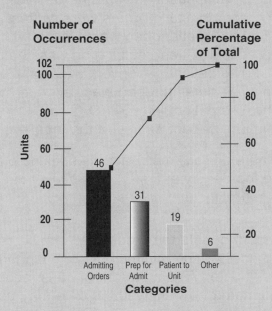

Number of Occurrences — Cumulative Percentage of Total

Units

Admitting Orders 46
Prep for Admit 31
Patient to Unit 19
Other 6

Categories

Document Tagging Worksheet										

Value Stream: Dispo-to-Admit   Start Date In: 4/10
Process: ED Dispo to Chart Prep   Start Date Out: 4/10

		In		Out			Time in Minutes				
Step	Name/Dept.	Date	Time	Date	Time	Task/Activity	Delay/Wait Time from Previous Step	Cycle Time	Elapsed Time	Value-Added Time	Non Value-Added Time
1	Doctor	4/10	0823	4/10	0833	Write Dispo/Admit Order	0	10	10	10	0
2	Doctor	4/10	0833	4/10	0838	Perform medication reconciliation	0	5	15	5	0
3	Doctor	4/10	0840	4/10	0841	Not Dispo (Admit) Order in chart	2	1	18	0	3
4	ED Clerk	4/10	0857	4/10	0859	Process Admit Order in IT system	16	2	36	0	18
5	ED Clerk	4/10	0907	4/10	0908	Place face sheet in chart	8	1	45	0	9
6	ED Clerk	4/10	0912	4/10	0925	Copy ED chart for IP chart	4	13	62	0	17
7	ED Nurse	4/10	0932	4/10	0936	Complete Med/Allergy form	7	4	73	4	7
8	ED Nurse	4/10	0936	4/10	0946	Complete charting record for IP unit	0	10	83	10	0
9	ED Nurse	4/10	0946	4/10	0949	Refer to chart when IP unit is called	0	3	86	3	0
10	ED Tech	4/10	0952	4/10	0955	Complete clothing check form in chart	3	3	92	0	6
11	ED Tech	4/10	0957	4/10	0958	Note vital signs in chart	2	1	95	1	2
12	ED Tech	4/10	1001	4/10	1004	Call transporter, note in chart	3	3	101	0	6
13	ED Nurse	4/10	1007	4/10	1010	Note last vital signs	3	3	107	3	3
14	ED Clerk	4/10	1012	4/10	1014	Place chart, face sheet, wst band, und. matt.	2	2	111	0	4
15	ED Nurse	4/10	1019	4/10	1020	Note call to IP Ns. Mgr. when patient leaves	5	1	117	0	6
16	Transporter	4/10	1023	4/10	1024	Check chart is ready to travel w/ patient	3	1	121	0	4
						TOTALS	58	63	121	36	85

Notes:
Delay/Wait Time is calculated by subtracting the In Time from the Out Time of the previous step.
Cycle Time is calculated by subtracting the beginning time of the step from the end time of the step.
Elapsed Time is the Delay/Wait Time plus the Cycle Time accumulated from each step (running total).
Value-Added Time is the time required to physically (or electronically) transform the service into value for the patient or customer (other healthcare provider or department). It typically is the cycle time minus any delay or wait time for that step.
Non Value-Added Time is calculated by adding the Delay/Wait Time plus any Cycle Time that does not add value to the patient (or customer).

Analysis:
Total chart activity time, from Dispo written to patient leaving, was 121 minutes or 2 hours, 1 minute (from 0823 to 1024). Note: this is less than the 170 minutes total lead time for the Dispo-to-Admit value stream because the Document Tagging ends when the patient leaves the ED.
The value-added time was 36 minutes.
Therefore, the chart was being used approximately 30% of the time, with the other 70% of the time being inactive.
This demonstrated the amount of information that must be ready prior to the patient being transferred to the inpatient bed from the ED. More importantly, it validated much of the information from the Cycle Time Table and other data collection tools used to create the current state value stream map. It also provided additional insight (and possible solutions) to the delays that were occurring.
This information was used to provide more detail to the current state value stream map. **It will not match exactly the Cycle Time Table because the focus of this data was the chart information process.**

The Document Tagging Worksheet presents information relative to a series of process steps in relationship to each other as well as the delays between each step.

The Document Tagging Worksheet confirmed the delay time as represented on the current state value stream map. The detailed process steps (and subsequent delays as indicated with this worksheet) allowed the team additional process activity information that would assist the team in further analyzing this part of the process.

Now Let's Answer Those Questions

1. What data do I collect?

Remember that the goal is to gather data that accurately reflects the process being observed to the level of detail that is helpful in analysis. Start with the highest level that will be helpful - in the case of the ED, you may want to start with breaking the overall value stream down into the three value streams of Door-to-Doc, Doc-to-Dispo, and Dispo-to-Admit (which includes the patient arriving into the hospital bed). When you have decided to delve deeper into one particular area, collect data along the MAJOR points that will help you decide which area to further focus on. For example, in the ED's Dispo-to-Inpatient Bed project, good collection points may be the times that:

    a. The Disposition was written
    b. The inpatient bed was requested
    c. The admitting orders were written
    d. The inpatient bed was available
    e. The inpatient registration was completed
    f. The patient paperwork was completed (belongings, etc.)
    g. The nursing report was called to the inpatient unit
    h. The patient left the ED
    i. The patient arrived at the inpatient unit

Note: There are still many activities taking place within these major areas - however, it is best not to delve too deeply at first. Let this level of data tell you where to further focus attention.

2. How much data do I collect?

The amount of data to be collected should be enough to give you a good representation of the actual process. The minimum recommended number is 30 samples - that is, 30 patients in the ED case. (Note: A sample size of 30 is recommended because of the distribution patterns of data; no matter how skewed the data may be, as the sample size grows larger, the data begins to take the shape of a normal distribution. If statistical testing is going to be included in the project, you may need to run a power and sample size test to determine exactly how many samples you need.) Collecting fewer samples may give a distorted view of the process. Should more data be collected? The number of data points for a statistically significant sample size is determined by a formula. If it is possible to collect that much data - so much the better. If not, collect as much as is reasonable but 30 should be the minimum. This will give you a valid mean (average) and standard deviation (representing the distribution of data around the mean).

It is also important to collect data that is random in nature. That is, do not collect the first 30 patients to come in on Monday morning. Try to collect data in a way that is representative of the time for the overall process. For example, divide each 24-hour period into 4-hour blocks, then select 1 or 2 patients from each of those time blocks, representing 4 to 8 patients a day or 28-plus patients in a week. If the first 28 patients were truly representative of the process and were truly random, that would be sufficient.

3. Who will collect the data?

Typically, data collection assignments are divided up between the team members, so that everyone has an equivalent "homework" assignment. When the data collection is divided up in this way, be sure everyone knows exactly what to collect and how to collect it, so that the team can do an "apples-to-apples" comparison. For example, if the time of disposition is to be taken from a particular part of a physician documentation form, ensure that all team members know where to find it and what to document.

If data can be captured from computer reports, or by chart review, it is useful to have a "dry run" with the entire team present, so that any questions can be resolved before starting the data collection process. If direct observation will be used, it is equally useful to have a "practice" session so that the team members have confidence in their assignments.

A cautionary note: Using data from computer reports may look like an easy method, but it is important to find out: Who put the information into the computer system? How was it collected? Do the times reflect the actual time of activity or do they reflect the time the data was entered? Making an assumption about computer-based data can lead to an inaccurate perception of how the process really works.

4. Will the data be easy to collect?

Collection by computer-generated reports can be "easy" if the information can be validated as representing real-time activities in the process.

Collection by chart review can be problematic if data is found to be illegible, missing, or in the wrong part of the chart. The data collection form should include areas for questions or observations on the part of the reviewer.

Collection by observation is the most time-consuming, as the observer is constrained by the actual time of the process. It is always best to observe one patient at a time as he/she flows through the process. In some cases, however, necessity dictates that each piece of the process be observed - for example, collect 30 samples of data on dispo-to-inpatient bed request on one day and then 30 samples of inpatient bed request-to-admit orders written on another day. The team will need to decided the representative sample size for each project.

When the team is putting together their data collection plan, each type of data collection method should be considered for each part of the process under scrutiny. The team should balance the ease of method with the time available for data collection. When in doubt, use the method that will give the best picture of the process, rather than an "easier" method that may yield an inaccurate perception of the process.

5. If the data is not accessible and cannot be observed, can I rely on process workers?

Process workers may be asked to help with data collection, using the following guidelines.

    a. The data collection process must be very quick - for example, making a check on a checklist or writing a time down on a form. Lengthy or cumbersome data collection instructions will most likely not be followed.

b. The data collection should be for a very defined period of time - one shift, one day, one week - so that the workers are well aware of the amount of time they will have to contribute this "extra" effort.

c. The data collection process should ideally be done on a form the worker is already using. Second-best would be a checklist or form that was easy to use, but remember that the workers will have to carry it or keep it available throughout the study period.

d. The workers should be asked to participate as partners - give them the explanation of what the project is about and how it will benefit them. Ask for ideas and feedback about the data collection and incorporate them where possible. Share the information after it has been collected and plan for recognition of those who participate.

e. Where possible, match some worker-collected data with other objective measures, to evaluate validity.

Data will need to be collected, before, during, and after the improvement event.

Oakview summarized their data collection methods by creating the following chart.

Data Collection Protocols ED/Admit Value Stream			
WHAT are we collecting?	WHERE are we getting the data?	HOW are we collecting it?	WHAT ELSE do we need to know or be aware of?
Time stamps from Ecare - N=200 Observations of clock time versus documented times on forms	ED documentation: Nurses' T sheet, Physicians' T sheet, Admit Log, Face sheet, Sign-in sheet	Team members will audit these sources each day after ED visit (charts are in Registration area)	Need to ensure all clocks are at the same time. Use first full week of data with second week used for comparison.
Staff/scheduling	ED schedules for Nursing, Techs, Physicians, and Health Unit Coordinator (HUC)	Schedules and records from ED Manager and Physician Director	Cannot account for length of breaks and lunches; can compare delay data to short-staffed shifts.
Sources of delays: - Patient Flow - Equipment - Supplies - Charts - Lab/Rad Consults - Transport - Admit Bed Availability	Observation Guide for ED staff VOC Survey for Inpatients	Nurse/Physician/HUC Tech Patient	Need to compare this to other data collected.

Note: There are numerous methods in which to collect data and/or obtain the appropriate sample size. Systematic, random, and stratified sampling methods can be used in this process. Please refer to a statistical expert for advice if this is required for the Lean project.

Brainstorming, Cause and Effect Diagram, and 5 Why Analysis

Once a current state value stream map has been created, populated with additional data, and a Waste Walk conducted, the quality improvement tools of brainstorming, Cause and Effect Diagram (Fishbone), and 5 Why Analysis can be used to assist teams in further understanding the root causes of why the waste is occurring.

Brainstorming

Brainstorming is a technique to generate a high volume of ideas around a common theme with team members' full participation. It is free of criticism and judgment. Brainstorming can be used anytime throughout a project or activity.

Brainstorming will:

- ✦ Encourage open thinking and assure new ideas are presented
- ✦ Allow all team members to contribute and thus actively be involved
- ✦ Allow ideas from team members to build upon each other

Note: In brainstorming, there is one cardinal rule:

> No idea is criticized!

There are two basic methods to brainstorm - structured and unstructured.

Structured - A method in which each team member contributes his or her ideas in order.

Unstructured - A method in which team members contribute their ideas as they occur (or come to mind).

Structured Brainstorming

Structured Brainstorming should be used if:

- ✦ The meeting will have a dominant team member
- ✦ The unstructured approach was used and numerous team members did not contribute their ideas
- ✦ The time element is critical

Approach a Structured Brainstorming session as follows:

1. Find a quiet room with a flip chart or whiteboard.

2. Verbally state the problem, gain a consensus, and write it down so everyone can see it. It is critical that everyone understands the issue or problem. The facilitator should get a visual or verbal confirmation from each team member that the problem is understood. Further clarification of the problem at this stage may lend insight into potential solutions. Do not rush this step.

3. Each team member provides an idea in a round robin fashion. *Round robin is receiving one idea from each person in a circular manner until everyone has stated their idea.* If a team member does not have an idea for their turn, then they can pass. This rotation process encourages full participation. It may also increase some team members' anxieties about having their ideas exposed. The facilitator should acknowledge this and be helpful to any person that seems shy.

4. The team facilitator or scribe writes down each idea. Each idea should be written large enough for everyone to see. It should be exactly how the person stated the idea, without any interpretation.

5. Collect the ideas until everyone has spoken, thus indicating all ideas are exhausted. This process should take between five and fifteen minutes, depending on how well the problem was stated.

6. Review the entire list once everyone has passed. Remove any ideas that are identical in nature. If there are subtle differences keep them as separate ideas.

7. Show appreciation to everyone for their contributions. The facilitator should acknowledge that this was a very beneficial exercise for the team even though it may not have been easy for some.

Unstructured Brainstorming

There are two methods to conduct an unstructured brainstorming session. Method 1: The facilitator writes down any and all ideas from the team members on a whiteboard or flip chart in no specific order or fashion. Method 2: The facilitator provides Post-it Notes to each team member. Each team member will then write their ideas on the Post-it Notes and place them on the whiteboard, flip chart, or wall. Method 2 is preferred when there is concern that some people find it difficult to speak in a public forum. Allow a maximum of 15 minutes for either method.

A brainstorming session starts with a clear question and ends with a raw list of ideas. Some ideas will be good and some will not be good. Once brainstorming is complete, duplicate (or similar type) ideas should be consolidated. Additional Lean tools and exercises will help to determine which of the ideas have the greatest impact on the identified problem.

One of the additional Lean (or quality improvement) tools that can assist to prioritizing, combining, and analyzing results of the brainstorming session is the Cause and Effect (or Fishbone) Diagram.

Note: You can also conduct the brainstorming session by directly inputting ideas on a Cause and Effect Diagram.

Cause and Effect (or Fishbone) Diagram

*A **Fishbone Diagram** is a visual representation of all the potential factors affecting a process with varying levels of detail.* This will assist in determining the true root cause(s). The problem, waste, issue, or why a measurement is not being met is identified on the right side of the diagram and brainstorming and/or other data collection techniques are used to identify and prioritize all possible causes. If done properly and completely, the cause(s) of the problem should be located on the diagram and therefore, the appropriate Lean tools can be applied.

Be flexible in the major "bones" or "skeleton" categories that are used. Many times the main categories of Man, Method, Machine (Information Technology), Material, and Mother Nature (Environmental Factors) are used. Different categories that relate to the hospital and value stream can also be used. Even though the goal is to focus on the process, it may be appropriate to have categories such as physicians, nurses, aides, clerks, etc. as they would be considered as groups of people and not as any one individual. However, isolating specific groups can be seen as finger pointing. There is no ideal set of categories or numbers; however, typically there will be 4, 5, or 6 main categories.

Approach creating a Fishbone Diagram as follows:

1. Write the 4 or 5 main categories on a whiteboard or flip chart as shown in the case study example to follow.

2. Write the effect of the problem as the "head" of the Fishbone.

3. List all possible causes of the problem (or effect) in the various 4-5 categories. Use brainstorming techniques to ensure all ideas are explored and documented on the Fishbone. Or, if brainstorming was done previously, consolidate, prioritize, and place those ideas on the appropriate location on the skeleton of the "fish".

4. Prioritize those causes that need to be investigated further via data collection, beta test, etc. Allow each team member 1-2 votes on the 1 or 2 main causes.

5. Circle the top 1, 2, or 3 items and use for further analysis.

6. Continue with the VSM methodology.

The Fishbone was used to further give analysis to the Pareto results and confirm the results from the ED/Inpt Delay Summary Worksheet. The Waste Walk (and Audit) as applied to the current state value stream map, the Observation Guide, and the information from the ED/Inpt Delay Summary Worksheet were used to provide clarification and prioritization to the delays in admitting. The following is their Fishbone Diagram.

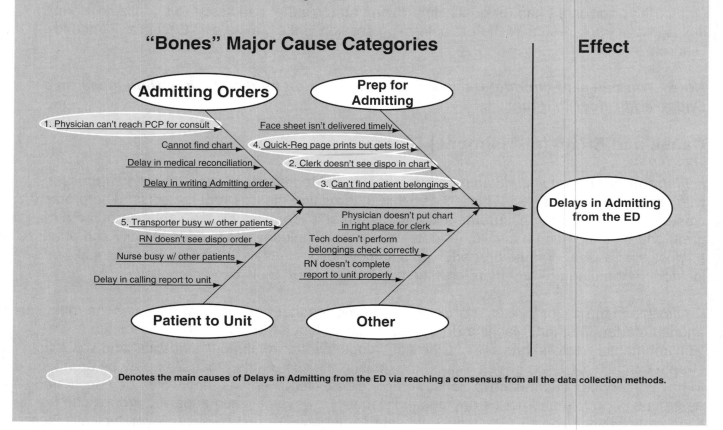

Once the Fishbone is completed, it is recommended that the team reach a consensus on the top 2, 3, or 4 causes. You cannot chase every possible problem (cause) that is listed. It is most likely that once the top 2, 3, or 4 causes are resolved, it will also resolve the other ones (remember the 80/20 rule). The 80/20 rule (or also known as the Pareto principle) states that, for many events, 80% of the effects come from 20% of the causes.

Discussion: As you use these different Lean and quality improvement tools, you will most likely find trends occurring (i.e., the same issues but stated a bit differently). For example, the ED/Inpt Delay Summary Worksheet listed "Delay in writing admitting orders", which on the Fishbone above was listed as "Physician can't reach PCP for consult". This is OK. So, as you continue with the application of Lean and the 5 Why Analysis (next tool), "common" trends and problems that are closely linked will be simply solved due to having been made aware of them through these various analysis tools. Another example; one of the key reasons for Delays was "Quick-Reg page prints, but is lost" and can be a contributing factor to the "Delay in calling report to unit" (which can be a simple fix). It is good to have confirmation of why the issues or problems are occurring from these different perspectives - as this is all part of the Diagnosis phase of the VSM methodology.

5 Why Analysis

The **5 Why Analysis** *is a simple problem solving technique that will help a team arrive at the root cause or causes of the problem quickly without statistical analysis.* It is closely linked to the Cause and Effect (or Fishbone) Diagram. The 5 Why Analysis involves looking at a potential cause of a problem and asking "Why?" and "What caused this problem?" as many times as it requires to discover the root cause(s). Very often, the answer to the first "why" will prompt another "why" and the answer to the second "why" will prompt another and so on; hence the name the 5 Whys.

Approach the 5 Why Analysis as follows:

1. List all potential causes of the problem (or waste identified) from the Fishbone (top 1-3) and/or Pareto analysis (80% rule).
2. Ask "Why" five times for each potential cause to get to the root cause. Note: Asking Why 5 times may or may not be required for each potential cause of the problem; the probable root cause may be identified after only 2 "Why?" questions.
3. Consider if the final "Why" is because of an inadequate standard, not following a standard, or no standard at all. Knowing this will create the basis for discussion on which Lean tools can be utilized.
4. Continue with the VSM methodology.

In order to understand the 5 main root causes as identified from the Fishbone analysis the team performed a 5 Why Analysis. Before the exercise team members were guessing reasons for the delays, but afterwards, the team found several additional avenues to explore that no one had thought of.

The following is one 5 Why Analysis from Oakview Hospital's Lean project.

5 Why Analysis

Problem: Delay in patients being admitted from the ED to IP bed

Cause 1. Physician can't reach PCP	Cause 2. Clerk doesn't see dispo in chart	Cause 3. Patient belongings missing	Cause 4. Quick-Reg page gets lost	Cause 5. Transporter busy w/ other patients
Why? PCP doesn't answer page	**Why?** Chart not given to clerk for filing	**Why?** Belongings misplaced in Triage	**Why?** No way to flag Quick-Reg page from others	**Why?** Not enough transporters to handle calls quickly
Why? PCP doesn't receive page	**Why?** Doctor busy, doesn't want to walk to clerk	**Why?** Hurry to get patient back to ED, no check	**Why?** Can't color code, all pages the same	**Why?** Budgeting/financial reasons
Why? Wrong pager number	**Why?** Doctor is focused on other patients	**Why?** Focus is on future, as more patients arrive	**Why?** Not a vendor change programming option	**Why?** Transporters considered non-direct care positions
Why? Information in computer listing not up-to-date	**Why?** Doctor perfers ownership of writing notes	**Why?**	**Why?**	**Why?** Transporters costs hit expenses directly; patient wait does not
Why? No standard audit process to ensure info is up-to-date	**Why?**	**Why?**	**Why?**	**Why?**

The team came up with the following Kaizen activities to be completed that relate directly to the 5 Why Analysis (1 - 5).

1. Verify the accuracy of the computer listings for the top 100 PCPs for admitted patients and create communications and standards for updates. Initially start with high-volume admitters.
2. Determine the chart placement location with the ED Medical Director. Create a new chart rack and clearly identify each phase of the patient process. IT will review the way the EMR/EMS system can accommodate color folders denoting patient process through the ED.
3. Create standard work, train, and audit, patient readiness to transport to the inpatient bed, and add a Check-off for Belongings statement to the Triage form.
4. Install a separate printer in Registration just for ED Admits with an audible signal when printing to alert Registration. IT requested to create automatic page and text message to Registration computer and unit clerk as a possible option. Communicate with the computer vendor to determine the costs of programming changes to change the EMR/EMS form in appearance (for example, by printing a black bar at the bottom of the Quick Reg notification form).
5. Determine transporter expense and possible improvements to their capacity planning. Request pilot/trial of adding 1.0 FTE transporter for two weeks to study impact on ED LOS. Also, the pilot/trial to dedicate one elevator for ED patients only.

The project team felt that they could not have come up with this list if they had not created the Fishbone Diagram as well as performed the 5 Why Analysis exercise; they would probably have thought that people were simply not doing their jobs correctly.

Note: These were not all the improvements that the team implemented within their project, however, the above listed activities should give you (the reader) a good idea of the simple-to-complex solutions that were entailed in this part of the Lean project.

Financial Analysis

The key to any successful Lean project will be eventually judged by its overall improvement to patient care and safety, staff/physician satisfaction, and cost improvement. With regards to cost improvement, it will be important to work with someone from the Finance Department with the data that has been collected, as well as the proposed changes, to ensure that true cost savings can be achieved and validated.

The following are some examples of the type of savings Lean projects have attained:

- ✦ Reduction in overtime for nurses and other staff
- ✦ Reduction in percent of patients leaving "Against Medical Advice" (AMA) when admissions are delayed
- ✦ Reduction in maintenance costs (need to repair equipment less frequently)
- ✦ Reduction in pharmacy/dietary charges to the ED, due to reduced LOS in the ED (reimbursed at a lower rate than for inpatient care)
- ✦ Savings in forms/printing
- ✦ Savings in supplies (need to order less)
- ✦ More efficient disposition of observation-status patients within 23 hours, with streamlined processes
- ✦ Better documentation of treatment resulting in more efficient coding and improved reimbursement for ED patients
- ✦ Higher percentage of ED patients meeting internal criteria for admission within a shorter time period
- ✦ Higher percentage of patients meeting expectations for clinical treatment within defined time periods (such as EKG for possible myocardial infarction) leading to more efficient use of clinical resources

Many other types of savings can be achieved depending on the type and length of the project as well as the team resource capacity.

The Oakview ED team met with their Director of Finance to determine what financial savings could be expected from an improvement in the ED-to-Admit process. Data was gathered from the budget analysis and variance reports generated by the Finance Department. Financial impact was identified in the following areas:

Increased Revenue

1. Decrease in the number of patients with status "Left Without Being Seen" because of increased capacity from 4% to 2%, leading to:
   - More discharged patient visits with an estimated revenue of $8,824 annually
   - More admitted patient visits with an estimated revenue of $27,118 annually

2. Decrease in the number of ambulance diverts, because of increased capacity by 50%, leading to:
   - More admitted patient visits with an estimated total revenue of $42,500 annually

3. Increase in the number of patients admitted because of improved throughput, leading to:
   - More discharged patient visits with an estimated revenue of $40,000 annually
   - More admitted patient visits with an estimated revenue of $65,000 annually

Decreased Costs

1. Decrease in agency nursing costs to cover patient care while being held for admission - est. $150,000 annually
2. Decrease in overtime and extra straight time to cover patient care while being held for admission - est. $45,000 annually

The Finance Director also agreed that there would be additional cost savings to the ED budget due to other miscellaneous reasons (for example, needing less dietary support for patients being held), but no data was available, so some figures were not included in the estimates.

The total increase in revenue is estimated at $183,442 annually and the decrease in costs is estimated at $195,000 annually.

The team had a further discussion with the Director of Finance about the costs and savings that were spread across various cost centers. Using the dietary department as an example, if patients were held less in the ED, they would still need dietary support but up on the nursing units, not in the ED. Therefore, there would be a savings to the ED but it might be balanced by increased costs on the units. The team also talked about admissions - since revenue from admissions does not accrue to the ED cost center, it might not be apparent from the ED budget alone that increased revenue was being achieved.

For non-financial benefit, the team re-evaluated the Goal Card to see whether any of those metrics needed to be adjusted. They agreed that the following would be measured for their project, as many were noted on the Goal Card:

- Patient hold hours in ED, per month
- % PCP contact prior to admit
- % Bed ready within 15 minutes of request
- % Medication reconciliation documented
- % Admission orders written in ED
- % Dispo-to-Admit within 1.5 hours
- Patient OBS hours, per month
- % Case Mgr involved
- % Clothing check documented
- % Report called to unit, documented
- % LOS within 4.5 hours
- % LWBS/AMA

The following spreadsheet was created.

Oakview Hospital ED Admitting Project Dispo to Inpt Bed - Financial Impact

Green Dollars* - Keeping LWBS Patients
Based on: Decreasing LWBS by 50%

LWBS visits (last year)	228	Source: ED Tracking
Kaizen Visits Opportunity (50%)	114	
Net Avg Revenue Per Visit	$114.81	Reimbursement = 25.19%
Direct Avg Cost Per Visit	(37.40)	Source: Operating Budget
Avg Contribution Per Visit	$77.41	
Total Green Dollar Opportunity	$8,824	

(Kaizen Visits Opportunity x Avg Contribution Per Visit)

Light Green Dollars - Discharged Patients (OP)
Based on: Increased capacity which will allow discharged patient volume to increase by 10% without adding additional staff

Overall Mean LOS for Disch Pts (minutes)	270	Source: ED Tracking System
Unadjusted Annual ED Visits	28,659	Source: Finance
Adjust for LWBS (above)	(114)	
Subtract admitted patients	(6691)	
Adjusted Annual ED Visits	21,854	
Kaizen Visit Opportunity	2,185	10% of disch patient volume
Net Revenue/Average OP ED Visit	$292.56	Source: Operating Budget
Direct Cost/Average OP ED Visit	$97.88	
Contribution/Average OP ED Visit	$194.68	
Visit Light Green Dollar Opportunity	$425,376	

(Kaizen Visit Opportunity x Avg Contribution Per Visit)

Light Green Dollars - Admitted Patients (IP)
Based on: Decreased ambulance diversions, which will allow admitted patient volume to increase by 5%

ED Admits (last year)	6,691	Source: Finance
ED Admits as % of Visits	23.3%	
Kaizen Admits Opportunity	335	5% of adm patient volume
Net Revenue per IP case	$5,711	
Operating Cost per IP case	$3,625	
Contribution per IP case	$2,086	
Admit Light Green Dollar Opportunity	$698,810	

(Kaizen Admit Opportunity x Avg Contribution per IP case)

Total Green Dollar Opportunity, 100% confidence	$8,824
Total Light Green Discharged Opportunity, 50% confidence	$425,376 x .5 = $212,688
Total Light Green Admit Opportunity, 50% confidence	$698,810 x .5 = $349,405

Total Kaizen Project Opportunity = $8,824 + $212,688 + $349,405 = $570,917 expected additional annual revenue

NOTE: Light green dollars are adjusted for a 50% confidence, because increased capacity does not, by itself, guarantee that increased patient volumes will be realized.

* Green Dollars explained on next page.

The team, along with representatives from the Finance Department, determined that revenue opportunities existed in three areas.

First, by reducing the number of patients who Left Without Being Seen (LWBS), the net revenue would be increased as these patients stayed and received treatment. The team thought that an achievable goal would be a 50% reduction from last year's 228 LWBS visits. If the number was reduced to 114, the "staying" 114 patients would generate an additional $8,824 of revenue (based on the past year's average contribution, or revenue - expense amount).

Second, by opening up capacity in the ED, the team thought that an additional 10% of outpatient (discharged patient) volume could be accommodated, without adding staff or other major expenses. Increasing the number of visits from the past year by 2,185 would yield additional revenue of $425,376 (using the past year's average contribution for an outpatient ED visit).

A third opportunity was seen to exist because of additional capacity in the ED. The team thought that an additional 5% of admitted patient volume could be accommodated, again without adding staff. Increasing the number of admitted patients from the past year by 335 would yield $698,810 (using the past year's average contribution for admitted patients).

The Finance Department classified savings into two types, "Green Dollars" or hard savings that could be removed from future budgets, and "Light Green Dollars" that represented potential increases in revenues, which might or might not be achieved.

When the finance representatives looked at the figures, they expressed some doubt about whether opening capacity could "guarantee" that this number of patients would actually be seen. They said that they had a 50% confidence level that those "Light Green" revenues would be realized. Therefore, they adjusted the total revenue expectation for discharged and admitted patients downwards by 50%. Combined with the Green Dollars savings from the LWBS patients, this gave an expectation that, following the Lean work on the ED Value Stream, the department and hospital would see an increase of $570,917 in revenue.

The team also tried to calculate cost savings for labor and supplies due to more efficient work (less overtime or external resource staffing), and fewer supply items used or wasted. At the beginning of the project, though, the team did not feel as though they could come up with concrete measures related to wasteful processes. They agreed to track the following throughout the project, note that these costs were already monitored through the budget variance process. However, certain line items would be pulled out and measured in comparison to the Lean process improvements to be implemented in the ED:

- ✦ Labor cost, broken down by position
    - Regular
    - Overtime
    - External resources
- ✦ Clinical (medical) supply cost, broken down by medical and non-medical expenses
- ✦ Office supply cost

Overall, this is exactly what the organization needed in financial understanding to continue with additional Lean-Sigma projects as part of their Operational Excellence program.

Readiness Guide for Diagnosis

The Readiness Guide for Diagnosis should be reviewed with the team to ensure all appropriate tools have been used. The team should spend approximately 10 minutes to reach a consensus on each of the items. This is also a good indication on how well the team understood the various tools contained in this chapter. At least fifty percent of the questions should be answered with a Yes before proceeding to the next chapter (or phase).

Readiness Guide for the Diagnosis Phase

If you answer No to more than half of these, then consider using additional tools in the Diagnosis phase.

1. Does everyone understand the 7(8) types of waste? ☐Yes ☐No

2. Have examples of wastes in healthcare been reviewed? ☐Yes ☐No

3. Has an elevator speech been created? ☐Yes ☐No

4. Has a Waste Walk been conducted? ☐Yes ☐No

5. Has the value stream map been updated with wastes? ☐Yes ☐No

6. Was everyone involved in the Waste Walk? ☐Yes ☐No

7. Has appropriate data been collected on the processes? ☐Yes ☐No

8. Has the value stream map been populated with recent data? ☐Yes ☐No

9. Has the data been displayed in a user-friendly form? ☐Yes ☐No

10. Has the team brainstormed the causes of the waste? ☐Yes ☐No

11. Has a Cause and Effect (Fishbone) Diagram been created? ☐Yes ☐No

12. Has a 5 Why Analysis been done? ☐Yes ☐No

13. Are all the team members contributing? ☐Yes ☐No

14. Are meetings run effectively? ☐Yes ☐No

15. Has a financial analysis of the project been proposed? ☐Yes ☐No

16. Has managment been comprised of the progess of data collected? ☐Yes ☐No

17. Are Idea Kaizens being captured? ☐Yes ☐No

Chapter 4:
Treat

Topics Include:

- ✦ 5S
- ✦ Just-In-Time (Continuous Flow, Pull System, and Kanbans)
- ✦ Pitch
- ✦ Work Load Balancing
- ✦ Standard Work
- ✦ Physical Layout
- ✦ Leveling
- ✦ Mistake Proofing
- ✦ Visual Production Board
- ✦ Lean Tools Applied to Oakview Hospital's Current State Value Stream Map
- ✦ Impact Map
- ✦ Gantt Chart
- ✦ Oakview Hospital's Future State Value Stream Map
- ✦ Readiness Guide for Treat

5S

5S is a process to ensure work areas are systematically kept clean and organized, ensure patent and staff safety, and provide the foundation on which to build a Lean healthcare system. It is often said, "If you can't do 5S, forget all the rest." 5S is an improvement process to ensure everything has a place and everything is in its place. This leads to improved patient and information flow, decreased cost for the facility, and the elimination of time spent searching for things, which is a waste. 5S is one of those programs that can have a tremendous impact on an entire organization in less than 6 months.

5S is a structured approach that is accomplished by:

- ✦ Placing a team of healthcare professionals in control of their own workplace
- ✦ Helping a team focus on the causes of waste and their subsequent elimination
- ✦ Establishing standards for basic organization and orderliness
- ✦ Demonstrating to patients and staff that a clean environment is a foundation for good work/patient flow
- ✦ Improving staff morale by ensuring the area is safe and clean

The 5 parts to 5S are:

Sort is the weeding out of items in a target area that have not been used for a period of time and/or are not expected to be used. It involves looking for replication of items in areas (i.e., crash carts, phlebotomy trays, etc.), and with the 2nd S, determining the most efficient location. The essence of Sort is found in the saying, ***"When in doubt, move it out."***

Set-In-Order involves arranging necessary items for easy and efficient access and maintaining them to stay that way. The essence of Set-In-Order is found in the saying, ***"A place for everything and everything is in its place."***

Shine involves cleaning everything, keeping everything clean, and using cleaning as a way to ensure that the areas are maintained as they should be. The essence of Shine is found in the saying, ***"To be Lean, you must be clean."***

Standardize involves creating guidelines for keeping the area organized, orderly, clean, and making the standards visual and obvious. The standards must serve as the basis for improvement. The essence of Standardize is found in the saying, ***"What you don't know, you can't improve."***

Sustain involves education and communication so that everyone uses the applicable standards. The essence of Sustain is found in the saying, ***"Maintain the gain and forget the blame."***

From its modest beginnings as a housekeeping tool, the 5S system has evolved into a method for initiating Lean-Six Sigma projects, reducing costs, improving work flow, and engaging all employees in reducing wastes.

Notes:
1. *The following pages contain examples of worksheets that provide guidance in each of the 5S phases. They should assist you in customizing a 5S program for your facility.*
2. *The following worksheets, plus additional ones, are available in Microsoft Excel at www.theleanstore.com/Etools/Forms and Worksheets.*
3. *5S can also be applied to your Desktop and networking environment utilizing the same principles. 5S for the Desktop (PC) Pocket Handbook is available at www.theleanstore.com/Etools/Books.*

Sort

The Sorting activity provides the guidelines and standards by which all employees in the target area will follow during the Sorting activities. The Sort Inspection Sheet, Tag Worksheet, and 5S Item Disposition Log (or similar type worksheets) allows everyone to be in agreement on what needs to be sorted. Post these in the department prior to any Sorting exercise.

Set-In-Order

The Set-In-Order activity establishes the locations where items belong, by visually marking the items or labeling them. It is recommended that an area diagram and flow chart be created of the physical area to identify conveyance and transport waste. A before and after map should be completed, along with the appropriate measurements.

Review the Waste Audit from Chapter 3 once an area map has been created. The Waste Audit may stimulate questions when deciding on the location and placement of items prior to any changes.

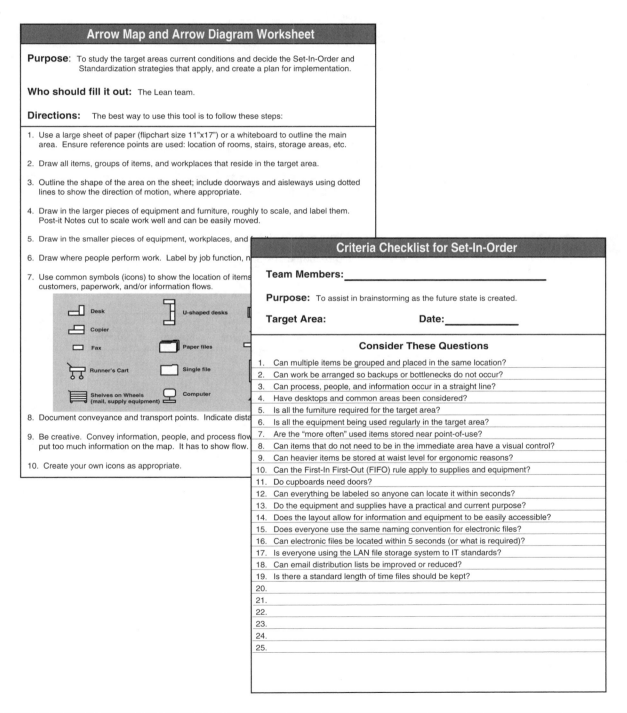

Shine

The Shine activity establishes the standard upon how an area should be cleaned on a regular basis. This ranges from cleaning the telephone receiver with an disinfectant to disposing of expired medications. The team should conduct a "spring cleaning" activity and then create standard daily and weekly activities to keep the area clean.

Criteria Checklist for Shine

Team Members: _____

Purpose: To assist in brainstorming as the future state is created.

Target Area: _____ **Date:** _____

Consider These Questions

1. Which areas are dirty and dusty?
2. Are current housekeeping duties not being performed?
3. Can someone be assigned to regular cleaning?
4. Are supplies available for cleaning?
5. Are personal areas involved?
6. If equipment has to be moved, will maintenance people be available?
7. Can walls be cleaned or will painting be required?
8. Will cleaning of this level make the area personnel proud?
9. Are there employees in the area not on the team available
10. Can a visual audit be performed regularly to ensure tidine
11. Are areas that require aggressive cleaning be clearly iden
12. Will someone create a procedure to ensure regular shine

Target Area for Shine

Purpose: To create an initial plan for cleaning the target area.

Who should fill it out: All target area workers should have input.

Directions: The best way to use this tool is to follow these steps:
1. Identify Target Points (specific areas) to be cleaned (1).
2. Determine Who, Method, and Supplies needed (2) - (4).
3. Add any Notes that may be helpful when the activity occurs (5).

(1) Target Points	(2) Who	(3) Method	(4) Supplies	(5) Notes

Standardize

The Standardize activity involves creating the guidelines for keeping an area organized, orderly, and clean. This includes making those standards visual and obvious.

Control Point Worksheet

Purpose: To ensure visual controls are linked to standards.

Who should fill it out: Selected members of the Lean team.

Directions: The best way to use this tool is to follow these steps:
1. Create categories for the target area (1).
2. Identify primary or physical things (Control Poitns) to control (2).
3. Create the standard for how control is to be established.

(1) Category	(2) Control Point

Five Minute 5S Checklist

Team Members: _____

Purpose: To assist the team in completing assigned duties on time.

Target Area: _____   **Date:** _____

Ex. John will put away extra supplies each day from Staples. (1 minute).

...will verify supply cabinets are stocked properly at the ... f the day (1 minute).

...nsure counters are clean in the supply room ...ute).

...vill walk through supply room and determine if ...nent is stored in the correct location (1 minute).

...vill sign-off on completing the Five Minute 5S Checklist.

5S Job List

Team Members: _____

Purpose: To designate specific duties ensuring the first 3 's are adhered to.

Target Area: _____   **Date:** _____

Job or Activity	SORT	SET IN ORDER	SHINE	STANDARDS	SUSTAIN	Start of day	End of day	Weekly	Monthly	Notes

Place a checkmark (✓) indicating the S for the activity.
For frequency, place initials of the person the Job or Activity is assigned to.

Sustain

Sustain involves providing the staff with the continued awareness (training) on the importance of the first 4 S's as well as the skills necessary to follow the standards set in the 4th S. Much of the Sustain success can be attributed to an audit being conducted on a regular basis. Audits should initially be done on a weekly basis until significant progress has been demonstrated, and then on a monthly basis. Audit team members should be rotated on a 6 month or yearly basis. Audit teams should be comprised of 3-5 individuals.

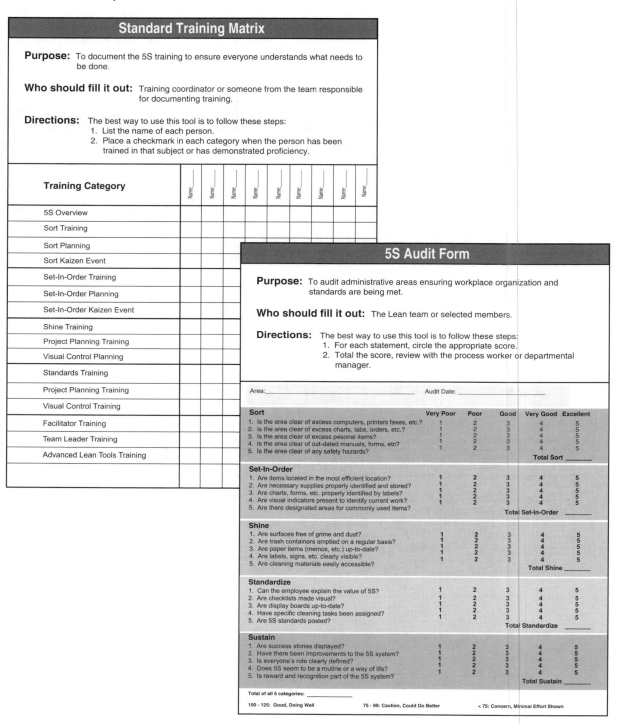

Many times a 5S seal will be used to visually convey completion of each 5S step. These are posted at either the individual work area or on the departmental bulletin board.

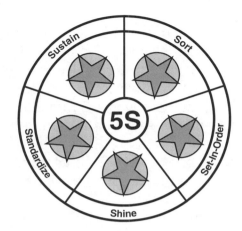

Healthcare facilities are like living organisms because they change and grow. 5S must be flexible in its delivery to adapt to these changes. Additional points regarding 5S are:

- ✦ Ensure it is part of everyone's job
- ✦ Make sure Sort is done well, as it will make the rest of the 4 S's go well
- ✦ Take before and after photos and post in appropriate location, as well as any area maps
- ✦ Obtain testimonials from staff on how things have improved and submit to newsletter or post on intranet
- ✦ Be creative and adaptive to the changes occurring within the organization
- ✦ Communicate the results of each step well
- ✦ Make reward and recognition part of the process
- ✦ Consider applying the same methodology to electronic files and folders

5S can be very instrumental in engaging employees in the Lean journey. Managers and supervisors now have the most basic methodology to effectively implement 5S as their foundation for Lean. 5S incorporates all of the Lean tools of waste elimination, standardized work, and respect for those who are closest to the process.

Oakview's ED team was responsible for a major 5S thrust during a two week period. 5S was a separate project to stabilize the ER environment. This was comprised of the following activities:

Sort - In the dirty utility room, the staff found old manuals and supplies for a blood glucose meter that had not been used for 2 years. One copy of the manual was sent to the Lab for archiving; the supplies were properly discarded. In the Triage area, the nurse found consent forms that were outdated and a typewriter used to type the patient names on forms "just in case" the computer system went down. The forms were discarded and a place for the typewriter was found in the Registration area.

In the patient rooms, posters were taped up to the walls with the patient Bill of Rights information. The posters were found to be outdated. They were replaced with new posters.

In the greeting area, the waiting area was filled with chairs. A two-week study was done to determine how many chairs were actually used. As a result, 10 chairs were removed, making room for a literature rack and water dispenser.

In a back hallway, old transport boards used by the EMS were found. Many were broken and subsequently discarded. The usable boards were returned to the EMS companies they originally came from.

In the clean utility room, it was found that there was a 3 month supply of 2x2 gauze squares. One month's of this supply was kept and the rest were returned to central supply.

In the main work area, some reference books were 2 - 3 years old. Newer editions were ordered as appropriate, with a reminder to discard the old ones as updated versions were received.

IV pumps that were cluttering the hallway were moved to the appropriate utility rooms.

Set-in-Order - In the clean utility room, the staff was proud to relate that every cabinet and cupboard was labeled. On further inspection, however, it became apparent that some of the items had been moved around, without the labels being changed. The staff held a quick meeting to determine whether the labels or the items should be moved. They decided to change the labels, since everyone knew where the items were stored.

In the physician documentation area, all charts needing action were placed in a rack. The clerk then had to look through each chart to determine what needed to be done. The staff decided to ask the physicians to help out by placing the charts in one of five labeled racks: New Orders, Pending Results, Pending Dispo, Ready for Discharge, and Pending Admit. The doctors agreed to try it, and after two weeks decided that it worked well enough to make permanent.

In the staff lounge, the refrigerator was always overcrowded, and some items were thought to be stale or outdated. The staff decided to try a new arrangement. They labeled the shelves in the refrigerator and freezer: Daily Lunches, Free For All, and Special Items. All items needed to be dated as they were placed in the refrigerator, and except for the "free" items, the initials or name of the person had to be added to the item(s).

Shine - Behind every computer there was a lot of dust. The staff held a "clean-up" day and not only dusted behind each PC, but used twist-ties to ensure that cords were neat and easily arranged for future cleaning. Computer screens and keyboards were also cleaned with wipes.

The ED staff asked Facilities Maintenance to strip and wax the floors on an evening where fewer patients were expected.

The ED manager sat down with the Housekeeping supervisor to work out a better schedule for cleaning in the ED. It turned out that the Housekeeping staff was afraid to touch most items for fear of being blamed if something did not work. The ED manager and Housekeeping supervisor were able to work out a schedule with definitions of what should and should not be cleaned and when to ask the ED staff for help with an item.

The ED staff was concerned about cleaning the ED rooms between patients. That task was usually done by the nurse since Housekeeping could not respond quickly to a stat call. The ED manager worked with the Housekeeping supervisor to set up a Housekeeping assignment for the ED during the busiest hours of the day. The Housekeeping manager agreed to a trial run and it was found that help was needed for 18 hours. However, during most of the midnight shift an assigned Housekeeper was not needed. When not cleaning the ED rooms, the Housekeeper kept an eye on the patient lounge and helped with clean-up issues there and in Registration.

A team of ED staff agreed to go through all of the papers tacked and taped to the walls in the staff lounge and triage area, updating and neatly typing all appropriate information, and replacing the information in sheet protectors to maintain a professional appearance.

The walls and doors showed many scrapes from equipment. The ED manager requested Facilities to install protective borders around doorways, high-use areas, and wall corners.

Standardize - In the unit clerk area, the chart racks were designated for each module, with the charts in alphabetical order by patient's last name. In the physician documentation area, charts were sorted by assigned doctor. In the new chart racks (New Orders, Pending Results, etc.) the charts were placed in no particular order. After discussion with the physicians, the staff agreed to place charts in alphabetical order in every rack. Although there was some doubt about the amount of time it would take to sort the charts, after a one-week trial everyone agreed that it was worth the small amount of time, due to the quickness with which a chart could now be located.

Blood glucose meters and other point-of-care supplies were stored in several places around the ED. A team decided to place all of the supplies in a central area, with manuals and handy phone numbers in the same place. At first there was resistance because it did not seem as convenient for staff members, but the advantages of knowing how many supplies were on hand and where to find them was significantly more convenient.

Sustain - In the staff lounge, it was agreed to clean out the refrigerator once a week, on a rotational basis; the schedule was posted on the refrigerator for the entire year. All undated items, items more than 2 weeks old, and unnamed items would be discarded.

A "5S Audit" was initiated, with the goal of ensuring that the new, improved ED area would be maintained. The audit was performed once every week by rotating staff teams. When a variance was found, it was brought to the weekly staff meetings as a standing item, so everyone could review and remember what the team agreed on. If new ideas came up, to make other improvements or to help sustain prior changes, they could be discussed and agreed upon at the team meetings.

It was decided to meet with Housekeeping once a month to ensure that proper attention was being paid to the area and to maintain good communications between the Housekeeping and ED staff. Following the Lean philosophy, variances and problems found were not used for blaming, but led to an open a discussion on how activities could be coordinated to resolving issues.

The ED team had chosen ED Patient Satisfaction Survey as one of their non-financial measures. The team was pleased to see an improvement in scores after their Kaizen Event - much closer to achieving their goal of 4.0 in all categories.

The team compiled the following measurements throughout the month of June. The team believed, since everyone was involved in the 5S project, that the project had an impact on these scores. The numbers reflect all the improvements that were made during that time. The following is their ED Patient Satisfaction Scores.

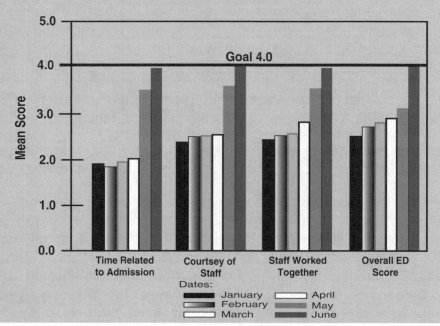

Mini Case Study for Radiology

The Radiology staff was motivated to implement 5S in their department after hearing the benefits of a successful team effort that had implemented 5S in the ED. They spent a week red-tagging the items not in use. They thought they would find a few items, but to their surprise, they found that almost 50% of the items in their storage area were no longer in use. These items were being kept "just-in-case", but no one could remember the last time they were actually used. The team decided to discard most of those items and sent a few to the warehouse with a review date of 6 months; if never needed, they would be discarded.

Once "Sort" was done, the "Set-In-Order" phase went quickly. With so much room freed up by the removal of old items, the team was able to move boxes and supplies out of hallways and off of countertops. "Shine Week" went well also, with most staff members pitching in. The Radiology manager said the department had never looked so good! Patients made favorable comments as well. The team put together their Standards and created an audit checklist for "Sustain."

The entire effort took only five weeks, roughly one week for each phase, and staff members agreed to rotate the responsibilities for the audit. 5S became a standing agenda item on the monthly departmental meeting. Soon, it seemed hard to remember what the department looked like before the 5S effort.

The results were as follows:

Increase of 300 square feet of floor space

$10,500 worth of equipment taken off the books as not needed or was not found

Patient Satisfaction Survey was higher during the first three months upon completion of the 5S project, with 5 patients commenting on the survey regarding the tidiness and neatness of the Radiology department

Just-In-Time

Just-In-Time (JIT) *establishes a system to supply work (data, information, etc.) or services (patient care) at precisely the right time, in the correct amount, and without error.* Just-In-Time is the heart of a Lean system and is an overriding theme for Lean healthcare. JIT is attained through the understanding and application of continuous flow, the pull system, and kanbans.

Continuous Flow

Continuous Flow *is characterized by the ability of a process to replenish a single unit of work (or service capacity) when the customer has pulled it.* The concept of continuous flow is used to move work, patients or provide a service between processes with minimal or no wait (queue) time. It is further used to ensure the process is to perform the work required, no sooner or no later than requested, as well as in the correct quantity, with no defects. The goal is to not do any work or service that is not requested by the downstream process (or customer). It is synonymous with Just-In-Time.

Continuous flow will:

+ Eliminate transport, delay, and motion waste
+ Decrease lead times
+ Reduce queue times
+ Allow staff to identify and fix problems earlier
+ Provide the needed flexibility in meeting demand changes
+ Improve patient and staff satisfaction levels

True continuous flow in a healthcare facility will most likely not be achieved because of the staff and departmental interdependencies required in the various care pathways. Therefore, the tools of In-process supermarkets, FIFO Lanes, and kanbans can be used at certain times when cycle time differences between processes exist and flow needs to be improved.

In-process supermarket

The **In-process supermarket** *is a physical device between two processes that stores a certain quantity of work or service capacity that, when needed, is pulled by the downstream process.* Its origination came from the grocery stores and how the clerks replenish food items. Supermarkets do not typically have large storage areas for many of their goods. Every item is received and transferred straight to the shelves (especially the perishable items), where it is made available to the customer. No costly storage. No large storage areas. No waiting. Minimum inventory.

The In-process supermarket (i.e., the grocery store shelf between the supplier of the goods and the consumer) exists due to the variations in customer demand. The customer's lead time is minimal (the time it takes to remove something off the shelf), therefore, it would not be feasible to have just one item there. In order to establish the In-process supermarket, an ordering pattern, establishing minimum and maximum levels needs to be determined to create a balance between what the customer demand is and the frequency of delivery to the store (and shelf). In-process supermarkets can also be explained in terms of cycle time. A supermarket exists between two processes to accommodate the differences in the cycle times of those processes (i.e., the time for the removal of an grocery item from the store shelf to the time it takes to replenish those items from the warehouse). This is called the pull system. Only the amount that has been used by the customer for that day, week, or month (depending on the ordering pattern), or "pulled" from the shelf, is reordered. The maximum level is never exceeded.

For In-process supermarkets to be successful, the following will need to be in place:

- ✦ A quantitative understanding of the downstream requirements
- ✦ Known cycle times for the downstream and upstream processes
- ✦ Communication system between the upstream and downstream processes
- ✦ Minimum and maximum number of work units or service capacity assigned to the supermarket
- ✦ Standard work created explaining the operation of the supermarket
- ✦ Training of all process workers on the supermarket operation
- ✦ Adequate documentation and visual controls communicating to the downstream process when there is a disruption in the flow
- ✦ A signal or "kanban" triggers a "pull" from the downstream process to the upstream process to replenish with what was removed

For example, supplies in many healthcare departments can run out on a hourly, daily, or weekly basis. To minimize this disruption and maintain optimal care for the patient, In-process supermarkets for unit/floor supply areas may provide value. The supermarkets would limit extra supplies throughout the area and prevent the searching for needed supplies at critical times. The supplies at these locations would be located in an In-process supermarket, meeting the hourly and daily needs of the staff. Replenishment of the supplies would be through kanban cards (next section) when supplies reached a minimum ordering level.

It should be noted that information (i.e., charts, labs, consults, etc.) can also be considered a "supply" or "supermarket item" and the supermarket concept be applied as such. Toyota found the supermarket to be the best alternative to scheduling upstream processes that cannot flow continuously. As you improve flow, the need for supermarkets should decrease.

Kanban

Kanban is a card or visual indicator that serves as a means of communicating to an upstream process precisely what is required at the specified time. In Japanese, kanban means "card", "billboard", or "sign." Kanban refers to the inventory control card used in a pull system. It is used to regulate the flow or work in and out of supermarkets as a visual control to trigger action.

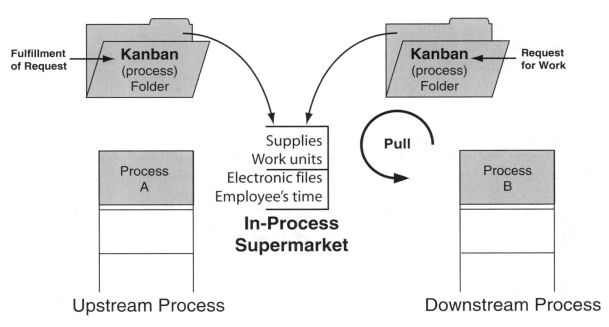

Kanban is a form of visual control (information that allows a process to be controlled). This information states when, who, what, and how many work units are needed for movement. A kanban can be anything from an actual index card, a file folder, or some type of electronic signal. There needs to be a mailbox or some repository for the kanban to be deposited in, as well as the signal system identifying it is there.

The most common use for the In-process supermarket is the ordering of supplies. Kanbans for supplies will ensure that the dollars allocated for supplies will be at the minimum required. The kanban system is used to create a "pull" of material, in this case a supply item, from the downstream process to the upstream process.

We will discuss a kanban system for supplies to further understand how a kanban system can be utilized. The eight steps are:

1. Conduct the supply survey.
2. Establish minimum/maximum levels.
3. Create the Supply Order Form.
4. Create the kanban cards.
5. Create standard work.
6. Conduct the training.
7. Implement the kanban system.
8. Maintain the standards.

1. Conduct the supply survey.

The team will need to create a standard list of supplies from which to draw upon. Distribute the list to all staff in the area requesting them to determine their usage level for a period of time (day/shift, week or month). The following is a sample Supply Survey Form.

Supply Survey Form

Please indicate from the list below the frequency of the items you will most likely use within a specific time period. (i.e., shift, day, week, or month). This data will be used to assist the Lean project team to establish the quantity of supplies to assure the item is there when you need it. Also, any items not listed, please add to the bottom of the form.

Item Description	Quantity Used/Time Period	Comments
Exam Gloves #7 (box)	0.5 box/shift (50 gloves)/shift	
Paper Drapes (50/box)	10/shift	
General Use Syringes - 3ml	50/shift	

2. Establish minimum/maximum levels.

Once the list and special requests have been collected, gain a consensus on usage and establish minimum/maximum levels. Include the following:

✦ Type of standard supply (there are numerous glove sizes, so agreement must be made on a certain quantity for each size)
✦ Weekly or monthly usage for the items
✦ Establish a minimum quantity to have on hand
✦ Establish a maximum quantity to have on hand

3. Create the Supply Order Form.

The Supply Order Form will list all the supplies represented by information obtained from the Supply Survey Form. The minimum quantity to have on hand is the quantity of items expected to be used during the time it takes to re-supply that item (plus some X factor or buffer). The X factor or buffer is to ensure no stock-out occurs at any time. The X factor is typically determined by the team and their experience with the supplies. It may be one day's worth of a particular supply, it may be a week's worth, again depending on the experience of the team. The maximum quantity to have on hand will be the minimum quantity plus the number of items that would be used during the supply or replenishment time. The following is a sample Supply Order Form.

Supply Order Form

Please fax this form to Central Supply, ext. 2234 by 1700 each day. The supplies will be delivered by 0800 the next day.

Delivery Location: __Pediatrics - Nurse Station__   Account Number: __PD5602__

No.	Item Description	Item #	Quantity Ordered Max - Min	Unit Price
1	Exam Gloves #7 (box)	GLEM70	2	$7.95
2	Paper Drapes (50/box)	DR33656	4	$17.68
3	General Use Syringes - 3ml	SP86A	100	$0.16
4				

Example for exam gloves size 7:

> Item: size 7 exam gloves, 20 used per shift, (3 shifts)
> Total usage of size 7 exam gloves for a day: averages 60 (20 per shift x 3 shifts)
> Order quantity: Size 7 exam gloves are purchased in boxes of 100. The additional 40 per box could be considered the built-in X factor or buffer per day. The buffer of 40 gloves would need to be reviewed monthly and adjustments to the order would need to be done to ensure of not overstocking the size 7 latex gloves.
> Re-order time from central supply: 2 days

Minimum Required: 1 box (100 gloves)
Maximum Number: 3 boxes (300 gloves)
Re-order time from Central Supply: 2 days

4. Create the kanban cards.

There should be one kanban card identified as the Supply Re-order Kanban for each supply item. It should be laminated and color coded, differentiating more than one supply ordering location (i.e., Baxter, Central Supply, Staples, etc.). Kanban cards should be affixed to the minimum re-order quantity item. For example, attach the kanban card to the last box of exam gloves size 7 on the shelf.

The card should be an appropriate size to visually convey all the pertinent information such as:

Item Name
Maximum Quantity on Hand
Minimum Quantity on Hand
Re-order Quantity (Maximum - Minimum)
Vendor Name
Catalog Page Number
Instructions as to what to do with the kanban card

The following is an example of a kanban card:

Supply Re-order Kanban Card

Item Name: Size #7 latex gloves

Maximum Quantity: 3 boxes - (100 pair/box)

Minimum Quantity: 1 box - (100 pair/box)

Re-order Quantity: 2 boxes **(Max - Min)**

Vendor Name: Central Supply **Catalog Pg. No:** N/A

Place this card in the Kanban Envelope

Note: Ensure a Special Order Kanban Card is created to be filled in by the staff for those special order items (e.g., latex-free band-aids). Typically there will not be a minimum/maximum number for the special items. Monitor the Special Order Kanbans to determine if they should be included on the standard Supply Order Form.

5. Create standard work.

Once the system has been designed and the process for re-ordering determined, create a Standard Work Chart. This should be posted at the supply cabinet and used to train the staff. A process flowchart can also be used as in the example provided.

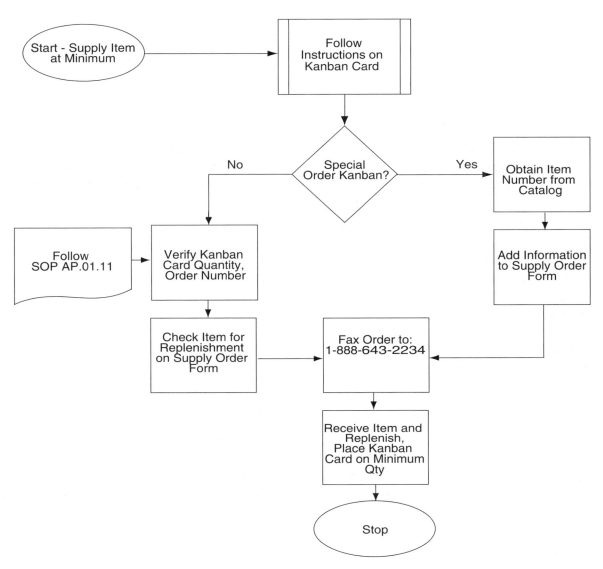

6. *Conduct the training.*

The training for the department should be done prior to implementation to ensure integrity of the system. The training should include the following:

- ✦ A brief explanation on the purpose of kanbans
- ✦ Explanation on how the minimum/maximum levels were established and convey appreciation for everyone's input when the Supply Survey was conducted
- ✦ Explanation of how the system will work (distribute process flowcharts)
- ✦ Explanation of the two types of kanbans: Supply Re-order and Special Order Kanban
- ✦ A demonstration at the supply cabinet on how the kanban system will work
- ✦ Acknowledgement of the key individuals within the team that contributed to this system
- ✦ Communication that this is a work-in-progress trial and improvement ideas from all staff members will be welcomed

7. Implement the kanban system.

Training and implementation should occur simultaneously. Once the training has been completed, the kanban for supplies will be ready to use.

8. Maintain the standards.

After a month or two of usage, review the appropriate budget supply line item, determine the cost savings, congratulate the team, and convey the success of the initiative to management. At all times during the kanban implementation, take suggestions on how the process can be improved.

The benefits of implementing a kanban system for supplies are:

- ✦ Ensures minimum inventory
- ✦ Creates staff awareness of the cost of supplies
- ✦ Easy tool to implement and train
- ✦ Encourages teamwork
- ✦ Minimizes transactions on ordering supplies
- ✦ Reduces stress
- ✦ Reduces excess inventory waste
- ✦ Allows staff to understand the concepts of flow and supermarkets
- ✦ Reduce costs
- ✦ Eliminates the waste of motion of searching through excess supplies

The responsibility to maintain the system should be rotated among the staff on a regular basis. This will help to ensure, as they take care of the system, that they will have an appreciation for how it works, and therefore, be more supportive of using the system as it was intended to be used.

First-In First-Out (FIFO)

FIFO is a work-controlled method to ensure the oldest work upstream (first-in) is the first to be processed downstream (first-out).

For example, in central supply areas, sterile materials are continuously rotated, replacing them with the up-and-coming expiration dates to the front of the shelf. This can also apply to work requests in pharmacy, pathology, radiology, medical records, etc.

The FIFO lane has the following attributes:

- ✦ Located between two processes (supply and demand)
- ✦ A maximum number of work units (written orders, lab requests, etc.) are placed in the FIFO lane and are visible
- ✦ Is sequentially loaded and labeled
- ✦ Has a signal system to notify the upstream process when the lane is full
- ✦ Has visual rules and standards posted to ensure FIFO lane integrity
- ✦ Has a process in place for assisting the downstream process when the lane is full and assistance is required

The team can be creative in establishing the signal method, within the FIFO system, to indicate when the system is full. This could be a raised flag, a light, a pager code, an alert email, or text message to the upstream process. The important point is to ensure the signal established will work effectively. When the signal is released, the upstream worker lends support to the downstream worker until the work is caught up. There is no point in continuing to produce upstream when the downstream process is overloaded. When this happens, it becomes an overproduction waste, which is considered the greatest waste of all.

FIFO lanes help to ensure smooth work flow between processes with little or no interruption. The following illustrations demonstrate the overall principle of FIFO, in that, the upstream (left part of the illustration) process only provides a certain quantity of work (FIFO Lane) to the downstream (right part of the illustration) process. This must be regulated by some type of visual control as indicated by the Lane Full flag on the bottom illustration.

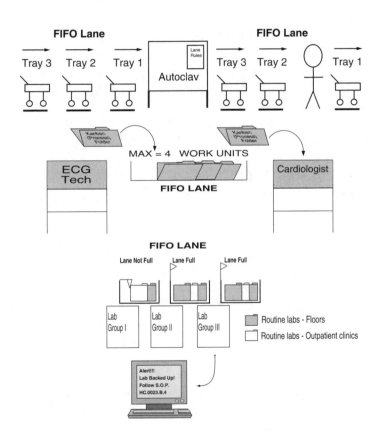

For example, when ECGs (electrocardiograms) are completed on several patients by the technician, they are then set on the desk of the cardiologist to be read. The reports are read, not in the order of test completion, but as they are placed in the pile of documents to be reviewed. Creating a FIFO lane (as shown in the middle illustration above) could be used in this situation. As a result, the first ECG test that was placed in the FIFO lane would be the first read by the cardiologist. A maximum number of tests to be placed in the FIFO lane would need to be determined as to ensure lane integrity.

Keep in mind that In-process supermarkets and FIFO Lanes are compromises to true continuous flow. They should be viewed as part of a continuous improvement system and efforts should be made to find ways to reduce or eliminate them in the quest for continuous flow.

The ED staff complained that they were always running out of items, even though there was someone assigned every day (on the midnight shift) to count and replace inventory. In some cases, small items such as pulse oximeters, were taken with the patients to the inpatient units. In other cases, the last item in stock would be taken, and the next person who needed it would be out of luck. The midnight shift stated that they had a hard time counting everything because there were so many places in the ED where items might be stored. The day shift said they had to stock extra supplies around the ED to make sure they would not run out. It seemed to be a vicious cycle.

The ED manager decided to spend a week to conduct a supply survey. Each team member was asked to document the amount of each item used, and whether any item was not available when needed.

After looking at the data, a small "Kanban" team determined standards for what (non-medication) items should be stocked in each ED room, and what should be kept in the Clean Utility Room or other appropriate areas. They discussed the ideas and received additional input from the staff at the weekly staff meeting. The team emphasized that an X factor (or buffer) would be kept so that the staff would not run out. Special attention was paid to any items that had expiration dates, to ensure that a surplus would not result in the wasting of these items.

The Kanban team posted minimum and maximum amounts for each item to be stored and labeled all the areas in the ED rooms where small amounts of material were to be kept on hand. They also created Re-Order and Special-Order Kanban cards for the storage areas and then put together a supply order form with all of those items listed, plus leaving space for special items to be added. The Kanban standard work was posted in the Clean Utility Room. These activities took about three weeks.

Training was done at a weekly staff meeting and the Kanban process was started that day. The Kanban cards were placed at the minimum inventory level (placed between items or taped to the next item), and when visible, would be placed in a special In Box for the midnight shift person designated to do the ordering. The order form would be completed and processed appropriately, i.e., sent via interdepartmental mail or faxed to the vendor before the end of the shift. The order forms were kept in a designated file folder in the Clean Utility Room for easy reference.

When supplies were received, they were processed as usual with the invoices and receivers being signed and sent to the appropriate department. The concept of FIFO was used to make sure that the oldest items would be used first. The Kanban cards were replaced (or attached) at the point of minimum inventory.

The ED staff agreed to review the process on a monthly basis to ensure that it was working as designed. At first the team found a few "hiccups" as some Kanban cards were not placed in the In Box, but after a review of the new process at the weekly meeting, the process was smoothed out. The Kanban team was later recognized at a monthly leadership meeting.

The results after 3 months were:
1. Reduction in $1,256.00 per month in purchased supplies, totalling $3,768.00.
2. Decrease in expired medications, from 1.8% to less than 1% per month, equating to a cost savings of $476.00 per month, totaling $1,428.00.

Pitch

Pitch is the time frame that represents the most efficient and practical work (or patient) flow throughout the value stream. It can be a multiple of takt time. Since takt time, for many healthcare practices (i.e., blood draws, charting, dispersing medications, etc.) typically will be too small of a unit of time to move the work or information to the next process immediately, pitch is a solution that can be used. Pitch is the optimal flow of work at specific times through the value stream. Pitch is the *adjusted* takt time (or multiple of) when takt time is too short of a time to realistically move something. Typically, each value stream (or process-to-process timed movement) will have its own pitch.

Pitch will:

+ Assist to determine the optimal patient or work flow
+ Set the frequency for movement of the patient or work to the next process
+ Assist in reducing transport and motion waste
+ Allow for immediate attention when interruptions to work flow arise
+ Reduce wait (or queue) times

Note: Each value stream may require a separate pitch.

How to Calculate Pitch

Pitch is used to reduce wait time and other wastes that exist within and between processes. For example, a medical office found it was constantly calling in refill prescriptions every time a request from a patient had been called in that day. Pitch was used as a tool to reduce some of the wastes that existed in that process as explained in the following example.

Use the following steps as a guideline when determining pitch increments.

1. Calculate takt time. (See previous chapter on takt time)

2. Determine the optimal number of patients or work units to move through the value stream (i.e., number of labs to be drawn, number of patients to be seen within a specified time period, number of charts to be processed, etc.).

3. Multiply takt time by the optimal number of work units.

Pitch = takt time (x) optimal number of work units

For example:

(1) Prescription requests to pharmacy 20 prescriptions per day. Time is an 8 hour day (or 480 minutes).
Takt time: Time/Volume = 480 minutes / 20 prescriptions = 24 minutes
(Approximately every half-hour a patient is requesting someone from the office to call in a script for them.)

(2) Optimal number of prescriptions to be moved = 10 (Ten scripts can easily be called in at one time as agreed to by the staff)

(3) Pitch = 24 minutes (takt time) x 10 prescriptions (optimal number of work units) = 240 minute pitch or 4 hours

This means every 4 hours, 10 prescriptions will be moved to the next process within the value stream (i.e., the pharmacy).

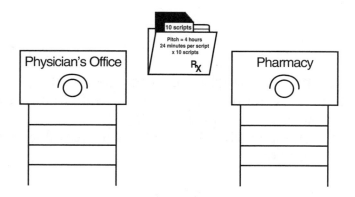

Do not confuse pitch with the cycle time. In this example, it only takes approximately 1 minute of cycle time (relaying the script to the pharmacy tech). The total cycle time it takes to complete the 10 scripts would be 10 minutes, plus 2 minutes to go to a phone and make the call, for a total cycle time of 12 minutes. If each script was called in separately, then there would be 20 minutes of going to the phone and making the call (each trip 2 minutes x 10 trips). From this example, the waste motion and transport of those other 9 times (or 18 minutes of staff time) would be eliminated. The cycle time would remain the same for each script. (The patient would have been notified of the time that the scripts were to be called in.)

Pitch increments must be monitored to ensure they are being met. If an interruption of work arises, a system should be in place to address why the work is behind schedule. There are different ways this can occur:

- ✦ The group leader communicates the need for assistance when pitch cannot be met
- ✦ The employee who cannot meet the next pitch work increment communicates the need for assistance
- ✦ The runner (see next section) communicates the need for assistance

The communication signal required for assistance can include:

- ✦ A pager code or text message to the supervisor or departmental manager
- ✦ An alert email, text message, etc. can be sent to all employees for a pre-defined round-robin type of support
- ✦ A phone call to the supervisor
- ✦ A physical meeting with the departmental leader or supervisor

Creating a visible pitch board will allow employees to think and work differently about the process that is being improved. *A **visible pitch board** is a bulletin board, whiteboard, etc. displaying the pitch increments and/or associated work that is required to be done for that day or week.* The simple fact of having a visual board at a location where the work is being done will be a motivating factor for employees to meet the goal (or pitch increment) that has been determined. This will create a sense of satisfaction each time the work (or pitch increment) is completed.

The benefits of a visible pitch board are it:

+ Begins to remove the work from desks and to make it known
+ Allows managers/supervisors to monitor hourly/daily progress and be aware of situations when work is getting behind
+ Provides a foundation to advance to a more sophisticated scheduling system (i.e., Leveling system) at a later date

If an employee gets behind (say more than 1 pitch increment) of what is required there should be a standard procedure to follow (i.e., notify supervisor, request assistance from another staff member, etc.).

The important point regarding pitch is to group work that can be aligned around a specified value stream, thereby reducing the queue time and other wastes that exist between two processes. Making the pitch increments as a visual cue is a great way to get everyone involved to a work rhythm (i.e., takt time). It places emphasis on completing a certain quantity of work in an allotted time to meet customer demand and further provides the team a common purpose of maintaining this "demand." After approximately two months of using visible pitch for a value stream, and as other value streams use the visible pitch board tool, then they all can be incorporated into a Heijunka or Leveling system. (See Leveling later in this chapter.)

The ED team looked for ways to use the concept of pitch in their workflow. They discussed whether they could determine an optimal work unit for copying records (no), sending records to the Medical Record room (these could be sent at the end of each shift), checking patients' personal belongings (no), lab draws (no), checking for new lab results at the printer (probably not), and bringing wristbands over from Registration (no). In most cases, the team thought that any type of grouping of work in ED could lead to delays in the process and their goal was to go for the ideal "one-piece flow." However, the team did think of a use for pitch outside of the Dispo-to-Admit process. After charts are copied for the patients being admitted, they were either being walked to the ED Chart room (outside of the ED) one at a time, or held until the end of shift. Neither system was very efficient, since in the first scenario the clerks did a lot of walking, but in the second scenario the chart room staff would be waiting for the end of the shift and then receive work that they could not process the same day. The ED unit clerks agreed to place the copied charts in a labeled tray in the ED and bring them down to the file room every 4 hours - giving the chart room staff enough work to process, while minimizing the walking of the ED clerks.

Mini Case Study for Phlebotomy

Laboratory phlebotomists drew "sweeps" for blood specimen collection each morning at 6 am. They usually collected all the samples and then came back to the Lab to drop the samples off at around 8 am. Physicians were complaining, because they wanted the test results back before morning rounds at 9 am. With usual process, the Lab had no chance of meeting the physicians' needs. Pitch was calculated as 6 minutes (takt time) x 5 specimens (optimal number of work units) = 30 minutes. Subsequently, the Lab leadership decided to ask the phlebotomists to send specimens through the pneumatic tube system every time they had collected 5 patient samples, about a half-hour's worth of work, and, in this way, were able to keep up with the testing so that 95% of results were available by rounding at 9 am.

Mini Case Study for Facilities

When beds are changed on the nursing units, the dirty linens are placed in a cart for pick-up. One nursing unit could generate 6 full carts per day, leading to problems if they were left for a single pick-up at the end of the shift. The Facilities manager worked with the Nursing Director to calculate takt time - in 24 hours, 6 carts were filled, so the takt time = 4 hours. One linen tech could move two carts at a time. Pitch was calculated as 4 hours (takt time) x 2 carts (optimal number of work units) = 8 hours.

Work Load Balancing

Work load balancing is the optimal distribution of work units throughout the value stream to maintain takt time or pitch. Also known as employee/staff balancing or line balancing, work load balancing assures that now one worker is doing too much or too little work.

Work load balancing begins with analyzing the current state of how work relative to the value stream is allocated and ends with an even and fair distribution of work, ensuring that customer demand is met with a continuous flow mentality.

Work load balancing will accomplish the following:

✦ Determine the number of staff needed for a given demand (or value stream)
✦ Evenly distribute work units
✦ Ensure cycle times for each process are accurate
✦ Assist to standardize the process
✦ Assist in creating the future state value stream (or process) map
✦ Improve productivity
✦ Encourage teamwork through cross-training

The best tool to perform the work load balancing is an Employee Balance Chart. *The **Employee Balance Chart** is a visual display, in the form of a bar chart, that represents the work elements, times, and workers for each process relative to the total value stream cycle time and takt time (or pitch).*

The seven steps to work load balancing are:

1. Visually display the list of processes from the current state value stream map.
2. Obtain individual cycle times for the various process activities.
3. Add the individual cycle times to obtain the total cycle time for each process.
4. Create the Employee Balance Chart of the current state.
5. Determine the ideal number of staff for a value stream.
6. Create the Employee Balance Chart of the future state.
7. Create standard work procedures and train staff.

1. Visually display the list of processes from the current state value stream map.

Be very clear about identifying each process, its beginning and end as well as the process's parameters. The team should have a good understanding of the processes from previously creating the current state value stream map.

2. Obtain individual cycle times for the various process activities.

Cycle times should be derived from the current state value stream map and the Document Tagging Worksheet and/or observation data. Revisit these times to ensure accuracy. Members of the team may want to use a stopwatch to time any process activities that may be questionable, evaluating the processes as they check the times. Take time to analyze the processes.

3. Add the individual cycle times to obtain the total cycle time for each process.

Each process's total cycle time should match the process times located on the step graph at the bottom of the current state value stream map.

4. Create the Employee Balance Chart of the current state.

The Employee Balance Chart is bar chart identifying each process and staff, along with the various individual cycle times as derived from the current state value stream map. This may be the entire current state value stream map or sections of it where it is known that duties can be shared or consolidated to improve the overall flow. It is recommended that you visually display the chart on an easel with a flip chart so the team can review it as a group and comment. Use Post-it Notes to represent the tasks associated with the processes. Make the Post-it Notes proportional to the time element for each individual task. Draw a horizontal line to represent takt time.

The following is the Oakview Employee Balance Chart for the entire Dispo-to-Admit value stream. The processes, (a) - (i), and cycle times used are from the Cycle Time Table (page 82). Note: In-process delays are identified in bold. In-process delays may or may not be included on the Employee Balance Chart. However, the team decided to display the delays on their chart.

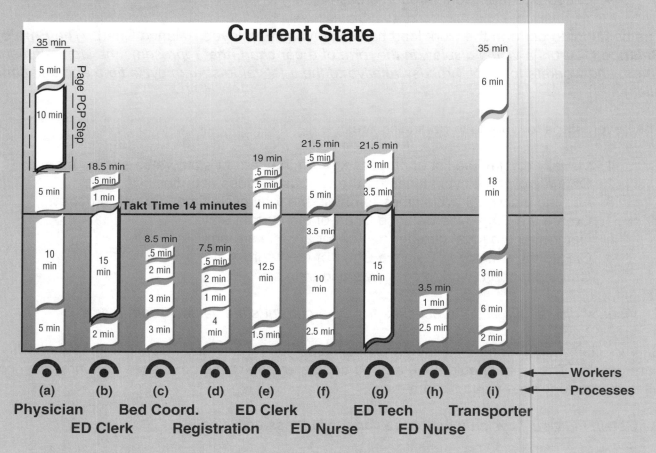

The team found that the visual display of data from the Cycle Time Table was very enlightening. The Cycle Time Table clearly identified which areas could be further analyzed to improve times to meet the takt time of 14 minutes.

5. Determine the ideal number of staff for a value stream.

When determining the ideal number of workers needed to operate the process or processes for the value stream, keep in mind that staff will most likely have multiple value streams they are responsible for throughout the day. The ideal number of staff is determined by dividing the total process cycle time by the takt time (or pitch). For example, in the lab, if an average blood draw took 5 minutes (total cycle time) and the demand (takt time) was determined to be 5 minutes (12 patient draws per hour), then the ideal number of staff needed would be 1 person (5 minutes total cycle time / 5 minute takt time). However, it rarely comes out that evenly. Use this to *assist* in determining staffing levels.

The ED is a bit more complicated due to its takt time for each 4 hour shift, as well as specific duties for each staff. The team decided to calculated the ideal number of staff using the Cycle Time Table data, however, they did not include any of the wait times. The following Staffing Levels Worksheet is their analysis of takt times and number of staff required per 4 hour blocks of time.

Staffing Levels Worksheet

Time (4 hour blocks)	Takt Time (Time / Volume)	Physician	ED Clerk	Bed Coordinator	Admitting	ED Nurse	ED Tech	Transporter	Physician	ED Clerk	Bed Coordinator	Admitting	ED Nurse	ED Tech	Transporter
		Total Process Time (Less Delays)							Ideal Staff Level (Total Process Time / Takt Time)						
0000 - 0400	60	22	3.5	5.5	7	18.5	6	27	.37	.01	.1	.12	.31	.1	.45
0400 - 0800	27	22	3.5	5.5	7	18.5	6	27	.81	.13	.2	.26	.68	.22	1
0800 - 1200	14	22	3.5	5.5	7	18.5	6	27	1.6	.25	14	.5	1.3	.43	1.93
1200 - 1600	9	22	3.5	5.5	7	18.5	6	27	2.8	.39	.6	.88	2	.67	3
1600 - 2000	8	22	3.5	5.5	7	18.5	6	27	2.8	.44	.7	.88	2.3	.75	3.4
2000 - 0000	14	22	3.5	5.5	7	18.5	6	27	1.6	.25	.4	.5	1.3	.43	1.93

Note: If the decimal number from the calculation is less than X.5 workers required, balance the value stream to the lesser whole number. Ensure each worker is balanced to takt time and allocate any excess time to one worker. Utilize the excess time to improve standard work procedures and conduct kaizen activities, attempting to reduce additional wastes within the processes. Once the employee's efforts are no longer needed on the original project, that person can be placed in another continuous improvement capacity or position in the organization. Lean is not about reducing the number of people, it is about eliminating waste. Without this understanding, Lean will never be accepted. (To work on reducing process cycle times to meet takt time, the Standard Work Combination Table on pages 189-189 can be used.)

If the decimal number from the calculation is equal to or greater than X.5, then balance to the larger whole number.

6. Create the Employee Balance Chart of the future state.

Work with team members to move the Post-it Notes around to balance the various work elements with each employee balanced to takt (or pitch) time, while maintaining the flow of work.

The team realized that everything in an ED cannot be ideally balanced to takt, however, it was a target for the team to try and get as close as possible. Using this tool, they realized the tremendous wait times that were included in the total times for each process/worker. Here are *some* of the changes that were made by the ED team:

1. Physician: Eliminated the wait time for PCP (Primary Care Physician) call-back from "undetermined amount of time" (typically they did not call back) (saving 13 minutes)
2. ED Nurse: Simplified chart copying procedure (less re-copying of information in other parts of the chart) (saving 8.5 minutes)
3. ED Unit Clerk: Created standard work for chart copy and belongings form resulted in less time looking for those items when patient was being picked up (saving 8 minutes)
4. Transporter: Identified a designated elevator and created transporter response guidelines (saving 8 minutes)

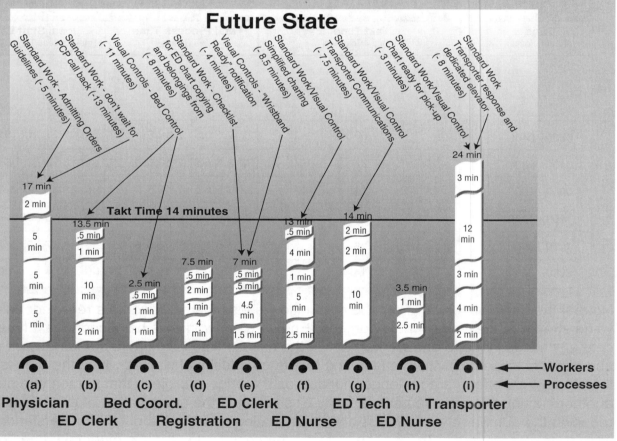

7. Create standard work procedures and train staff.

Once a consensus has been obtained on balancing, redistributing, and/or modifying the process activities, update all necessary standards and then train staff to those standards.

The future state Employee Balance Chart creates a clear, visual target. If there are difficulties in reallocating the work duties, or the takt time cannot be met within the current cycle times, the tools in the next section on standard work can be used.

Standard Work

Standard work establishes and controls the best way to complete a task without variation from the original intent. These tasks are then executed consistently, without variation from the original intent. Standard work offers a basis for providing consistent levels of healthcare productivity, quality, and safety, while promoting a positive work attitude based on well-documented work standards. Standard work, done properly, reduces all process variation. It is the basis for all continuous improvement activities.

Creating the standard work procedures is comprised of using two main tools: the Standard Work Combination Table and the Standard Work Chart.

*The **Standard Work Combination Table** is the visual representation displaying the sequential flow of all the activities related to a specific process.* The Standard Work Combination Table will:

✦ Document the exact time requirement (i.e., cycle times) for each work element or task in the process
✦ Indicate the flow (or sequence) of all the work in the process
✦ Display the work design sequence based on takt time (ideally)
✦ Demonstrate the time relationship between physical work (patient care, dispersing meds, charting, etc.) to the movement of the patient or work (transporting patients, retrieving equipment, checking doctors' orders, etc.), queue times, and computer access time

The Standard Work Combination Table is an important tool for allocating work within the value stream when total cycle times are greater than takt time. Capturing the motion of the process that is being reviewed is a good method to accurately document the times of each work element.

The 7 steps for creating the Standard Work Combination Table are:

1. Break the process into separate work elements (record motion to obtain accuracy).
2. Time each work element from step (1) by observation or EMR/EMS database retrieval.
3. Complete the Standard Work Combination Table.
4. Review each work element (task). Question whether it should be eliminated or if the time can be improved.
5. Gain a consensus on any changes.
6. Create a new Standard Work Combination Table. Update the standard work procedures.
7. Train everyone on new standard work procedures and audit.

The Standard Work Combination Table is a powerful tool and should be used as the basis for all improvement activities. It does require time to thoroughly complete, but will be well worth the effort in the long run.

By reviewing the process map and the Cycle Time Table (page 82), the team realized that there may be opportunities to reduce some of those times, especially for the wristband process. They decided to observe someone doing the activities related to the wristband process and then use that data (along with that person) to complete the following Standard Work Combination Table. Subsequent analysis and Kaizen activities would reduce this overall cycle time.

Standard Work Combination Table

Date	4/18
Daily Reqt.	105
Takt Time	14 minutes (avg)
Process Name	ED Clerk processes dispo order to wristband on patient

Value Stream	Dispo-to-Admit
Work Instruction No.	1
Page	1 of 1

Work (physical)	———
Walk/Transport	∿∿∿
Computer Interaction	– – – –
Wait/Delay/Queue Time	←——→

Processing Times (minutes)
Wrk - Work Physical   Wlk - Walk/Transport   CI - Computer Interaction   WT - Wait Time

Step #	Task/Activity	Wrk	Wlk	CI	WT
1	ED Clerk notes dispo in chart	0.5			
2	ED Clerk calls Bed Coord	1.0			
3	Bed Coord receives request	0.5			
4	Bed Coord checks bed status			2	
5	Bed Coord waits for bed avl				15
6	Bed Coord cks Ns Mgr/Hskp	3.0			
7	Bed Coord confirms bed/IP	1.5			
8	Bed Coord notifies ED Clerk	1.5			
9	ED Clerk process Admit order			2.0	
10	Reg receives Admit order			0.5	
11	Reg changes pt status			2.0	
12	Reg prints new wrst/face sh	1.0			
13	Reg takes wrst/face sh to ED		4.0		
14	ED Clerk rec wrst/face sh	0.5			
15	ED Clerk places face sh	0.5			
16	ED Clerk gives wrst to Ns		4.0		
17	Ns places wrst on patient		0.5		
Totals		10.0	8.5	6.5	15.0

Grand Total (not including parallel waiting time, Step 5 from above) = 25.0 minutes

The **Standard Work Chart** illustrates the sequence of the work being performed. It provides a visual training aid for employees. Employees who may not interact with a certain process regularly can refer to the chart and be confident if they had to complete that process. It should be updated as improvements are made. The Standard Work Chart can be a detailed flowchart with digital photos, step-by-step instructions, etc.

The 4 steps for creating the Standard Work Chart are:

1. Draw the area layout or process flow on the chart. Label all items.
2. Designate work element locations by number to correspond to items listed in (1).
3. Use arrows to show movement of patients, information, staff, and any special instructions or safety concerns.
4. Post the chart in the work area and use as basis for continuous improvement.

It will do little good to improve a process if it is not from an existing standard. If you do not work from some type of standard, you will be attempting to improve to a moving target, one of process variation.

The Standard Work Chart will:

✦ Display the work sequence, process layout, and work-in-process in relationship to each other
✦ Display the worker movement for each activity, task, or operation
✦ Identify quality standards, safety concerns, and/or critical opportunities for errors

Using a typical Standard Work Chart for ED did not seem practical. Because staff members are caring for multiple patients in different locations (rooms), it is hard to track movement as a standard protocol. Since there are hundreds of activities involved, no ED is going to prepare work charts for all of them, let alone post them all over the ED. However, the ED team decided to create a Standard Work Chart for those activities that needed to be done after the Disposition order had been written. They drew a map of the ED and listed the activities in order, gaining consensus on the ideal model. They then posted the Standard Work Chart (as shown below) in the staff lounge and asked for comments during the week, which could be discussed at the next team meeting.

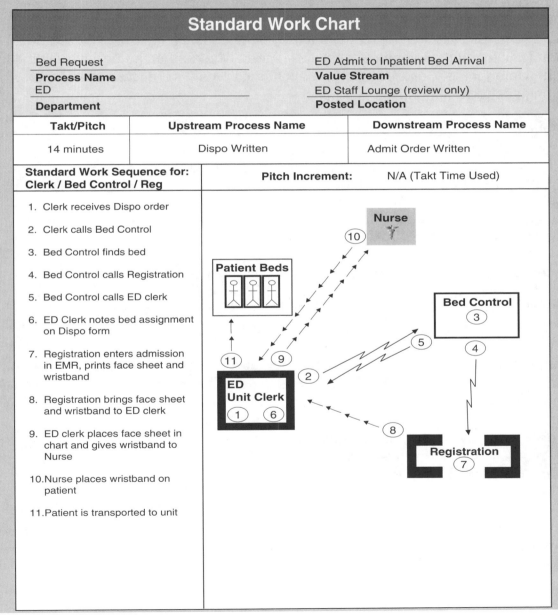

Standard Work Chart

Bed Request	ED Admit to Inpatient Bed Arrival
Process Name	**Value Stream**
ED	ED Staff Lounge (review only)
Department	**Posted Location**

Takt/Pitch	Upstream Process Name	Downstream Process Name
14 minutes	Dispo Written	Admit Order Written

Standard Work Sequence for: **Clerk / Bed Control / Reg**	**Pitch Increment:** N/A (Takt Time Used)

1. Clerk receives Dispo order
2. Clerk calls Bed Control
3. Bed Control finds bed
4. Bed Control calls Registration
5. Bed Control calls ED clerk
6. ED Clerk notes bed assignment on Dispo form
7. Registration enters admission in EMR, prints face sheet and wristband
8. Registration brings face sheet and wristband to ED clerk
9. ED clerk places face sheet in chart and gives wristband to Nurse
10. Nurse places wristband on patient
11. Patient is transported to unit

Nurse

Patient Beds

Bed Control ③

ED Unit Clerk ① ⑥

Registration ⑦

The ED team considered the following processes for creating improved standard work procedures:

> Triage (will vary with patient condition)
> ED bed assignment
> Nurse assessment (will vary with patient condition)
> Chart preparation
> Clinical protocols for MI, stroke, pneumonia, others
> Call to PCP by ED physician
> Clothing/belongings check
> Report to unit (Admissions Report)
> Chart management (dispo rack)

The ED team realized not all of them could be done within one Kaizen Event. Therefore, they prioritized the areas and implemented the following standard work procedures.

Belongings Form

The ED had a form for patient belongings, but it was not consistently used. When queried, the staff said that they found it easier to just ask the patient whether he/she had everything they came in with. Unfortunately, even when the patient said "yes," there were often times when patients belongings were left behind.

The team held staff meetings to ask how the form could be improved. After gathering everyone's feedback, they revised the form to include questions to ensure the belongings are with the patient and/or family, as well as a space for comments. The staff agreed to try the form for two weeks as a pilot. After that time, there was a 50% reduction in missing belongs and form usage with proper documentation was up by 75%.

Report to Unit (Admissions Report)

ED nurses called the Admissions Report to the receiving unit when all the expected test results, admission orders, and other work was completed. (Occasionally, the receiving unit requested that the patient be held in the ED because of staff breaks or short-staffing.) Once the receiving unit agreed to take the patient, the transporter was called.

The ED team met with nursing leadership and came to a consensus that unless a patient was coding on the receiving unit the ED should always expect that the receiving unit would take the patient when the Admissions Report was called in.

In order to prevent delays from special equipment not being available on the receiving unit, the Bed Control nurse started to include notification for special equipment when she was confirming that a bed was available on the unit. Since the admission process was expected to take an hour, it gave the receiving unit that hour to find and deploy the special equipment, if needed.

The nursing leadership agreed to incorporate those steps as part of the standard work for the ED Admitting process.

Mini Case Study for Housekeeping

When linens were returned to the department for cleaning, the department staff checked them for wear and tear, literally checking for items that needed special cleaning, repairs, or should be discarded. A supervisor had to be called every time the item was in question. The supervisor called the staff together to create standard work definitions for wear and tear conditions, and said that if these standards were followed, the supervisor would only have to be called when an item looked like it should be discarded. A visual standard was created and posted at the location where the linens arrived. The staff could work more quickly and the supervisor could use his/her time more effectively. This saved 11.5 hours per month of staff time.

Mini Case Study for Housekeeping

The Housekeeping department found that every staff member stocked their carts differently. They would often spend as much as a half-hour "getting ready." The manager brought the staff together to do a 5S project for their carts and supply room, and the team developed a standard way of stocking the cart, along with taking ergonomics into consideration. Because each cart was now restocked in a standard fashion at the end of each shift, the subsequent shift could get started to work as soon as they got their assignments, requiring less preparation time.

Physical Layout

A **Lean physical layout work area** *is a self-contained, well-ordered space that optimizes the flow of patients and work.* Typically, many facilities have areas or departments separated by physical walls that may impede the efficiency of work flow. Eliminating walls may be difficult to achieve, but once people understand some of the efficiencies that can be gained, they become engaged in tackling the challenges. Many different methods can be used, such as the computer and visual controls simulating these walls coming down. It is important to realize that there are delays in many processes due to the physical separations.

The graphic illustrates the comparison between the current physical arrangement with walls and a future Lean state designed without walls. Lean designs without walls remove any and all barriers that impact work flow, improving all types of communication and movement; no design should ever compromise patient safety or confidentiality.

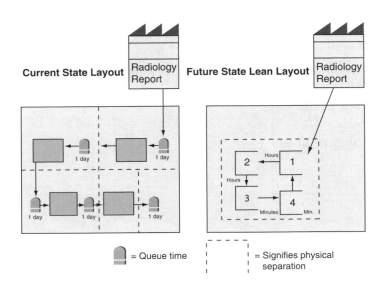

In the Old Physical Layout current state (see adjoining page), the ED's triage room had one entrance. When patients needed quick treatment or diagnostics, such as an EKG or medication within a certain timeline, it was very difficult to get the patient into care quickly. An additional door was put in the Triage room so that the patient could 'flow' over to a "Quick Treatment" room where a tech could be posted to give rapid treatments, EKGs, or other physician approved advanced protocols. This allowed for more timely patient care. (1 - New Physical Layout - adjoining page)

In the current state, the Psych Observation room was not located near any staff whose responsibility it was to observe the patients. It was moved to the former physician director's office, who transferred to an office at the rear of the ED, which was much quieter. (2)

In the current state, the four exam rooms were used as overflow rooms. Along with the former Psych Observation room, the other exam rooms were modified to include two OB exam rooms, placing the casting room up front near the exit for easier departure, and a lounge for the Ambulance drivers (EMS) (much appreciated by the Ambulance companies and helpful for new business). (3)

Other changes were made to accommodate the new chart racks located near the ED clerk's area. (4) The physician's work area had always been small and crowded. Moving the physicians into the former Clean Utility Room gave them more space and privacy. (5) Communications were maintained by installing two windows into the room facing the ED desk and beds, so they could be signaled quickly if needed. (6)

The Clean and Dirty Utility rooms were moved down one room, and the lounge was moved to a new space created by two cubicles that were being used for only storage (which the 5S program had cleared out). (7)

Finally, near the entrance, the current state layout had an unused office nearest to the main ED door that was being used as a supply room, but which had deteriorated into a "junk room." The space was cleaned out in the 5S project and was now used for the Financial Counseling Room. The former Financial Counseling Room could now be turned into a Family Counseling room, which could be used for family members in difficult circumstances or when loved ones were severely injured and the families needed a space for privacy. (8)

These changes helped the flow of patients through the various treatments, placed rooms in a more logical layout for their function, and opened space for areas such as the Family Counseling Room and Quick Treatment rooms.

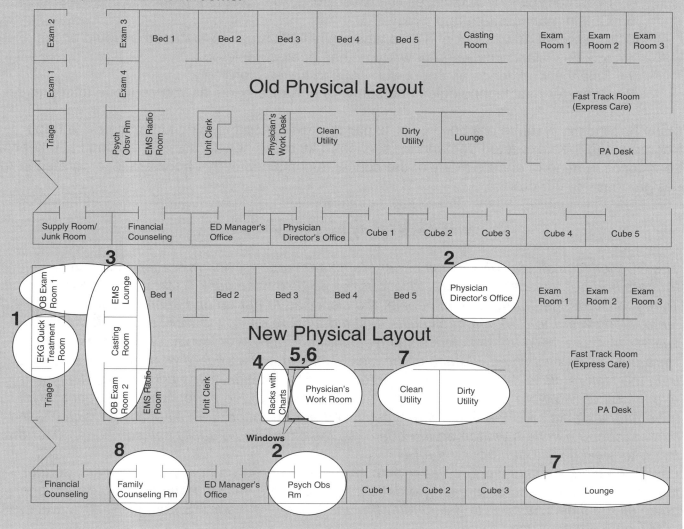

A few reasons to consider a new physical layout are:

- ✦ Process knowledge can be better shared among the staff to allow everyone to be better trained
- ✦ Improved communications will occur between processes
- ✦ Wastes of delay, motion, and transport will be reduced or eliminated
- ✦ Most efficient use of equipment, people, and materials will be ensured
- ✦ Greater job flexibility will occur if someone is absent
- ✦ Less floor space will be required
- ✦ Work throughput will be increased as well as overall productivity

The following guidelines can be used when determining a new physical layout.

1. Review the current physical layout and associated process tasks to determine which wastes occur due to the current layout in terms of travel, motion, and delays.
2. Brainstorm to consolidate where to reduce or eliminate the wastes identified in (1). Processes may need to be modified or standardized and may require additional cross-training.
3. Determine if an In-process supermarket or FIFO lane is required.
4. Prepare a plan, including result expectations, to implement proposed changes.
5. Obtain management approval.
6. Implement new layout at a time when minimal disruption to the area would occur. Post any new standards when new layout has been completed.
7. Balance work loads amongst workers and train accordingly.
8. Consider new technologies and software enhancements as you continue to improve.

Many healthcare systems are building or expanding their facilities to accommodate the Baby Boomers and their expected demand for services. As these new facilities are being built, keep a Lean focus in mind to ensure many of the concepts contained in this book are incorporated in the design phase of the project.

Mini Case Study for ED Clerk's Desk

The ED clerk's desk was always full of papers, charts, reports, and miscellaneous items. Printers had been placed in several locations, some below the desk so they were hard to reach. To reach charts, get forms, or find people, the clerk had to get up and search for items. The ED team, along with the clerks from all shifts, first did a 5S Audit on the work area. After some space had been freed up, the clerk's suggested a better physical layout for the items. Charts were put in racks within easy reach of the clerk's station and standard work was developed to train the staff to place the charts in the appropriate rack location. One printer was eliminated, and the other two were placed on racks above the desk with the paper flow (and paper trays) towards the clerks. A dry-erase board was placed at the station, with all of the physician's and nurses' phone numbers written on the board, so the clerks could easily call someone rather than trying to search for them around the ED.
Lastly, the clerk's chairs were replaced with sturdy task chairs on heavy-duty casters, so that they could roll back and forth easily to get charts and forms, rather than having to get up and down all the time. As one clerk said after the changes were made, "Sure feels like my work is 100% easier than it used to be!"

Leveling

Leveling *is a system that balances (allocates, distributes) the volume and variety of work among the staff during a period of time - typically a day.* It is also known as Heijunka. Leveling is the combination of *several* value streams to ensure each process has the capacity to meet the demand.

The purpose of leveling is to ensure:

+ Work is evenly distributed among staff by volume and variety
+ Work is distributed efficiently, eliminating transport and motion waste
+ No work is waiting in queue
+ No work is released upstream that is not required downstream
+ A pull system of work is established
+ Continuous flow is achieved
+ A visual aid identifies where and when work is behind schedule

Leveling is a simple concept, but it can be difficult to understand and implement. The main principle of leveling is scheduling. Initially, leveling and scheduling may seem similar, but they are distinctly different. Scheduling is allocating work units throughout processes for one value stream. Leveling is allocating work units throughout processes for multiple value streams. Leveling is a sophisticated form of scheduling. Leveling is the distribution and allocation of the work units or services to fulfill numerous customer demands over a defined period of time. The difference may not seem like much, but it is significant. Scheduling does not take into consideration customer demand and, most importantly, the application of Lean principles to meet that demand. For example, a lab has a schedule to provide blood test results (routine) every four hours to the hospital floors throughout the day. Everyone in the lab is working hard and there is no problem meeting the schedule. However, there has been an increase in demand from the outpatient clinics in a effort to provide lab results to their patients with 24 hours. Previously the outpatient clinic labs were always done when time permitted, usually within 48 or 72 hours. The concept of leveling could be used to balance both the hospital floor's lab results with the outpatient clinics. The pitch for the hospital floors would be every two hours and the pitch for the outpatient clinic could be every 4 hours. Scheduling the work throughout the lab to meet these *two* pitch times (2 hours and 4 hours) would be using the concept of leveling. See page 199 for visual representation of this.

Note: Typical Lean-Sigma project focus is on one value stream. After improvements have been sustained for over 30 days for that value stream, then additional value streams can be identified and thus "leveled" into the Lean system.

COMPARISON OF SCHEDULING AND LEVELING

Scheduling	Leveling
✔ More commonly used	✔ New tool for departments
✔ Capacity fixed	✔ Capacity based on customer demand
✔ Based on volume	✔ Based on volume and variety
✔ Lean tools not used	✔ Lean tools used
✔ Continuous flow not key to improvements	✔ Continuous flow required

The steps to leveling are as follows:

1. *Calculate takt time for each value stream.*

Takt time = $\dfrac{\text{Available daily work time}}{\text{Total daily volume required}}$

Example: The lab has the following takt times:

Takt Times for Lab (routine)				
Customers (i.e., value streams)	Monthly Time Available (minutes)	Monthly Volume of Work (units)	Time/Volume	Takt Time (minutes)
Walk-Ins	14400	720	14400/720	20
Pediatrics	14400	480	14400/480	30
Outpatient Clinics	14400	960	14400/960	15
Hospital Floors	14400	1440	14400/1440	10

2. Determine pitch for each value stream.

Pitch is a multiple of takt time that will allow you to create and maintain a consistent and practical work flow throughout the value stream or area. To calculate pitch, multiply the takt time by the number of work units to flow through the value stream.

Pitch = takt time x practical number of work flow units (patients, charts, labs, orders, etc.)

Pitch Times for Lab (routine)			
Customers (i.e., value streams)	Takt Time (minutes)	Optimal Number of Work Units to Flow*	Takt Time x Optimal Number of Work Units
Walk-Ins	20	12	20 x 12 = 240 minutes
Pediatrics	30	4	30 x 4 = 120 minutes
Outpatient Clinics	15	16	15 x 16 = 240 minutes
Hospital Floors	10	12	10 x 12 = 120 minutes
* Determined by historical demand as well as asking their downstream customers.			

3. *Create a sequence table or chart.*

A **sequence table or chart** *is a matrix which shows each value stream pitch as grouped work elements, when it is required, by whom, and in what quantity.* The table illustrates the customer's demand at a glance and should be posted by the heijunka box. *The **heijunka box** is a physical device similar to a group of mailboxes dedicated to holding the work units or kanban cards for that day (or week).* Time slots on the heijunka box should correspond to the pitch increments of the work. This is a useful tool to visually "see" when work is not going according to the schedule (pitch increments). Standard processes should be in place to address when work is behind schedule. The sequence table should be updated as customer requirements change. The time elements (pitch increments) do not account for any breaks, daily meetings, or other diversions from the work day. The times represent the actual time the work must be moved to the next process. Breaks, meetings, etc. must be considered when determining pitch times.

Leveling Sequence Table (routine)

Customers (i.e., value streams)	Pitch (minutes)	Daily Pick-Up Times with Number of Units (Day Shift)								
		0800	0900	1000	1100	1200	1300	1400	1500	1600
Walk-Ins	240					12				12
Pediatrics	120			4		4		4		4
Outpatient Clinics	240				16				16	
Hospital Floors	120		12		12		12		12	

4. *Determine the runner's route or other method for distributing work.*

A **runner** *is an employee who ensures and maintains pitch integrity.* Using a runner frees transport or motion time for the people directly involved in value-added activities. The runner covers a pre-defined route within the pitch time period, picking up work, patients, etc. and delivering them to their appropriate areas.

If a work unit is not ready for pickup at the heijunka box or location (which could be a pre-exam or waiting room) or from the upstream process, the problem is immediately apparent. The runner should immediately notify the appropriate person to remedy the problem.

The qualifications of a runner are:

✦ Understands value stream requirements
✦ Communicates well
✦ Understands Lean concepts
✦ Understands the importance of takt time and pitch
✦ Works efficiently and effectively
✦ Is innovative and resourceful to continually improve the route

Runners play an important role in proactive problem solving of the value streams that have been connected via leveling and the heijunka box. Runners must continuously monitor the flow of work and be attuned to any changes that may be occurring throughout the value stream. They are in a unique position to assist by preventing small problems before they become big problems that may negatively impact the customer. A runner's duties most likely will not require a full-time person, therefore, once the duties (route and times) have been defined, there should be a schedule to rotate those duties weekly, bi-monthly, or monthly.

5. Create the heijunka box.

The heijunka box is the post office for the value streams, and the runner is the mail carrier. There are many different ways to create a post office or heijunka box. It should be kept simple (e.g., a common location with a stand or rack identifying the times for pick-up). Also, a heijunka box could be a location (i.e., waiting room for different types of surgical patients).

6. Create the Standard Work Chart and post on box at at the location. (See previous section.)

The work that is to be moved in the value streams are placed in the slots corresponding to the pitch increments in which they are to be released to the downstream process.

7. Load the heijunka box.

Set a date and time for beginning the use of the heijunka box. Ensure training has been completed on the purpose of the box.

8. Implement and adjust as necessary.

Monitor the leveling system and make adjustments as necessary

Note: We are not stating that patients should be placed in any type of box or queue, but rather use this overall concept of leveling to minimize any delays for the patient when multiple value streams are competing for hospital resources. .

In order to complete the disposition, physicians frequently had to look for lab and radiology results that might have come in, but were not yet placed in the chart. The ED manager decided to use one of the techs, present on the afternoon and night shifts, to serve as a "runner" for the reports that were received. She called the position "Disposition Tech" and gave them the assignment to collect reports from the printers in the ED, and then place them in the charts. Techs would rotate into this role twice per week. At first there was resistance, as the techs did not see report distribution as essential work. But once it was tried on a pilot basis, the physicians were very happy with their completed charts and the ED made the assignment a part of the tech's standard work (and had their job description updated by Human Resources).

Mini Case Study for the Lab

The laboratory serviced a number of local nursing homes as well as outpatient clinics. Couriers were sent out throughout the day and evening to pick up specimens as calls were received. The laboratory looked at their call frequency to see if they could use a leveling or pitch strategy to better service the demands that were occurring throughout the day and make more efficient use of the courier service.

Takt Times for Lab Pick-ups				
Value Stream	Daily Time Available (day + afternoon shifts)	Daily Volume of Work	Time / Volume	Takt Time (minutes)
Nursing Homes	960	17 specimens from 12 nursing homes	960 / 17	56
Outpatient Clinics	960	60 specimens from 6 outpatient clinics	960 / 60	16

Pitch Time for Lab Pick-ups		
Value Stream	Takt Time (minutes)	Optimal Number of Work Units to Flow	Takt Time X Optimal Number of Work Units to Flow
Nursing Homes	56	4	224
Outpatient Clinics	16	15	240

The lab team decided that if they picked up specimens every 4 hours (240 minutes) they would usually have 3 - 5 specimens to pick up from the nursing homes, as well as 25-30 from the outpatient clinics, which made a courier run worthwhile. The first pick-up would be done with the morning blood specimen collection, at 0700 - 0800, so the rest of the routine courier pick-ups could be spaced 4 hours apart, 1100, 1500, 1900, and 2300. (The latter two times would not be scheduled for the outpatient clinics.)

The leveling sequence table looked like this:

Heiunka Box (or Leveling Visual)						
Value Stream	Pitch Time (minutes)	Daily Pick-up Times with Number of Units (Days + Afternoons)				
		0700	1100	1500	1900	2300
Nursing Homes	224 (approx. 4 hours)	3-5	3-5	3-5	3-5	3-5
Outpatient Clinics	240 (4 hours)		25-30	25-30		

The courier runs were minimized, and the nursing homes and outpatient clinics no longer had to call for each specimen, since the pickup runs were made regularly. They subsequently standardized the daily pick-up times to be 1100 and 1500. This reduced the number of those additional trips by 10 per month, at an average cost of $154.00 per trip, for a cost savings of $1540.00 per month.

Mistake Proofing

Mistake proofing is a system designed to ensure that it is impossible to make a mistake or produce a defect. Mistake proofing is also known as error proofing or by its Japanese name of Poke-yoke. It is derived from "Poka" - inadvertent mistake and "yoke" - avoid. A Poka-yoke device is any mechanism that prevents a mistake from being made or ensures the mistake is made obvious at a glance. These devices, or processes, are used to prevent those circumstances that cause defects. In addition, mistake proofing can also be used to inexpensively inspect each item or work unit that is produced, created, or modified. The ability to find mistakes at a glance is essential. The causes of defects lie in process errors, equipment and material errors, and worker errors and defects are the results of those errors. These mistakes will not turn into defects if these errors are discovered and eliminated beforehand. Defects occur because errors are made; the two have a cause-and-effect relationship. However, errors will not turn into defects if feedback and action take place prior to the error stage. Many times visual controls will play a large role in reducing the opportunity for errors to occur, thereby ensuring that no defects result from the process.

Defects vs. Errors

To be a defect:

- The process or service must have deviated from specifications or standards of service

- The process or service does not meet customer (internal or external) expectations

To be an error:

- Something must have deviated from an intended process

- All defects are created by errors, but not all errors result in defects

---

The four steps to mistake proofing are:

1. Shift your paradigm.
2. Conduct analysis.
3. Standardize the work.
4. Create appropriate visual controls or error-proofing devices.

1. Shift your paradigm.

Errors can be prevented! Begin looking for the source of defects, not just the defects themselves. At the same time look for opportunities to eliminate them at their source. Everyone must understand that they are playing by a new set of rules. The root cause of defects is in the process, not the people.

2. Conduct analysis.

To analyze the problem you must be able to identify and describe the defect or potential error in depth, including the rate that it may have been occurring over time. A Failure Prevention Analysis Worksheet (FPAW) can assist in this process. ***Failure Prevention Analysis*** *is a technique that allows the team to anticipate potential problems in the solution before implementing it, permitting the team to be proactive to prevent the solution(s) from going wrong.* The subsequent processes of mistake proofing would be the procedures, visual controls, alarm notifications, etc. that would prevent a mistake from being made or to ensure the mistake, if made, is obvious at a glance.

The following guidelines will assist you in using the Failure Prevention Analysis Worksheet (See example next page):

    a. Create a list of potential failures for each improvement activity that has a probable cause-effect relationship with an opportunity for error.

    b. Rank the potential failures by rating the potential and consequence for each possibility for each item going wrong on a scale from 1 to 5.

    c. Multiply the potential and consequence together for each of the potential failures to give the overall rating.

    d. Rank each potential failure from highest to lowest (1 - XX).

    e. Brainstorm with the team to modify any/all activities to lessen the likelihood of causing a problem.

    f. Continue with the VSM methodology.

There are two points in a Lean project where the FPAW may be useful. When developing the solutions, the FPAW can help the team to determine whether any of the proposed solutions may cause unforeseen consequences. After the solutions have been implemented, the FPAW can be used to determine whether some activities happen with more frequency or with more severe consequences than anticipated. In either case, the goal is to identify potential issues that may require updated standard work procedures with appropriate visual controls and/or some type of error management.

The Failure Prevention Analysis Worksheet is most useful when there is a need to:

    ✦ Study the current process to point out the most problematic areas of the current state and determine which problem areas would be the most important to fix

    ✦ Develop the future state to imagine what problems might occur if the process was changed

    ✦ Review the standard work after the change has been implemented to analyze the mistakes and problems that are apparent based upon observation and feedback

The ED team wanted to know how to avoid any problems in the processes that they were looking to improve. They started by listing all the things that could still go wrong with the process and, after a few minutes, agreed to focus on those failures that might occur normally, not "once-in-a-blue-moon" scenario.

The team based their list on the Fishbone Diagram and the 5 Why Analysis findings. After developing their list they came to a consensus on the potential for each error to occur and the consequence of the error if it did occur. After calculating the scores, they ranked the scores from 1 (lowest) to 5 (highest). The team subsequently used the information in support of the improvement activities.

The following is Oakview's Failure Prevention Analysis Worksheet for their top 5 ranked items.

Failure Prevention Analysis Worksheet

Directions:
1. List all potential failures.
2. Assign a number from 1 to 5 for the potential and consequence of an activity going wrong.
3. Multiply the potential and consequence and rank from highest to lowest.

Potential Rating

1 - Very unlikely to occur - once a year
2 - Might occur rarely - once a month
3 - 50/50 chance to occur within five days
4 - Good chance to occur at least once a day
5 - Excellent chance to occur several times a day

Consequence Rating

1 - Very little or no risk to the patient
2 - Some risk to the patient, but easily corrected
3 - Moderate risk to the patient, needing some action
4 - Severe risk to the patient, requiring action
5 - Most severe consequence to the patient, possible death, requiring immediate action

Potential Failure	Potential	Consequence	Overall Rating	Ranking
A. Physicians can't reach PCP for consult (after 15 min. from first call)	3	1	3	5
B. Clerk doesn't see dispo in chart, even though Dr. places it there	1	4	4	4
C. Pt belongings missing, even though form used when pt was in ED	2	4	8	3
D. Quick Reg page prints but is not seen; printer is dedicated	3	4	12	2
E. Transporter still busy with other patients when called for by ED	3	5	15	1

Improvement Solutions:

A. The ED physician would continue with patient care (and admit process) without waiting for PCP call back. When (and if) the PCP would call back the ED physician would at that time discuss patient care.
B. The team asked the computer support group to investigate whether they could "broadcast" a message to all registrars computer terminals that an ED Admit had been ordered, to assure that the registrars would know that an admit order needed to be processed.
C. The team discussed the possibility that the patient might have additional items of value, besides clothing, that were not noted at the time the form was started; for example, a necklace that was not removed initially, but was then removed for an X-ray. The team decided that training was needed for all staff that came in contact with the patient and the belongings form needed to travel with the patient rather than being placed in the chart.
D. A separate printer had been placed in the Registration area to handle admitting requests from the ED. However, there was still a possibility that a busy registrars might not see the forms immediately, and the audible signal (B) might not be heard in a busy environment.
E. The team added to the unit reporting form a checkbox for transporter being called to remind the nurse to do that right away. Earlier notification would help the transporter prioritize the work. The team had also piloted the use of a dedicated elevator, which did not seem to be a significant factor at this time, so they discontinued that trial.

3. Standardize the work.

Create standard work instructions and train the staff to the standards. The standard can be written documentation already in existence (i.e, policy manuals, service standards, work instructions, etc.).

4. Create appropriate visual controls or error-proofing devices.

See next section: Visual Control.

It is not always possible to fully prevent mistakes from happening. Even computer systems can be over-ridden and bar codes ignored. However, the goal must be to reduce the number of defects that are likely to occur. In healthcare, that may mean a system of rechecks such as, a surgical time-outs, two-party processing (where two individuals have to sign that something was done), technology-assisted processes (such as bar codes and passwords), or checklists (for imaging test preparation).

Patient safety will always be of paramount importance. The concept of clinical bundles, or groups of tasks that must be performed to ensure positive outcomes, is an example of an error-reduction strategy. Wherever these concepts can be used to support a positive outcome they should be developed to "make it easy to do the right thing and hard to do the wrong thing."

Additional Points to Consider

   ✦ The goal of error proofing is zero defects.
   ✦ All staff must understand the importance of error proofing and believe that all errors can be prevented.
   ✦ Error proofing reduces cycle times and prevents the following wastes: defects, waiting, transportation, inventory, motion, and overproduction.
   ✦ Always focus on the process and not the staff (or person).

Mini Case Study for Lab

When blood specimens were ordered and collected by non-lab personnel, the bar-code labels were printed on the nursing units. Unfortunately, to be read by lab instrumentation bar-code readers, the labels had to be placed a certain way on the tube. There were numerous times that the labels had to be reprinted and replaced on the tubes which caused delays in getting the test results. The lab team brainstormed ways to resolve the issue, and then worked with their Lab Information System staff to add a small arrow with the word "UP" on the label. The team then in-serviced all the nursing units that the arrow needed to point toward the cap. In this way, they reduced the number of "defective" labels (which had to be removed and replaced before testing) from 45% to 7% within two weeks.

Mini Case Study for Pharmacy

The hospital introduced an automated-delivery system for medications. Each nursing unit had a dispensing module that was run by the hospital's computer system and linked into the Pharmacy Information System. Pharmacy would stock the dispensing module with medications that had been ordered for patients on that unit. To obtain the medication, the nurse entered the patient's account number, then the correct drawer would open and the nurse could retrieve the meds.

However, as a precaution against a possible emergent need, the nurses had been given a password to access the module without a specific patient account number. Over time, nurses found it easier to use the password than to bring the account number with them in the form of a chart, patient form, or note. Eventually, almost 25% of the withdrawals were being done via that password, rather than specific account numbers. The nurses did not see any difference, but the non-specific password made it impossible for the medication billing to be processed correctly and also had an impact on the accuracy of the electronic Medication Administration Record (MAR).

The Pharmacy staff studied the number of times withdrawals were made in actual emergency situations and concluded that there had been none since the inception of the dispensing module. While the Pharmacy believed that an override function should still exist, they limited that functionality to the nursing leaders on the individual units, utilizing their ID badge bar-codes. Pharmacy performed in-service training to all of the nurses, pointing out the advantages of an accurate MAR (which meant less work in the daily reconciliation that was performed). The percentage of over-ride withdrawals after this change was less than 2%.

Visual Production Board

A **visual production board** is a physical device located at (or near) the process that displays the work requirements for the day, as well as being updated every hour or two (or at some other pre-defined interval). These boards are a simple conversion of the customer demand and a nature extension of the Just-In-Time concept. They instill a sense of urgency for the processes.

These boards can be of many types, some of which are:

- ✦ Magnet boards with various styles and shapes to display the processes, times, and goals
- ✦ Peg boards that use clipboards with data shown as appropriate
- ✦ Whiteboards that are inexpensive and easy to update
- ✦ Computer screens that are group accessible and/or larger computer screens displaying relevant information in a secure environment

When considering use of a visual production board, the following questions should be answered:

1. Can the work that is required be quantified easily?
2. Can hourly, daily, or some portion of a day be reasonably evaluated?
3. Has a daily goal been established?
4. Who would be responsible for updating the board?
5. Are there procedures in place for when a goal is not met?
6. How often is the board checked by the supervisor or manager?
7. Is the data that is updated on the board easy to collect?
8. Is there a central location for the board to be placed for everyone to see?

Work with the team to determine if a visual production board will assist the overall objectives of the value stream project. A visual production board can be a very powerful Lean tool if everyone is in a consensus of its purpose and usage.

The ED team discussed the use of a visual production board. With the ED clerk's input, they decided that they would place a small dry-erase board near the clerk station, where the ED clerk could note the Dispo status of each patient and the time of Dispo. The ED staff could check the time as the patients went through the process. When the nurse handed off the patient to the transporter, he/she would erase the name.

The ED team knew that an electronic tracking system would soon be implemented and would display all the phases of ED care on one screen, demonstrating elapsed times, so they did not create a full visual production board at this time.

Lean Tools Applied to Oakview Hospital's Current State Value Stream Map

Once a team has understood the Lean tools and concepts, it is recommended that those tools and concepts be connected to the Waste Audit that was applied to the current state value stream map. This activity would bridge the concept of waste identification to specific and actionable activities in the elimination of the wastes with the use of Lean tools.

This is accomplished in the following way:

1. Distribute different color Post-it Notes to each team.
2. Ask team members if they need clarification on any Lean tool or concept.
3. Allow 15 minutes for each team to write the top 3-5 Lean tools that would assist in the elimination of the waste that was earlier identified in the Waste Audit and apply it to the current state value stream map.
4. Direct each team to place their Post-it Note on the area of the value stream map corresponding to the waste to be eliminated. If this map was created via a laptop and LCD projection unit, if at all possible, project the map (updated with the Waste Audit information) on a whiteboard so the physical placement of the Post-it Notes can be done on the image. The practice that we are recommending is not the computer practice, but the wall version.

The ED team decided to return to their initial ED Arrival to Inpatient Bed Current State Value Stream Map and placed Kaizen bursts in the process areas that the Lean tool applied (next page). This was done mainly for management to see the big picture of not only what this team was working to improve, but what could be additional Kaizen opportunities.

The team reviewed all their previous work, including the 5 Why Analysis and Failure Prevention Analysis Worksheet, to make sure they were focusing on the right areas for improvement. The Employee Balance Chart was found to be one of the most useful tools to assist in visualizing their future state and was used in determining Kaizen activities.

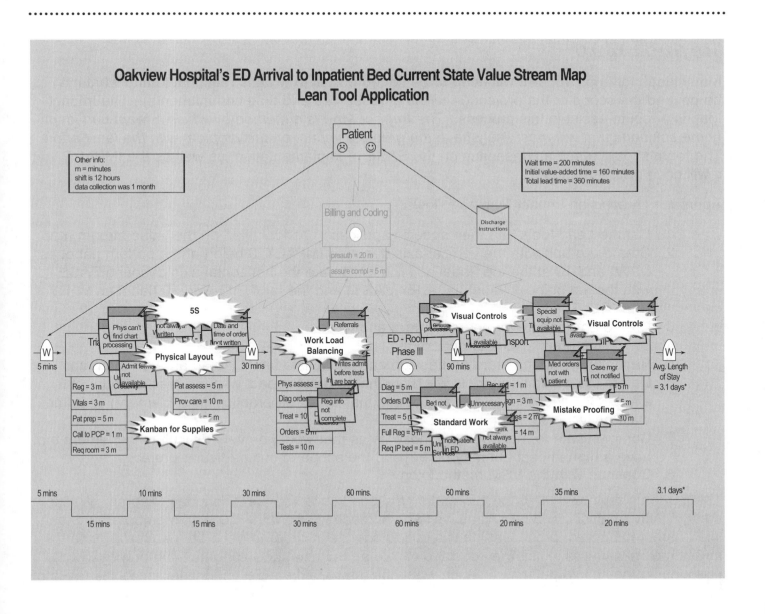

Oakview Hospital's ED Arrival to Inpatient Bed Current State Value Stream Map
Lean Tool Application

Impact Map

Many ideas for improvement will need to be sorted out as to what is reasonable and what may be beyond the scope of the project (in terms of resources and time commitments). The Impact Map is a tool to assist in this process. *The Impact Map is a method by which a team can identify the solutions that will most likely have the greatest impact on the problem with the least effort.* The team should reach a consensus on the EASE of implementation, as well as the IMPACT that it will have on the result.

Approach creating an Impact Map as follows:

1. List the Lean tools and their specific application as identified on the value stream map.
2. Create a graph with the vertical-axis denoting IMPACT; 0 being at the bottom (label as LOW) and 10 at the top (label as HIGH). Create the horizontal axis denoting EASE with the left being 1 (label as VERY EASY) and the far right being 10 (label as VERY DIFFICULT).
3. Create appropriate numbers 1-10 for each axis.
4. Divide the graph into four quadrants.
5. Brainstorm with the team and assign each item listed in (1) to an area on the map.
6. Determine which Lean tools will have the greatest impact with the least amount of effort. Consider these (and any others that would be practical to implement) as immediate activities for improvement.
7. Communicate to management those items that would be very difficult to implement that have a high impact but may be beyond the scope of this particular project.
8. Continue with the VSM methodology.

The ED team reviewed all of the information they had collected (i.e., Fishbone Diagram, Waste Walk, 5 Why Analysis, and FPAW, as well as the feedback from the ED staff members) and identified numerous areas (processes) that required change in order to become "Leaner". Since they had come up with a long list, they decided to use an Impact Map to prioritize the proposed changes so they could determine which would be the most feasible. The following is the result of their Impact Map.

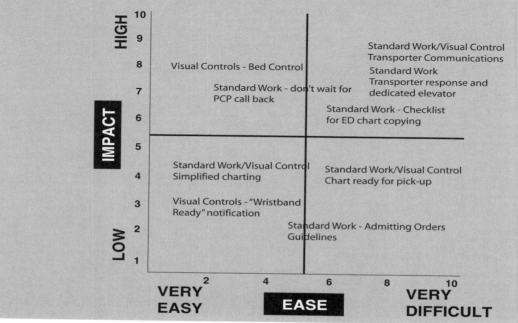

Gantt Chart

A *Gantt Chart* is a table of project task information as a bar chart type that graphically represents all the scheduled tasks and progress in relation to time. It is similar in nature to a timeline that denotes actions over time. Gantt Charts should be updated regularly.

Note: Microsoft Project and Visio have effective Gantt Chart programs.

Approach creating a Gantt Chart as follows:

1. List all the main steps that need to be completed for a Kaizen Event.
2. Organize listed tasks in sequential order.
3. Assign a person or a group of people to be responsible for each step.
4. Decide how long each step will take, when it can be started in relation to the other steps, and when it should be completed.
5. Develop a horizontal bar chart to portray the above steps, including sequencing and overlapping of the steps as needed.
6. Document assumptions and develop contingency plans to implement if any of the assumptions proved wrong.
7. Continue with the VSM methodology.

The Gantt Chart should be posted in the department, or the area the improvements are being conducted, to ensure project communication continues with everyone involved.

The ED team decided to map out their project timelines and that awareness sessions would help staff members to understand and support the process. They had a choice of doing the 5S activities within the Kaizen Event, or outside of the Event, and eventually determined that a 5S project should be done prior to the Event. The other issue was scheduling: the ED could not make staff scheduling changes without adequate notice (schedules were made 6 weeks in advance as discussed previously). The ED team decided more time would be required to study the scheduling situation prior to moving to the Kaizen Event. They also had to schedule some preparatory meetings with the Kaizen team. Even after the Kaizen Event week, there would be follow-up meetings that would need to be scheduled. The following is their Gantt Chart.

Gantt Chart Worksheet

No.	Task Name	Duration	April	May	June	July
1.	Intro to Lean for ED staff - Basics	1 week	▬			
2.	5S ED area	4 weeks	▬▬▬			
3.	Work load balancing and cross-training	2 weeks		▬		
4.	Kaizen Event prep training	3 weeks		▬▬		
5.	Kaizen Event	1 week		▬		
6.	Kaizen Event follow-up	8+ weeks			▬▬▬▬	

Oakview Hospital's Future State Value Stream Map

A future state value stream map should be created once all the improvement activities have been defined. Future state value stream maps can be created for 6 months, or 1 - 2 year implementation plans. The important point is to communicate the Lean vision so everyone can visually "see" the plans for future state improvements.

The following is Oakview Hospital's ED Dispo-to-Admit Future State Value Stream Map (Level II).

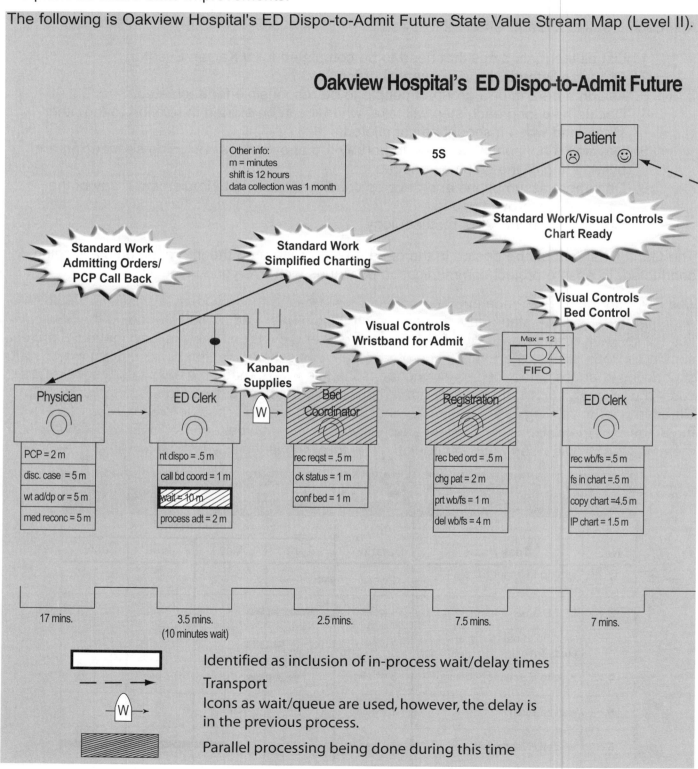

State Value Stream Map (Level II)

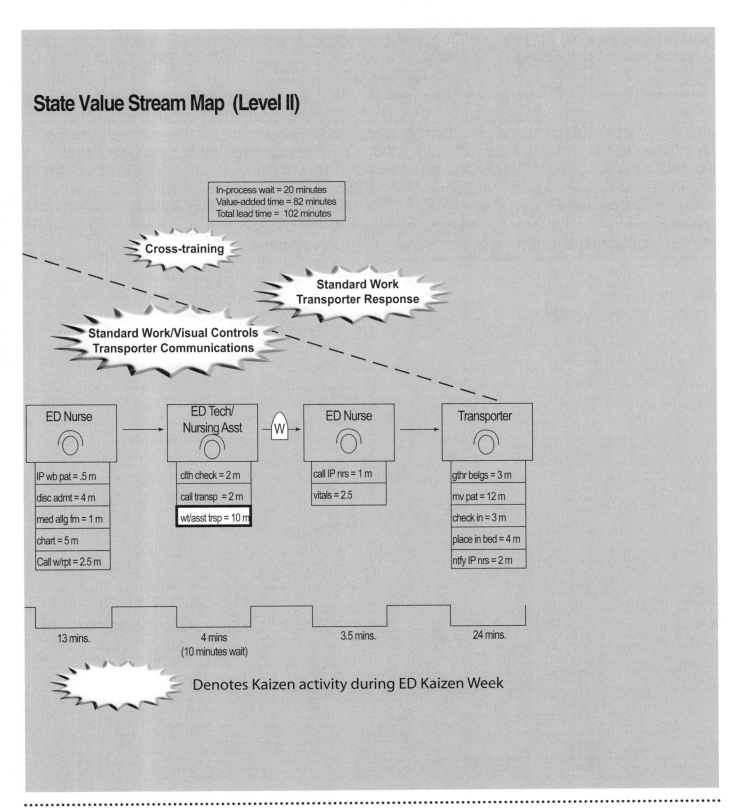

In-process wait = 20 minutes
Value-added time = 82 minutes
Total lead time = 102 minutes

Cross-training

Standard Work
Transporter Response

Standard Work/Visual Controls
Transporter Communications

ED Nurse	ED Tech/ Nursing Asst	W	ED Nurse	Transporter
IP wb pat = .5 m	clth check = 2 m		call IP nrs = 1 m	gthr belgs = 3 m
disc admt = 4 m	call transp = 2 m		vitals = 2.5	mv pat = 12 m
med allg fm = 1 m	wt/asst trsp = 10 m			check in = 3 m
chart = 5 m				place in bed = 4 m
Call w/rpt = 2.5 m				ntfy IP nrs = 2 m

13 mins.   4 mins   3.5 mins.   24 mins.
             (10 minutes wait)

Denotes Kaizen activity during ED Kaizen Week

The future state conveys the following:

	Current State Map (from pp. 104-106)	Future State Map (from pp. 212-213)
Wait Times	40 minutes	20 minutes
Value-Added Times (Cycle Times as it includes parallel processing times)	130 minutes	82 minutes
Total Lead Time	170 minutes	102 minutes

The team knew that the specific identified Kaizen activities accounted for the reduction of 68 minutes (page 188) (5 + 13 + 11 + 8 + 4 + 8.5 + 7.5 + 3 + 8 = 68). Even though the goal from the Team Charter was for 90 minutes, the team felt very satisfied with the results with a 40% reduction in the ED Dispo-to-Admit cycle time. They also realized with all the improvements there would most likely be additional time savings from other hidden wastes that were eliminated. The team focused on implementing the proposed changes, standardizing the processes, and monitoring the improvements over time to ensure everything is sustained.

Readiness Guide for Treat

The Readiness Guide for Treat should be reviewed with the team to ensure all appropriate tools have been used. The team should spend approximately 10 minutes to reach a consensus on each of the items. This is also a good indication on how well the team understood the various tools contained in this chapter. At least fifty percent of the questions should be answered with a Yes before proceeding to the next chapter (or phase).

Readiness Guide for the Treat Phase

If you answer No to more than half of these, then consider using additional tools in the Treat phase.

1. Does everyone understand the importance of 5S? ☐Yes ☐No

2. Have 5S practices been initiated? ☐Yes ☐No

3. Has the team determined if a kanban system can be used? ☐Yes ☐No

4. Has pitch been determined? ☐Yes ☐No

5. Has work load balancing been completed? ☐Yes ☐No

6. Has standard work been incoporated into all improvement activities? ☐Yes ☐No

7. Has the new physical layout been reviewed? ☐Yes ☐No

8. Is the concept of leveling understood by all team members? ☐Yes ☐No

9. Has the team analyzed the improvements for potential errors? ☐Yes ☐No

10. Has mistake proofing been included into new standards or controls? ☐Yes ☐No

11. Is a visual pitch (or production) board needed? ☐Yes ☐No

12. Has the team connected the Lean tools to the wastes? ☐Yes ☐No

13. Has an Impact Map been created? ☐Yes ☐No

14. Has a Gantt Chart been created? ☐Yes ☐No

15. Has management been made aware of any project changes? ☐Yes ☐No

16. Has a future state value stream map been created and posted? ☐Yes ☐No

17. Are Idea Kaizens being captured? ☐Yes ☐No

Chapter 5: Prevent

Topics Include:

✦ **Lean Chronicle**
✦ **Paynter Chart**
✦ **Run Chart**
✦ **Visual Control**
✦ **Storyboard**
✦ **Yokoten**
✦ **Readiness Guide for Prevent**

As healthcare professionals work with patients in post-treatment roles, such as physical therapy and health and wellness programs, so too must Lean apply tools, such as Paynter Charts, Run Charts, Storyboards, Visual Controls, and Yokotens be used to ensure that the process improvements are sustained and controlled over time. These improvements should also be well-documented to share the knowledge.

Lean Chronicle

A **Lean Chronicle** is the record or narrative description of the activities that comprise the Kaizen (or continuous improvement) Event and is a form of knowledge management. A Lean chronicle can be one of the following:

1. A database repository of the Kaizen activities on the organization's intranet or website
2. A newsletter that is distributed monthly to all staff
3. Postings of the Kaizen Event in the departmental bulletin boards and central areas (cafeteria, media center, website)
4. 5-10 minute presentations of the Kaizen Event at departmental meetings

The Lean Chronicle can be any and all of these communication channels as they each allow the information (successes and failure) to be shared throughout the organization. The following types of information should be conveyed in a Lean Chronicle.

Executive Summary - 1-2 sentences explaining the overall purpose and mission of the continuous improvement project (similar to what is contained at the beginning of the Team Charter)

Expected Deliverables - the specific measureables that were identified in the Team Charter (reducing, eliminating, improving, etc.)

Recommendations to Management - the listing of issues that management needed to be made aware of (resource commitments, costs, financial gains/losses, etc.)

Recommendations to Team Members - the listing of specific activities that would benefit other teams when conducting an improvement activity (data collection methods, team composition, meeting times, pilot project issues, etc.)

Accomplishments - the listing of what the team accomplished, as well as the time frame in which it was completed (should correspond to the expected deliverables)

Issues - the listing of internal and external factors that affected the team (departmental boundary problems, lack of team participation, staffing issues, etc.)

Team Members - the listing of all team members as well as their email addresses and phone numbers

Summary - the listing of any plans to roll out improvements enterprise-wide, how to control and sustain the improvements over time, and how the organization benefited

Visual Support - the inclusion of any digital before and after photos, relevant Gantt Charts, Paynter Charts, Storyboards, etc.

Paynter Chart

The **Paynter Chart** is a visual representation of defects over time relative to the subgroups based on information from the Pareto Chart. The Paynter Chart is a further analysis of what is comprised in the bars of the Pareto Chart in a simply graphical form and allows you to determine the composition of each bar for determining trends and areas for improvement efforts. The Paynter Chart is also used to track defects over time (similar to a Run Chart) relative to corrective action.

Approach creating a Paynter Chart as follows:

1. List the main categories from the Pareto Chart on the x-axis. This does not need to be only what is compromised of the 80%.
2. List the number of defects on the y-axis in equal segments representing the total population of defects.
3. Graphically represent the number of defects relative to to the various Pareto Chart categories.
4. Use this to monitor continuous improvement efforts.
5. Continue with the VSM methodology.

The ED team decided to track the reduction of defects by using a Paynter Chart and posting it next to the value stream map in the Staff Lounge. Summarizing the ED/Inpt Summary Delay Worksheets, they chose to focus on three types of defects: Admitting Orders, Prep for Admit, and Patient to Unit. The chart clearly showed that the number of defects was decreasing over time, especially after the Kaizen Event in May. A similar worksheet was used as part of the 30-60-90 day follow-up report to management.

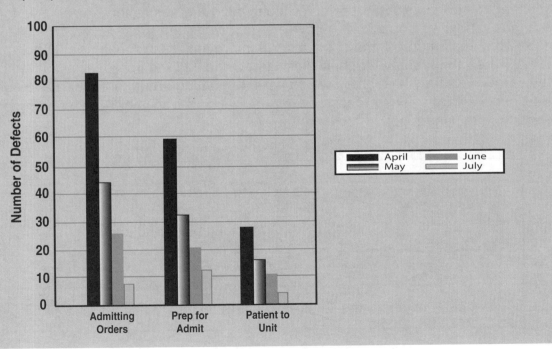

Run Chart

A **Run Chart**, in its most simple form, is a method to display serial data points over time. Because our minds are not good at remembering patterns in data, a visual display will allow you to see the measurement(s) of an entire process. This will enable you to see trends over time and to make adjustments accordingly. Improvement activities must be tracked to determine their overall effectiveness. For example, if an improvement activity did not result in having an impact on eliminating a waste, then that should not be part of any long term or enterprise-wide solution.

Run Charts will allow a team to compare performance measurements before and after implementation of a solution to measure its effectiveness. Run Charts are a powerful tool in demonstrating whether the vital changes made to the current state value stream had the intended impact to the future state value stream.

Approach creating a Run Chart as follows:

1. Label each main improvement activity.
2. Create a graph denoting the vertical axis as 100 Percent of the problem being solved. Use the goal or benchmark number established in the Team Charter. Create the horizontal axis with the dates from the Gantt Chart.
3. Use the data collected from the trials (i.e., pilots) and plot on the graph the specific label from (1).
4. Look for trends to ensure all improvements are on schedule and adjust as necessary.
5. Continue with the VSM methodology.

The ED team created a simple Run Chart to track the cycle time for Dispo-to-Admit. The team was pleased to see that the 5S project, which was done before the Kaizen Event (second week in May), had a positive impact on the cycle time. When the Kaizen Event was held and the new standard work implemented, they saw a large improvement in the June numbers, and even better in July, when they nearly reached their target when all the improvements had been implemented. However, they knew they would have to continue monitoring to make sure the process did not slip backwards. The process owner had taken responsibility for creating and updating this important tracking tool.

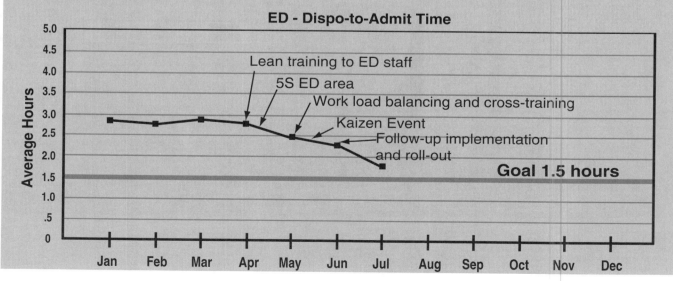

Visual Control

Visual control *is a technique employed whereby control of an activity or process is made easier or more effective by deliberate use of visual signals (signs, information displays, maps, layouts, instructions, alarms, and poka-yoke or mistake proofing devices).* These signals can be of many forms, from different function keys on the keyboard, to various types of measurements relating to a problem or departmental goal, to kanbans and heijunka boxes, and many more; these signals can also be audio. A visual control will effectively communicate the information needed for decision making.

Visual controls are one part of an overall communication system (one picture is worth one thousand words) of an organization to ensure standards are met, work is completed on time, and can continue to the next process without errors. Visual controls should be used (or at least considered) at every juncture of the Lean project.

Visual controls will accomplish the following:

- ✦ Reduce confusion in completing a process
- ✦ Reduce opportunity for errors and defects (using mistake proofing)
- ✦ Assist in adhering to a process standard
- ✦ Involve the staff
- ✦ Improve productivity
- ✦ Improve staff/patient satisfaction

Visual controls are used to identify conditions that may cause an error, or if an error occurs, what must be done to prevent it from becoming a defect. There are three levels of visual control which also support error proofing devices (previous section). They are as follows:

Level 1 - Indicators - providing information about the immediate environment, area, department or process. These are passive and people may or may not notice them or respond to them. A Level 1 visual control may be a sign displaying the "Triple Check" procedure for dispersing medications. Another example would be ensuring "Allergy Alert" is highlighted in red on the patient's chart and ID bracelet.

Level 2 - Signals - causing a visual or auditory alarm that should grab your attention and is a warning that a mistake or error is about to occur. People still may ignore these, but they are very aware that something may be wrong. A Level 2 visual control may be typing in the patient's medications on the computer and a visual or auditory alert would occur if there was a potential for a drug interaction. If codeine is ordered for a patient, and the patient is allergic to codeine, the pharmacy computer program would issue "med/alert" on the computer screen.

Level 3 - Physical or Electronic Controls - limiting or preventing something from occurring due to its negative impact it will have on the process (or area) (most likely referred to as mistake proofing devices). A Level 3 visual control may be the mechanical wall connections for medical gases, such as oxygen and nitrogen. Each of these devices has access ports that will only fit the appropriate gas, oxygen for oxygen and nitrogen for nitrogen.

When you create the device or physical/visual control, you will need to decide which level is most appropriate for the situation. Clearly, Level 3 is most comprehensive in terms of ensuring that an error or mistake cannot occur, but not always possible or cost effective.

The following steps can be used to create a visual language throughout the facility:

1. Form and train the visual controls team.
2. Create an implementation plan.
3. Begin implementation.
4. Standardize visual measurements.
5. Standardize visual displays.
6. Standardize visual controls.

1. Form and train the visual controls team.

This may be a subset of the Lean project team. Creating this part of the Lean project can be fun to do, but it will require additional time; many Lean project teams do not allocate sufficient time to create visual controls. It will be the team's responsibility to:

✦ Create the locations where visual displays and standards will be posted
✦ Understand the various parts of a Lean communication system of visual measurements (VM) (i.e., bar charts, pie charts, goals, outcomes, etc.), visual displays (VD) (i.e., banners, placards, signs, etc.) and visual controls (VC) (i.e., alarms, lights, color-codes, etc.)
✦ Create standards for all visuals (location, updates, themes, etc.)

2. Create an implementation plan.

The core team must designate target areas with a timeline for training and implementation to ensure everyone understands why new or enhanced visuals are being used.

3. Begin implementation.

Once a plan has been determined for using visuals to improve an area or process, immediately deploy it. Distribute Idea Kaizen forms to all staff for input on ideas to improve the visual control.

4. Standardize visual measurements.

The Lean project should have identified appropriate measurements or other performance measurements critical to the facility.

Visual measurements must have the following attributes:

✦ Directly relate to strategy
✦ Be non-financial
✦ Be location-specific
✦ Be easy to collect and post
✦ Provide for fast feedback
✦ Foster improvement initiatives

5. Standardize visual displays.

Visual displays communicate important information about the facility in terms of goals, outcomes, safety, environment, or other related activities. Signboards are often used as a visual display.

6. Standardize visual controls.

The goal of the team would be to integrate visual measurements, visual displays, and visual controls to ensure process stability and control. Visual controls at this level are similar to mistake proofing devices. This would include task lists, checklists, and computer programs to ensure that a process does what is expected, and if not, what must happen.

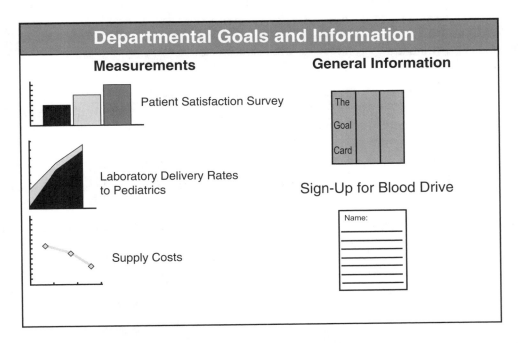

For example, medications are being administered to a patient on the floor: To help eliminate the potential for errors, a Level 1 visual control may entail posting the 7 Rights and Triple Check at various locations where the medications are dispensed. The 7 Rights are:

1. Right patient
2. Right medications
3. Right dose
4. Right route
5. Right time
6. Right technique
7. Right documentation

Many times an 8th Right will include patient education.

A Level 2 may be having each person sign off that they acknowledge the following Triple Check:

1. Check medication as you take it off the shelf
2. Check medication as you prepare it
3. Check medication as you replace it on the shelf

A Level 3 may be verifying your fingerprint with your ID card on a reader prior to accessing the medications.

The following chart lists the various types of visual displays and controls that can be used.

General Purpose	
Storyboards	Share information about projects or improvements Educate and motivate
Signboards	Share vital information at point-of-use
Maps	Share actual processes, standard operating procedures, directions, etc.
Kanbans	Control the withdrawal of work (or supplies) in and out of supermarkets, work areas, etc. Can be used to regulate work in FIFO lanes
Checklists	Provide an operational tool that facilitates adherence to standards, procedures, etc.
Indicators, Color Codes	Show correct location, item types, amount, or direction of work flow
Alarms	Provide a strong, unavoidable sign or signal when action needs to be taken (email alert, text message, pager code, etc.)

The following illustration displays the progression of creating a visual communication system as well as the various types of visual displays and controls.

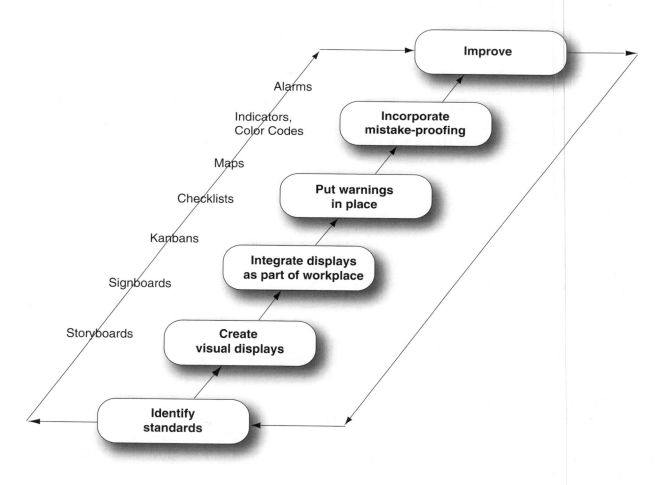

The ED team ranked (or prioritized) the potential failures from all their improvement suggestions. They created a chart with the type of visual control that would be needed for part of the solution (Description of Control). If the team found that their standard work lacked a visual control and/or error-proofing device, then they would modify the standard work to reflect the type of control needed. The team did notice that they had no Level 3 visual controls or true mistake-proofing devices. The following is their Potential Failure and Level Control Chart.

Potential Failure and Level Control Chart

Potential Failure	Ranking	Standard Work	Level of Visual Control	Description of Control
Physicians can't reach PCP for consult (after 15 min. from first call)	8	✔	2	ED clerk sets timer when PCP is paged – alerts physician if PCP does not call back within 15 mins. to proceed with orders
Clerk doesn't see dispo in chart, even though Dr. places it there	7	✔	1	Chart rack placed at eye level at clerk's desk
Pt belongings missing, even though form used when pt was in ED unit	6	✔	2	Std Work to ask patient whenever moved: Do you have any additional belongings that you want to have documented on our form?
Quick Reg page prints but is not seen; printer is dedicated	5	✔	2	Audible alert set on printer
Transporter still busy with other patients when called for by ED	4	✔	1	Transporter has Std Work to call Supv to notify of delay if it will be more than 5 minutes
Clothing checklist not performed	3	✔	1	Check of chart prior to patient transport by the nurse
Physicians don't date/time dispo order	2	✔	1	ED clerk to check when processing dispo order
Medication reconciliation not performed	1	✔	1	Check the chart prior to patient transport by the nurse

Level 1 - Indicators
Level 2 - Signals
Level 3 - Physical or electronic limitations

Note: There are many new products on the market that use the concept of visual controls in tracking patients and their status as well as coordinating crucial events from admission to discharge. These provide the real-time data and task coordination to increase hospital capacity at all levels.

Mini Case Study for Bed Control

The Bed Control manager wanted a better way to indicate to physicians that the hospital was nearing capacity. Although an email was sent each morning indicating the capacity status, not all physicians monitored their emails closely. A small team, including the Physician Relations manager, installed a visual "stop light" at two key physician locations: the physician lounge and the hospital entrance nearest the physician parking lot. Colored circles were placed on the stoplight as follows: Green, less than 75% of beds filled; Orange, 76 - 85% of beds filled; and Red, 86% or more of beds filled.

Mini Case Study for ED Charts

When ED patients were ready to be transferred to their inpatient units, or discharged, the nurses sometimes had difficulty locating charts, even though they were supposedly completed. It turned out that sometimes physicians or residents would take the charts to add a comment, or check results. A small group of ED team members created a "STOP - DO NOT REMOVE" sign to be placed on the chart when the ED documentation was completed. They asked for cooperation from the residents and physicians to add any comments or check results right at the patient's bedside, leaving the chart always near the patient for the nurse to find when needed.

Storyboard

*The **Storyboard** is a poster-size framework for displaying all the key information from the Lean-Sigma project.* The Storyboard is very similar to an A3 report and is a visual aid for communicating the progression of a Lean project. The Storyboard is organized into various areas that can be represented by a graph, illustration, and/or a simple sentence or two. The information is then displayed on a format that is graphically rich and engaging. The Storyboard will contain many of the tools used throughout the project.

The Storyboard segments may include some, if not all, of the following categories:

✦ Reason for Selecting the Project (Problem Statement)
✦ Data Chart of Present Condition (Pareto Chart, Fishbone, etc.)
✦ Target Goal
✦ Plan of Action (portion of Gantt Chart)
✦ Results (New Standards, Metrics, etc.)
✦ Team Recognition
✦ Next Target

The Storyboard should be posted in the area where the continuous improvement activities are occurring and should be updated frequently as new information is obtained. Storyboards should be fun in designing, many times taking on a graphical theme (eg., an ED department may display the various sections in comparison to an ambulance, an OR comparison to an operating table, etc.). Team members who are responsible for creating the Storyboard should make it engaging by using color, themes, etc.

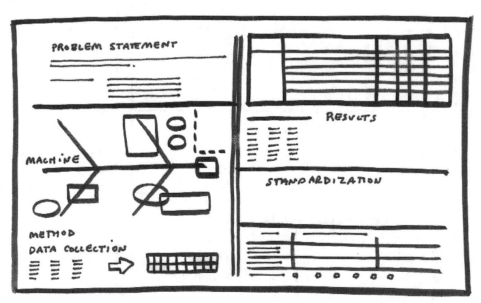

The Oakview Hospital's Storyboard is as follows:

Storyboard Report (A3)

PDCA Kaizen Project Name: ED Arrival to IP Bed Value Strea

Team Members: Drs. Abrahms/Kingsley, M. Hart, J. Dean, S. Richards, M. Ro

Problem Identification

Source of Complaints: External Customers (Patient Satisfaction Survey)
Impact on Customers: Delays in ED Admissions, from Dispo-to-Admit
Problem Statement: The process for admitting a patient is not efficient, leading to delays in admitting the patient to the unit, and extra care given in the ED environment
Time Measure: Average cycle time from Dispo written to Pt on Unit
Quality Measure: Percent of patient who are admitted to the unit within 90 minutes after the Dispo order is written to patient in hospital bed

Fishbone

"Bones" Major Cause C

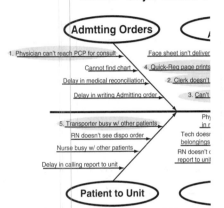

Data Chart(s)

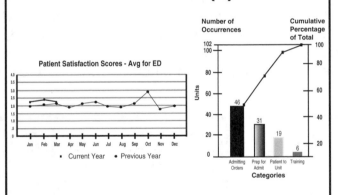

Goal / Standard

1. Reduced cyle time, Dispo-to-Admit by 50%
2. Improved Patient Satisfaction by 50%

Waste(s) Indentified

- ☐ Overproduction
- ☑ Waiting
- ☑ Motion
- ☑ Transport
- ☐ Overprocessing
- ☐ Inventory (Time)
- ☑ Correction (of defects)
- ☑ People's Skills

Measurement(s) Affected

Patient Satisfaction, ED LOS, LWBS/AMA

Counter

(Actions from the OLD PROCESS

Physicians
Page PCP then wait 20-60 minutes for PCP to call back

Wait for test and treat results

Write Dispo, then place chart near unit clerk

Registration/Bed Request
Bed Control waits for available bed and calls ED clerk when ready

Nurses
Call report and hold patient if receiving unit not ready

Unit Clerk
When bed assigned, call Registration to admit patient

Storyboard Report (A3)

m

Date: September 2nd

...driguez, B. Hagan, A. Calley, S. Schultz, J. DuBois, R. Simmons

Diagram

ategories   **Effect**

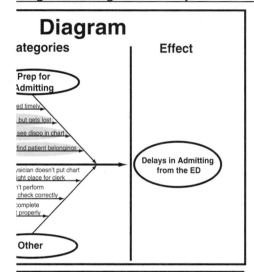

Prep for
Admitting

ed timely

but gets lost

see dispo in chart

find patient belongings

sician doesn't put chart
ight place for clerk

n't perform
check correctly

complete
t properly

Other

Delays in Admitting
from the ED

measures
5 Why Analysis)
NEW PROCESS

Physicians
Page PCP and if call not returned within 15 minutes, call to leave message for PCP and proceed with Dispo

Dispo tech watches for new results coming through printer and places them in chart, flagged for doctor

Write dispo, then place chart in Dispo rack

Registration/Bed Request
Bed Control contacts units and housekeeping if bed is not ready
Goal: find bed within 15 minutes

Nurses
Call report; send patient unless there is a Code in progress on receiving unit

Unit Clerk
When bed assigned, Bed Control calls Registration to admit patient

Results

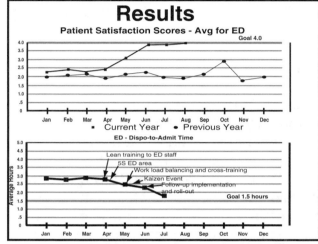

Patient Satisfaction Scores - Avg for ED
Goal 4.0

Jan Feb Mar Apr May Jun Jul Aug Sep Oct Nov Dec
■ Current Year ● Previous Year

ED - Dispo-to-Admit Time

Lean training to ED staff
5S ED area
Work load balancing and cross-training
Kaizen Event
Follow-up implementation and roll-out
Goal 1.5 hours

Jan Feb Mar Apr May Jun Jul Aug Sep Oct Nov Dec

Standardization

Process owners identified and standard work procedures created.

Visual Controls/Signals (just a few listed):
1. Chart racks for each ED value stream
2. Tracking board to time transport pick-up
3. Chart flags for results pending by physician

New Standard Work (just a few listed):
1. Streamline PCP consult process
2. Streamline bed assignment process
3. Streamline movement of patients to unit process

Yokoten Review Date

September 2nd - 1:00pm - 2:30pm in the Administration Conference Room

Recognition

Team lunch at The Seafood House and a $25.00 movie gift card.

Next Target

Doc-to-Dispo cycle time to be reduced by 50%.

Yokoten

Yokoten *means "best practice sharing" or "taking from one place to another."* It encompasses the methods of communicating, documenting, and distributing knowledge horizontally within an organization (peer-to-peer) about what worked and what did not work from an improvement project. Yokoten is a form of knowledge management. At its most basic level, Yokoten can be the notebook that a team keeps as a history of the problems/solutions encountered. Yokoten can also be the library of A3 problem reports (Storyboards) that a team or work group maintains for all to access. As a knowledge management device, the Yokoten process ensures information becomes part of the organizational knowledge base. At Toyota, there is an expectation that copying a good idea will be followed by some added "kaizen" to that idea (kaizen + copy = yokoten).

Approach Yokotens as follows:

1. Create a standard improvement methodology (i.e., the VSM methodology as it is customized to your organization) that problem solving, Lean, or Six Sigma teams will follow. Ensure adequate training is integrated.
2. Create standard forms and worksheets to be used. Inform employees where these forms are located on the Local Area Network (LAN).
3. Assign a certain date and time each month (or quarter) for groups and/or departments to share their project successes and failures. Allocate 10-15 minutes per group (or representatives) to share their improvement projects.
4. Document all completed improvements on the LAN.
5. Ensure each team completes a Yokoten Worksheet prior to their presentation and file accordingly.
6. Continually look for ways to improve the Yokoten process.

Yokoten standardizes a solution and shares it. Sharing of standards and/or best practice procedures across an organization promotes the development of associates and organizational learning.

The ED team believed that some of their ideas could be used by the Emergency Departments at other Oak Valley hospitals. They created a Yokoten worksheet to capture the tools used and the solutions implemented as a guide to other ED teams. The following is their Yokoten Worksheet.

Yokoten Worksheet

Problem: Delays in moving patient from ED at time of disposition to arrival in their hospital bed (unit)

Presentation Date: September 2nd

List team members that will present at Yokoten meeting.

Margaret Rodriguez and Sue Richards

Convey pre and post measurements in simple form.
Patient Satisfaction:
Pre – avg 2.3   Post – avg 3.9
Cycle time, Dispo-to-Admit:
Pre – avg 170 mins   Post – avg 102 mins (-68 min)

Place a checkmark (✓) by each waste that was eliminated.

	Overproduction		Overprocessing
✓	Waiting (Queues)		Inventory
✓	Motion	✓	Defects
	Transport	✓	People's Skills

Convey timeline in simple bar graph form.

April   May   June

Lean training
5S ED area
Cross-training
Kaizen Event
Follow-up

Place a checkmark (✓) by the tools used. Identify the main tools used by placing a cirlce around each checkmark.

(✓)	5S	✓	Effective Meetings	✓	Idea Kaizen	✓	Perf. Measurement	✓	Takt Time
✓	5 Why Analysis	(✓)	Effective Team	✓	Impact Map		Pitch	✓	Training Plan
✓	Accepting Change	(✓)	Failure Prev. Analysis		Just-In-Time	✓	Problem Identfication	(✓)	Value Stream Mapping
✓	Brainstorming	(✓)	Fishbone	✓	Kanban	✓	Pull Systems	(✓)	Voice of the Customer
✓	Continuous Flow	✓	Flowchart	(✓)	Mistake Proofing	✓	Run Chart	✓	Waste Audit
✓	Cycle Time	✓	Gantt Chart	✓	Pareto Diagram		Runners	(✓)	Work Load Balancing
✓	Data Collection	✓	Heijunka - Leveling	✓	Paynter Chart	(✓)	Standard Work	✓	Yokoten

List any Idea Kaizens that were generated.
1. Move printers from under counter for ED clerk
2. Change lab printer to green paper for easy ID of lab results

List recommendations to management.
1. Have Mgt attend monthly ED department meetings to ensure that communication continues
2. Continue working with Bed Control, Housekeeping, and Units to promote bed readiness

List a few experiences regarding the team process.
1. Initial meetings were difficult due to different perceptions and expectations of team members
2. Group development of the detailed value stream, and collection of data, helped team to move forward toward solutions
3. Upon implementing solutions, the team was supportive and enthusiastic among other staff members

List recommendations to other teams.
1. Need a cross-functional team including front line staff, supervisors, and downstream customers in the process
2. Allow team to come together through group exercises
3. Make sure to allow stakeholders a chance to give feedback on proposed solutions, prior to implementation

List overall benefits from the PDCA Kaizen Event.
1. Patients feel as if hospital wants to admit them – reflected in overall satisfaction scores
2. Staff feels less stressed in this portion of the work – easier to "get things done"
3. Physicians like the improved communication among staff

List contact person and email for additional information.
Sue Richards, Team Facilitator,
586-441-2244 sue.richards@oakviewhosp.org
Margaret Rodriguez, Process Owner
586-441-3426 margaret.rodriguez@oakviewhosp.org

The location of the electronic version of the Yokoten, as well as the supporting materials, can be found at:

http://www.oakvalley.oakviewhosp.org/yokoten/EDAdmit_Oakview

During the Yokoten, the following information was also conveyed. The team had numerous documents to present, however, the following measurements summed up results from all the improvement activities.

Project Goal Overview

Project Metric	Baseline	Mar	Apr	May	June	July	Target
Financial							
Pt hold hrs in ED, / month	450	405	327	205	175	178	180
Pt OBS hrs, / month	420	350	325	330	328	332	360
% PCP contact prior to admit	80	70	75	88	90	89	85
Case Mgr Involved, %	82	93	95	97	99	99	100
Bed Ready <= 15 min of request	72	75	80	87	92	92	90
Quality							
Clothing Check, % documented	85	87	89	94	96	98	95
Med Reconciliation, % documented	65	68	75	92	98	98	100
Call report to Unit, % documented	97	95	96	99	100	99	100
Admission orders, % written in ED	75	77	85	92	95	94	90
Service							
ED % Adm Pts LOS <= 4.5 hrs	72	61	70	76	86	85	85
Dispo-to-Admit % <= 1.5 hr	62	60	68	83	85	88	85
% LWBS / AMA	4.7	5.9	5.7	3.0	3.2	3.2	3.5
Satisfaction							
ED Pt Sat	2.8	2.3	2.4	3.1	3.9	3.9	4.0

Readiness Guide for Prevent

The Readiness Guide for Prevent should be reviewed with the team to ensure all appropriate tools have been used. The team should spend approximately 10 minutes to reach a consensus on each of the items. This is also a good indication on how well the team understood the various tools contained in this chapter. At least fifty percent of the questions should be answered with a Yes before beginning the VSM process again with another value stream or area of concern.

Readiness Guide for the Prevent Phase

If you answer No to more than half of these, then consider using additional tools in the Prevent phase.

1. Is there a database or repository for kaizen project information? ❏Yes ❏No

2. Has a Paynter Chart been reviewed, and used, if appropriate? ❏Yes ❏No

3. Has a Run Chart been reviewed, and used, if appropriate? ❏Yes ❏No

4. Has a Storyboard been created and posted? ❏Yes ❏No

5. Are visual controls part of the kaizen activities and any standard work? ❏Yes ❏No

6. Has standard work been incoporated into all improvement activities? ❏Yes ❏No

7. Has a Yokoten been planned? ❏Yes ❏No

8. Has the team completed a Meeting Evaluation Form? ❏Yes ❏No

9. Is the Kaizen Event Scorecard being used? ❏Yes ❏No

10. Has the team been congratulated by management? ❏Yes ❏No

11. Has the team accomplished their goals? ❏Yes ❏No

12. Has the team celebrated their success? ❏Yes ❏No

13. Has a detailed follow-up plan been created? ❏Yes ❏No

14. Are all visual aids, devices, and controls in place? ❏Yes ❏No

15. Has their been an impact on the Balanced Scorecard? ❏Yes ❏No

16. Have all team members fully participated? ❏Yes ❏No

17. Is there a plan to capture Idea Kaizens? ❏Yes ❏No

In Conclusion

Topics Include:

✦ **Key Aspects of the Value Stream Management for Lean Healthcare Case Study**
✦ **Final Thoughts**

Key Aspects of the Value Stream Management for Lean Healthcare Case Study

The following discussion represents an overview of the project timeline, additional team discussions, tools, worksheets, and forms on how all these were used in *this* particular case study. It should assist you in understanding how *this* team conducted *this* Kaizen Event. Please use the following as a review and guide when planning your Kaizen Event.

Three Weeks Prior to the Kaizen Week

The project began when Mary, Judy, and Sue had a meeting with the project sponsor (champion), process owner, ED physician director, and financial leader to review the ED Goal Card (pp. 68-69) as well as the Balanced Scorecard (p. 73). Further discussions led to completing a Project Prioritization Worksheet to better align everyone as to the focus on a new improvement team. Sue had data regarding the proposed area and created the Distribution/Volume Report (p. 77) and a more detailed 4 hour breakdown Distribution Report (p. 78). Also, the takt time information (p. 79) was calculated to determine the patient demand. A Cycle Time Table (p. 82) was initially created due to Sue's access and proficiency with the current hospital data management system. Mary, Judy, and Sue created an initial Team Charter (p. 88). A Meeting Information Form (p. 90) was sent out to all team members, executives, and appropriate managers announcing the first team meeting.

The team had their first meeting and kept to the meeting agenda. At the conclusion of the meeting, a Status Report (p. 91) was sent to the team champion to ensure good communication from the start. The team completed the Effective Meeting Evaluation Worksheet (p. 95) to provide feedback to the team leader and Facilitator for improvements to upcoming meetings.

The team discussed how to prepare for the Kaizen Event week to ensure the stakeholders would have a good understanding of the entire process. They considered that stakeholder buy-in was essential to long-term success. In order to introduce the basic concepts of the Lean approach, the team decided to do one-hour introductory sessions for the ED staff explaining Lean concepts and the elements of the Kaizen Event to follow. Several sessions were planned over the course of a week's time to ensure everyone received the Lean overview training.

The ED team held their second Kaizen Event planning meeting and listed the various hospital processes that impacted the ED (Brainstorming for pre-Value Stream Mapping, p. 97). With all the data that was available, the team created the Level I Oakview Hospital's ED Arrival to Inpatient Bed Current State Value Stream Map (p. 103). They subsequently created the Oakview Hospital's Dispo-to-Admit Current State Value Stream Map (pp. 104-105). As the team completed the maps, there were some questions regarding the registration process. A process map (p. 114) was created in about 15 minutes which allowed everyone to be on the same page for this process.

At this second meeting prior to the Kaizen Week, the team created an elevator speech (p. 125) to ensure everyone would be communicating the same message when they conduct their Waste Walk. The current state value stream map (p. 131) was updated with this information. They immediately related the wastes to actual hospital processes or problems via using different colored Post-it Notes (p. 132).

The team decided that additional data needed to be collected to verify much of the data that Sue had presented. An ED/Inpt Delay Worksheet (p. 135) was created, along with its results tabulated via the ED/Inpt Delay Worksheet Summary (p. 136). Since the charting process had an impact on the Dispo-to-Admit value stream, it was determined that a Document Tagging Worksheet (p. 139) was to be used to gather additional data about this process.

Someone from the team suggested that patients should be surveyed as to what they feel are the delays from the ED. A Voice of the Customer (VOC) ED/Inpt Survey was conducted (p. 141). This information was presented as a pie chart (p. 143).

By the third meeting prior to the Kaizen Event week, the team was ready for solutions. The team created a Fishbone Diagram (p. 150) and a 5 Why Analysis (pp. 151-152). At this time, Mark, an analyst from the Finance department, assisted the team to determine projected cost savings (pp. 154-156) derived from the stated goals on the Team Charter. 5S (pp. 167-170) had been going well, as certain team members were spearheading that effort for the past few weeks. There were some non-team members that had initiated a kanban system for supplies (p. 180) with very little assistance from the team. The ED staff were not only supporting the team in data collection and ideas for improvement, but also were taking the initiative on their own for improving their processes and work areas.

Although the awareness training, 5S, data collection, etc. were very successful, the ED manager discussed the staffing levels to the team. ED employee schedules could not be changed over the course of one day. Schedules were developed in 6-week blocks and employees had already made plans for their days off. In addition, by hospital policy, employees must be given at least two weeks notice prior to any schedule change. Staff began their shifts in a staggered manner to provide the best mix based on expected patient volumes. However, that meant that at any given time, there could be 2 - 6 nurses, 0 - 4 techs, 1 - 2 ED unit clerks, and 1 - 4 physicians present. Due to the changing nature of the staffing, many work duties were to be performed "by anyone available." Also, due to the variable numbers of staff present on the different shifts, tasks that were done by one set of employees on the day shift were done by a different set on the night shift. The ED manager wanted the team to be aware of this when potential solutions were being proposed.

The ED team took three weeks to examine all the information. The team immediately started using the visible pitch board (p. 183) to assist the ED unit clerks. This was accomplished by placing the copied charts in a labeled tray in the ED and bringing them down to the file room every 4 hours, giving the chart room staff enough work to process, while minimizing the walking of the ED unit clerks.

The team used the Employee Balance Chart (pp. 186-188) to tie all the proposed solutions together to better balance the work load to takt time. This assisted the team to determine where cross-training and/or standard work would be needed. The roles of the ED unit clerks, techs, and nurses were evaluated and it was decided to hold a departmental meeting to make the staff aware of the issue and to solicit their input. The response was surprising to the ED manager. She had expected a lot of resistance to the possibility of changing schedules (as well as some tasks), and while there was some concern expressed, the majority of the staff was relieved. There was a good discussion of nursing tasks compared to non-nursing tasks. The underlying foundation of respect and care for the patient was strengthened, and the staff was happy that they would have more role clarification as a result of this Lean approach.

The ED team held one final meeting prior to the Kaizen Week. The team created a Standard Work Combination Table (p. 190), as well as a Standard Work Chart (p. 191), to assist their training efforts during the Kaizen Week. At this time, even though it was beyond the scope of their Team Charter, the team created a New Physical Layout (pp. 194-195) to be conveyed to management for consideration of future-type improvements. The team summarized their improvement ideas and created a Failure Prevention Analysis Worksheet (p. 204) to ensure process integrity for critical changes that may impact the patient. A visual production board (p. 207) was installed to better track the patients that were to be admitted to the hospital.

The team revisited their current state value stream map (pp. 208-209) and placed Post-it Notes with the name of the Lean tool on the respective areas denoting the elimination of that problem (i.e., waste). An Impact Map (p. 210), as well as a Gantt Chart (p. 211), were created to further define specific activities for improvement. Oakview Hospital's ED Dispo-to-Admit Future State Value Stream Map (pp. 212-214) was created to reflect the proposed improvements.

During this final week prior to the Event, Margaret and Sue made a presentation to the ED Physician group to share the findings to date and to ask for feedback about the specific process (Dispo-to-Admit) that was targeted to be improved during the Kaizen Event. It was confirmed that any changes regarding the physician's role were to be reviewed with the ED physician director before implementation.

The Kaizen Event Week

Now the team was ready for the Kaizen Event week. Following the standard 5-day structure, on the first day the team validated their current state value stream map, all the data that had been collected, and the wastes they had identified. They prioritized their wastes and determined which wastes to attack. The future state value stream map was reviewed with some minor changes.

On the second day, solutions were created for the prioritized activities to eliminate the wastes. The team decided to standardize the usage of the chart racks, utilizing visual signals; create standard work among the physicians, nurses, techs, and unit clerks; develop a schedule based on work load balancing and cross-training; and set some time expectations in two areas: for the Registration clerk to process ED Admits and for receiving units to accept patients except when a code was in progress on the receiving unit. Standard work guidelines and training instructions were prepared. The solutions were reviewed with the ED physician director, who saw no problems or concerns with the new process. It was decided to begin using the new standard process at 8 am the following morning, when there was usually a lull in the incoming patient volume.

On the third day, the team arrived early so that training for the day shift could be done between 7 and 8 am. The team divided themselves up among the ED staff to provide support for the new process. Although there were a few mistakes and misunderstandings, the new process worked very smoothly. As patient volume increased and additional staff reported to work, the team members provided training and support throughout the day. When the night shift came on, additional training was done. The ED manager made sure her shift supervisors were clear on the new process before leaving for the day.

For the fourth day, the team again came in early to train any staff members who had not been there the previous day. When the full team met in the morning, they agreed on a few small changes to make the work flow better, based on comments from the ED staff and team members. They reviewed the data from Days 1 - 4 and prepared their final report. With the process owner, they developed a weekly reporting schedule.

On the fifth day, the final presentation was given in an open meeting for hospital leaders and staff. The response was overwhelmingly positive, with some very good questions from the audience about the need for scheduling changes (to be implemented on the next six-week schedule, with appropriate 2 weeks notice) and the standard work for physicians related to contacting the Primary Care Physician within a certain amount of time.

Following the report-out, the team was treated to lunch at The Seafood House and each team member was presented with a $25.00 movie gift card.

Over the next few months, the team submitted an article (i.e., the Lean Chronicle) (p. 218) that included the Paynter Chart (p. 219) and Run Chart (p. 220). The team decided to summarize a few of their Lean improvements relative to visual control levels and created a Potential Failure and Level Control Chart (p. 225). The team also created a Storyboard (A3) Report (pp. 228-229), along with a Yokoten Worksheet (p. 231), to concisely document and share the knowledge gained from the project.

The team presented a 90 day follow-up using the Project Goal Overview (p. 232). Even though they did not meet the goal of 1.5 hours for the Dispo-to-Admit cycle time, they were very close - averaging 102 minutes (1.7 hours) for Dispo-to-Admit total cycle time (170 minutes - 68 minutes) which was a significant decrease. The team did improve ED Patient Satisfaction scores to their stated goals, as well as contribute to the ED% of Admitted Patients Meeting Target for 4.5 hrs for the entire ED Arrival to Inpatient Bed value stream.

There was increased enthusiasm to try this same approach for other parts of the ED. The OR leadership was very interested in being the next focus for this Lean methodology (see the Appendix for an Operating Room case study). In conclusion, the ED staff felt more empowered in their jobs and the financial leader was able to validate most of the projected savings over the next quarter. Executive leaders saw that the combination of the Lean approach, employee involvement and ownership, and process owner accountability with patient care and safety always a priority, as keys to the success of the project.

No two projects will use the exact same sequence of tools. Keep in mind that a hospital's information systems are a reservoir of data. The intent of this book is to assist you to "tap" this reservoir of data so you can make the right decisions at the right time when implementing the improvement activities. How will you learn which tools to apply to your exact situation? Most teams embarking on their Lean journey use an experienced facilitator to lead the first Lean project. If you do not have access to an experienced Lean facilitator, or Sensei, in your organization, perhaps you have a sister organization or parent organization that have facilitators that can be "loaned" to you. Or, you might choose to hire a consultant as your first guide. If you are eager to try this approach on your own, remember that the success of Lean is not dependent on the number of tools that are used; it is dependent on how you engage the team members that are working the process to help identify waste, and then use the appropriate Lean or quality improvement tool to reduce or eliminate that waste.

The following illustration provides a quick overview of the various tools and worksheets used in each of the VSM phases. Remember, many tools may be used at numerous times throughout a Kaizen Event. By keeping that overall perspective of Assess, Diagnosis, Treat, and Prevent as your framework for improvement, you should do well in your Kaizen Event.

Planning Tools/Worksheets

Kaizen Event Daily Review	Kaizen Event Scorecard	Kaizen Event Preparation Schedule (3 Weeks Prior)	Kaizen Event Preparation Schedule (2 Weeks to Event)	Kaizen Event Daily Schedule Days 1-3	Kaizen Event Daily Schedule Days 4-5+	Idea Kaizen Form

Assess Phase

The Balanced Scorecard	The Goal Card	Project Prioritization Worksheet	Distribution/Volume Report	Distribution Report	Takt Time	Cycle Time Table
Team Charter	Meeting Information Form	Status Report	Effective Meeting Evaluation Worksheet	Brainstorming for pre-Value Stream Mapping	Current State Value Stream Map	Process Flowchart

Diagnosis Phase

Waste Audit/Walk	Elevator Speech	ED - Delay Worksheet/ Summary Worksheet	Document Tagging Worksheet	Voice of the Customer (VOC) ED/Input Survey	Brainstorming Fishbone 5 Why Analysis	Financial Analysis

Treat Phase

5S	Just-In-Time Supermarkets Kanbans	First-In First-Out (FIFO) Lanes	Pitch	Work Load Balancing	Standard Work Combination Table Standard Work Chart	Physical Layout
Leveling Heijunka Box	Mistake Proofing	Failure Prevention Analysis Worksheet	Visual Production Board	Impact Map	Gantt Chart	

Prevent Phase

Lean Chronicle	Paynter Chart	Run Chart	Visual Control	Storyboard	Yokoten

Consider the following:

- ✦ Apply the four phases of Assess, Diagnose, Treat, and Prevent to any process in any area of healthcare
- ✦ Use the Readiness Guides as you move through the various phases of process improvement
- ✦ Involve your staff to provide ideas for improvement and generate enthusiasm for the improvement
- ✦ Share best practices with your healthcare colleagues; you may spark a great idea from sharing
- ✦ Remember to stabilize your work environment with 5S as part of any Lean project
- ✦ Keep quality and patient safety at the forefront of any improvement activity

Most importantly, keep in mind the overall purpose of the four phases as explained throughout this book: Assess - determine what will be driving the improvement and obtain a visual representation; Diagnosis - gather reliable data and be able to present it logically; Treat - apply Lean tools to a process or area; and, Prevent - use the appropriate tools to ensure the process is controlled and improvements are sustained.

Final Thoughts

It is not easy to continually improve an organization's processes to a state of total wellness. The constant struggle to balance budgets, resources, and people to get the daily work done without allocating the time and effort needed for improvement initiatives, is the challenge for managers, directors, and supervisors - as well as the process worker. However, there really is no alternative. Organizations that do not actively pursue continuous improvement initiatives (and take the time) through Lean, Six Sigma, or Lean-Sigma on all levels of their organization are setting themselves up for loss of market share, cost and staff reductions, and eventually, loss of customer (your patient's) confidence.

The following questions may be rattling around in your mind as you read through this book. Where do you begin with so many issues to deal with? What difference will one project make? Questions like this can be answered with the following story:

A woman was walking on the beach in Venice, Florida one January morning. On that morning there were hundreds, if not thousands of starfish that had washed ashore due to a red tide. Without hesitation, she proceeded to pick one up and place it back in the ocean, saving it from eventual death. After continuing this for a few minutes, another woman came up from behind her and asked, "What are you doing? You cannot save them all." To her she responded, "I can save this one, (and as she picked up another starfish), this one too, and that one…." She continued on her way picking up as many starfish as she could. The other woman just stood there - wondering.

You have choices: to do something or not to do something. If you do something that improves, say 5 patient care experiences in one year, that would be commendable. If everyone did something like that, and focused on other processes that need to be improved, a major shift in healthcare can happen. It just takes the right attitude.

This book provides the framework and all the detailed steps required for a healthcare system (hospital, lab, clinic, or long term treatment facility) to either implement a system-wide improvement program or accelerate the one you currently have.

Begin by picking up your starfish!

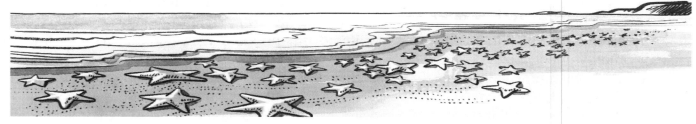

Appendix

Topics Include:

+ **OR Case Study**
+ **Executive Assistant's Email Case Study**
+ **Length of Stay (LOS) for Patients from E-Referral Case Study**
+ **Physician's Office Case Study**
+ **Selecting the Right Kaizen Approach for your Improvements**
+ **Integrating Lean with your EMR/EMS (Electronic Medical Records/Systems)**
+ **Applying 5S to Your Emails**
+ **Additional Sources for Finding Improvement Ideas in the Healthcare Industry**
+ **Glossary**
+ **Index**

OR Case Study

The following case study was shared by Trinity Health. A team was formed to first create an overall value stream map (VSM) in order to better understand the flow of patients, information, and resources through the value stream and to identify the opportunities for improvement. The team specifically mapped the total knee joint replacement pathway for an elective, surgical patient.

The Total Joint Replacement (Knee) Current State

Other info:
DOS - Day of Surgery
m = minutes
shift is 12 hours
data collection was 1 month

Surgical Prep Center

Physician's Office
- reg info = 3 m
- ins/DME = 2 m
- Xray = 15 m
- exam = 10 m
- Delays = 60 m

W 30 days

Surgical Prep Center
- H&P = 30 m
- pt educ = 70 m
- pre admit testing = 15 m
- chart prep = 15 m
- Delays = 30 m

W 7 days

DOS to Transport

Preoperative Prep (DOS)
- obt ID/reg = 5 m
- pt asst. = 5 m
- vitals, IV = 15 m
- validatation = 5 m
- anesth asst = 5 m
- Delays = 20 m

W 90 mins.

Surgical Procedure
- procedure = 120 m

W 5 mins.

Recovery
- educ pt = 10 m
- assess pt = 10 m
- pain ctrl = 15 m
- init therapy = 20 m
- disch ords = 5 m
- pat sleep = 60 m

Patient

Billing and Coding
- preauth = 20 m
- assure compl = 5 m

Timeline:
30 days — 90 mins. — 160 mins. — 7 days — 55 mins. — 90 mins. — 120 mins. — 5 mins. — 120 mins.

Data collection methods:
SPC = direct observation n=30
PP = review schedules
SP = EMR report
R = direction observation n = 100
IR = VOC
D = VOC

Legend:
Delays = XX — **Minor** delays
W / XX — **Major** delays — This will be the
— Electronic
* — Denotes care

Value Stream Map for Surgical Services

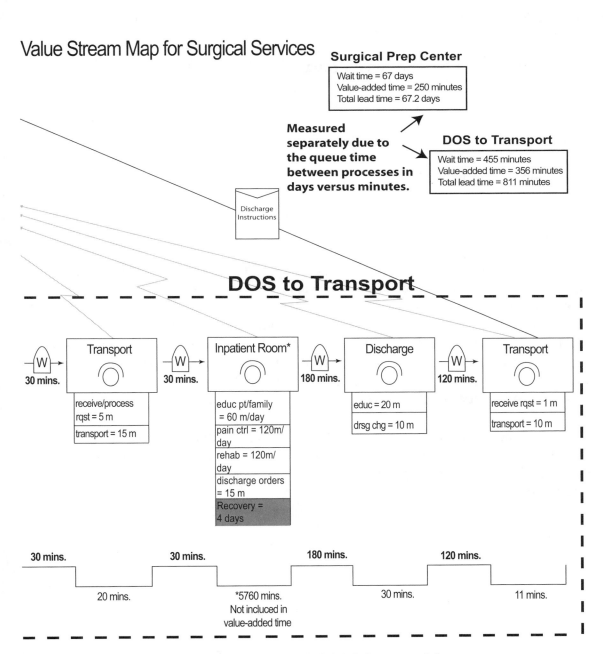

Surgical Prep Center

Wait time = 67 days
Value-added time = 250 minutes
Total lead time = 67.2 days

Measured separately due to the queue time between processes in days versus minutes.

DOS to Transport

Wait time = 455 minutes
Value-added time = 356 minutes
Total lead time = 811 minutes

Discharge Instructions

DOS to Transport

| Transport | Inpatient Room* | Discharge | Transport |

W 30 mins. → Transport
receive/process
rqst = 5 m
transport = 15 m

W 30 mins. → Inpatient Room*
educ pt/family = 60 m/day
pain ctrl = 120m/day
rehab = 120m/day
discharge orders = 15 m
Recovery = 4 days

W 180 mins. → Discharge
educ = 20 m
drsg chg = 10 m

W 120 mins. → Transport
receive rqst = 1 m
transport = 10 m

30 mins.   30 mins.   180 mins.   120 mins.
        20 mins.   *5760 mins.   30 mins.   11 mins.
                     Not inclued in
                     value-added time

which represent activities within a process that may be non value-added but included in the process cycle times.

which represent significant time delays between one process (or department) and another.
main reason why two processes are not connected on a value stream map.

information connecting current value stream process to another potential value stream or critical process.

pathway and is not included in the DOS to Transport times.

Following the mapping session, the team identified waste in the processes and then determined the appropriate resources that were to be allocated to eliminate that waste. The following areas were identified:

✦ Surgical Preparation Center: Defects were cancellations. Solution: Standardized Work
✦ Preoperative Holding Area: Preop patients were waiting due to elongated process. Solution: Work load balancing (Employee Balance Chart)
✦ Operating rooms: Outdated, wasted supplies were excess inventory. Solution: 5S
✦ Inpatient rooms: Patient falls were defects. Solution: Visual Cues

Process Step: Surgical Preparation Center

Assess

Waste: Overprocessing, Defects

Identification: Surgical cancellations

Project: To establish standardized criteria to identify those patients that should undergo an early pre-anesthetic evaluation

Current State: Physicians/surgeons refer patients to the Surgical Preparation Center (SPC) based upon their personal preference, resulting in inconsistencies in the preparation of surgical patients. In the current state, surgical patients are being evaluated and tested in an inconsistent, non-standardized manner, which is contributing to surgical cancellations and adverse outcomes. The improvement team determined that an analysis of cancellation data and chart audits would enable them to better understand which patients should be seen in the SPC. The team recommended testing requirements for all pre-operative patients that would then be aligned with those of the American Society of Anesthesiologists (ASA).

The Surgical Services team completed a retrospective chart audit for patients who had been cancelled on the day of their surgery; the time period covered in the audit was one calendar year. The team discovered that the cancelled patients were of the service lines seen in the following Pareto (80/20 Chart) illustration.

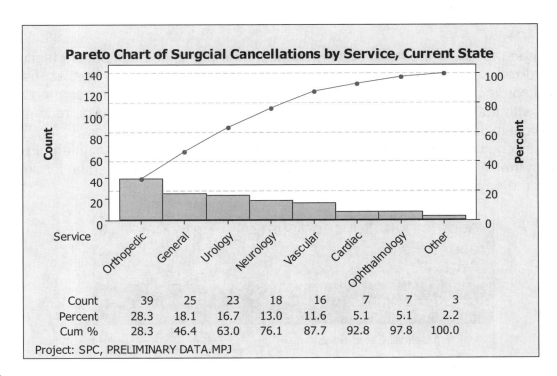

Pareto Chart of Surgcial Cancellations by Service, Current State

Service	Orthopedic	General	Urology	Neurology	Vascular	Cardiac	Ophthalmology	Other
Count	39	25	23	18	16	7	7	3
Percent	28.3	18.1	16.7	13.0	11.6	5.1	5.1	2.2
Cum %	28.3	46.4	63.0	76.1	87.7	92.8	97.8	100.0

Project: SPC, PRELIMINARY DATA.MPJ

Diagnosis

The team also investigated the reasons why the patients were cancelling. The Pareto Chart (shown below) indicates that nearly 22% were cancelled for Unknown reasons and 40% were cancelled for multiple miscellaneous reasons (i.e., the Other category), 38% of the patients were cancelled for reasons that appropriate pre-anesthetic testing could potentially prevent. The team felt that there was improvement opportunity to prevent and/or eliminate surgical cancellations in the areas of Patient sick, Rescheduled, Cardiac issues, Medical clearance, Patient no show, and Patient refused, to attain optimal patient preparation in the SPC.

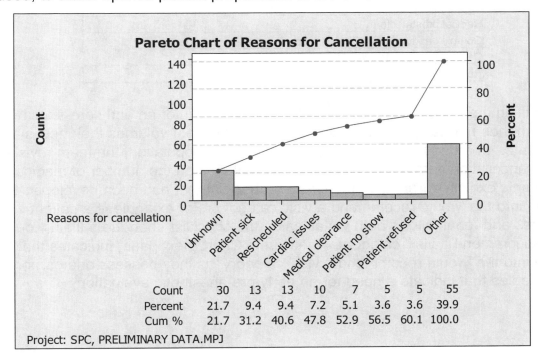

Pareto Chart of Reasons for Cancellation

Reasons for cancellation	Unknown	Patient sick	Rescheduled	Cardiac issues	Medical clearance	Patient no show	Patient refused	Other
Count	30	13	13	10	7	5	5	55
Percent	21.7	9.4	9.4	7.2	5.1	3.6	3.6	39.9
Cum %	21.7	31.2	40.6	47.8	52.9	56.5	60.1	100.0

Project: SPC, PRELIMINARY DATA.MPJ

Treat

The team agreed to follow the ASA recommendations for pre-anesthetic patient testing to create their standardized work; any further testing would be ordered by the SPC staff as they deemed necessary according to medical necessity. The team also used the ASA recommendations, in combination with their chart audit data, to determine which patients should be recommended for pre-anesthetic evaluations at the SPC. The following matrix was developed as their standard work and distributed to all surgeons. The team believed that the standardization of patients being seen in the SPC for standardized evaluations would lessen the potential for surgical cancellations on the day of surgery.

Recommendations for Surgical Prep Center Patient Visits

By medical condition:

Medical Conditions	Testing Required		
	Laboratory	EKG	Chest
Diabetes	BAS	EKG	
Complex Cardiac	BAS		CXT
Chronic Lung Problems			CXT
Renal Failure	BAS, Hct	EKG	
Sleep Apnea			
Morbid Obesity		EKG	
Hx. Of Difficult Intubations			
Children: Complicated History			
Hx: Malignant Hyperthermia			

By surgical procedures:

All vascular procedures (exception: varicose vein stripping)
Radical prostatectomy
Complex abdominal: Whipple, Liver, Pancreas, Large bowel
Carotid stents under anesthesia
Radiologic procedures under anesthesia: CT, MRI

Having identified the patient populations that should be seen for an early pre-anesthetic evaluation, the team then needed to determine what potential patient volumes their new standard work would generate. In order to estimate the potential patient population, the team revisited the chart audit cancellation data and looked for documentation on the number of medical conditions that the patients exhibited from the standardized checklist that had been developed that would placed them into the 'would recommend a visit' category. For example, if a patient was found to have diabetes and renal failure, both variables on the checklist, then the patient would fall into the 'would recommend a visit' category. The Pareto Chart (next page) indicates that 62% of the patients fall into the 'would recommend a visit' category, as they possess one or more of the medical variables that indicate a need for an early pre-anesthetic evaluation.

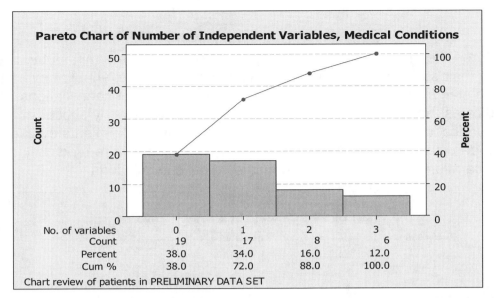

No. of variables	0	1	2	3
Count	19	17	8	6
Percent	38.0	34.0	16.0	12.0
Cum %	38.0	72.0	88.0	100.0

Chart review of patients in PRELIMINARY DATA SET

The team discovered through their chart audit that the number of patients that would be recommended for evaluation at the SPC did not increase when reviewed by surgical procedure as these patients, for the most part, fell into the 'would recommend' category covered by the medical variables.

The team developed the following model for scheduling to allow for optimization of the patient to arrive for their appointment; provide all testing within one environment, and reduce handoffs. The sections Teaching/FHA represent hour-long blocks (color coded, but not shown as such) for the nurse practitioner to complete the history, physical, and preoperative instruction. A technician who would work within the SPC would complete the EKG and blood work as indicated below. This schedule was color-coded (not shown). The scheduling model allows for patients to experience a full service 75-minute appointment with minimum exposure to multiple providers.

Time	Nurse Practitioner 1	Patient - NP 1	Patient - NP 1
8:00	Teaching/FHA	Teaching/FHA	
8:15	H & P	H & P	
8:30			
8:45			
9:00	Teaching/FHA	EKG, blood work	Teaching/FHA
9:15	H & P		H & P
9:30			
9:45			
10:00	Teaching/FHA	Teaching/FHA	EKG, blood work
10:15	H & P	H & P	
10:30			
10:45			
11:00	Lunch: 30 minutes	EKG, blood work	
11:15	Chart review: 15		
11:30	minutes		
11:45	Teaching/FHA		Teaching/FHA
12:00	H & P	Clerk lunch: 30	H & P
12:15		minutes	
12:30			
12:45	Teaching/FHA	Teaching/FHA	EKG, blood work
1:00	H & P	H & P	
1:15			
1:30			
1:45	Teaching/FHA	EKG, blood work	Teaching/FHA
2:00	H & P		H & P
2:15			
2:30			
2:45	Teaching/FHA	Teaching/FHA	EKG, blood work
3:00	H & P	H & P	
3:15			
3:30			
3:45	Teaching/FHA	EKG, blood work	Teaching/FHA
4:00	H & P		H & P
4:15			
4:30			
4:45			EKG, blood work
5:00			

Prevent

The team monitored their Day of Surgery (DOS) cancellations to determine if the implementation and execution of their standardized work surrounding which patients should have a pre-anesthetic evaluation with standardized testing would result in a reduction of cancellations. The Control Chart below indicates that the standardized work has been significantly successful in reducing the number of surgical cancellations, from 1.7% to 0.6% of all SPC patients evaluated. As a result of the standardization of pre-anesthetic evaluation, patients were medically optimized and the Surgical Preparation Center experienced less surgical cancellations.

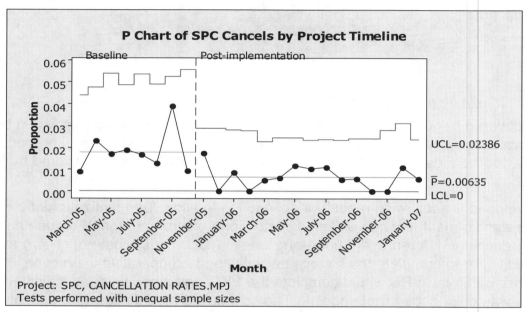

Fewer cancellations provide surgical departments to retain their expected revenues. The reduction in surgical cancellations demonstrated above was able to preserve $259,000.00 in retained revenues for the hospital as shown below.

	SPC HP Volume	Expected Cancels from Baseline Factor	Actual Cancels	Sugical Case Contribution Margin	SPC Savings
October-05	108	2	1	7,000	7,000
November-05	115	2	2	7,000	-
December-05	115	2	0	7,000	14,000
January-06	121	2	1	7,000	7,000
February-06	127	2	0	7,000	14,000
March-06	209	4	1	7,000	21,000
Pre-Realize	**795**	**14**	**5**		**63,000**
April-06	174	3	0	7,000	21,000
May-06	173	3	2	7,000	7,000
June-06	194	4	1	7,000	21,000
July-06	185	3	2	7,000	7,000
August-06	193	4	1	7,000	21,000
September-06	179	3	1	7,000	14,000
October-06	181	3	0	7,000	21,000
November-06	149	3	0	7,000	21,000
December-06	92	2	1	7,000	7,000
January-07	185	3	1	7,000	14,000
February-07	114	2	2	7,000	-
March-07	180	3	1	7,000	14,000
April-07	132	2	0	7,000	14,000
May-07	157	3	1	7,000	14,000
Realized Total	**2288**	**41**	**13**		**196,000**
Totals	**3083**	**55**	**18**		**259,000**

Process Step: Preoperative Holding

Assess

Waste: Waiting

Identification: Cycle time for patient preparation too long

Project: To establish standardized process for preparing the patient for surgery that eliminates delays in care through parallel processing

Project: To reduce the wait times experienced by preoperative patients

Current state: The team, in response to their value stream map, recognized that their patients were experiencing long wait times in the preoperative holding areas. The team mapped the process of prepping the patient from arrival to the hospital to when that patient departs for the operating room.

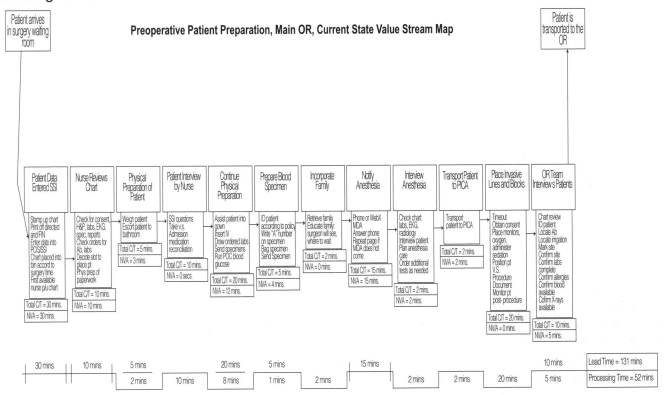

Note: The total cycle time is the total length of time; the non value-add time is the portion of time of the cycle time that is non value-added. These two will not add up - they are not supposed to.

*(Grafx® FlowCharter™ is a process analysis and modeling tool available to help organizations understand and improve business processes. A graphical representation of processes allows people to easily comprehend information and quickly focus on the bottlenecks and issues in a process. It can easily create: Flowcharts, Process Maps, Swimlane® Diagrams, Value Stream Maps, Cause & Effect Diagrams, FMEA Spreadsheets, etc. (other types of flowcharting/mapping software is also available in the market).

Diagnosis

The hospital's preoperative staff documented their work using an Employee Balance Chart and determined the length of time that it took for each step of the process. Microsoft Excel was used to create this simplified version of an Employee Balance Chart.

Minutes	Patient Data Entered SSI	Nurse Reviews Chart	Physical Preparation of Patient	Patient Interview by Nurse	Continue Physical Preparation	Prepare Blood Specimen	Incorporate Family	Notify Anesthesia	Interview Anesthesia	Transport Patient to PICA	Place Invasive Lines and Blocks	OR Team Interviews Patients	Total Minutes
1	1	1	1	1	1	1	1	1	1	1	1	1	12
2	1	1	1	1	1	1	1	1	1	1	1	1	12
3	1	1	1	1	1	1	0	1	0	0	1	1	9
4	1	1	1	1	1	1	0	1	0	0	1	1	9
5	1	1	1	1	1	1	0	1	0	0	1	1	9
6	1	1	0	1	1	0	0	1	0	0	1	1	7
7	1	1	0	1	1	0	0	1	0	0	1	1	7
8	1	1	0	1	1	0	0	1	0	0	1	1	7
9	1	1	0	1	1	0	0	1	0	0	1	1	7
10	1	1	0	1	1	0	0	1	0	0	1	1	7
11	1	0	0	0	1	0	0	1	0	0	1	0	4
12	1	0	0	0	1	0	0	1	0	0	1	0	4
13	1	0	0	0	1	0	0	1	0	0	1	0	4
14	1	0	0	0	1	0	0	1	0	0	1	0	4
15	1	0	0	0	1	0	0	1	0	0	1	0	4
16	1	0	0	0	1	0	0	0	0	0	1	0	3
17	1	0	0	0	1	0	0	0	0	0	1	0	3
18	1	0	0	0	1	0	0	0	0	0	1	0	3
19	1	0	0	0	1	0	0	0	0	0	1	0	3
20	1	0	0	0	1	0	0	0	0	0	1	0	3
21	1	0	0	0	0	0	0	0	0	0	0	0	1
22	1	0	0	0	0	0	0	0	0	0	0	0	1
23	1	0	0	0	0	0	0	0	0	0	0	0	1
24	1	0	0	0	0	0	0	0	0	0	0	0	1
25	1	0	0	0	0	0	0	0	0	0	0	0	1
26	1	0	0	0	0	0	0	0	0	0	0	0	1
27	1	0	0	0	0	0	0	0	0	0	0	0	1
28	1	0	0	0	0	0	0	0	0	0	0	0	1
29	1	0	0	0	0	0	0	0	0	0	0	0	1
30	1	0	0	0	0	0	0	0	0	0	0	0	1
31	0	0	0	0	0	0	0	0	0	0	0	0	0
													131

To validate the length of time documented in the value stream, the team also collected data, observing the patients as they went through the preparation pathway. The patient experience was then evaluated to determine if it was value added activity or waste. The following pie chart demonstrates the experience of the patient undergoing a total knee replacement. The patient experienced 61% waste, which was attributed to waiting.

Analysis of Patient Care for the Total Knee Replacement Patient Pathway

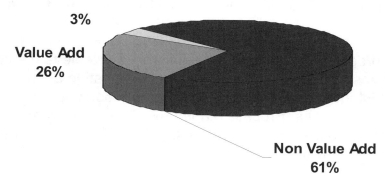

3%

Value Add
26%

Non Value Add
61%

To validate the length of time documented in the value stream, the team also collected data, observing the staff as they delivered patient care. RNs were evaluated via direct observation in 2 hour-blocks of time. This data (shown below) was for a preoperative nurse. The work activities were then evaluated for value-added activity or waste. The data demonstrates that the preoperative RN experienced 36% waste in her work.

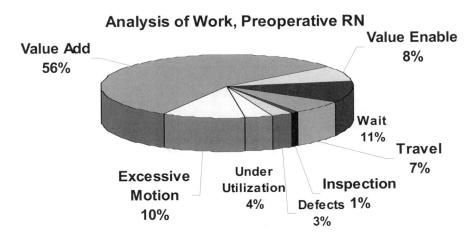

Analysis of Work, Preoperative RN

Value Add 56%
Value Enable 8%
Wait 11%
Travel 7%
Inspection 1%
Defects 3%
Under Utilization 4%
Excessive Motion 10%

Treat

The Surgical Services team redesigned the patient preparation pathway to eliminate waste, reducing the patient wait time. As part of the redesign, the team implemented a tracking board in the preoperative area, so that surgeons and anesthesia personnel would be aware of patient arrivals and locations. The tracking board would also be used to identify nurse staff assignments and alerts for patient testing and treatment needs. The future state value stream map is documented below.

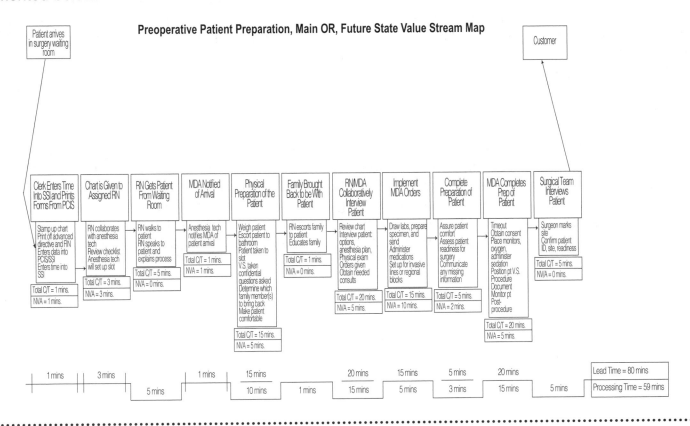

Preoperative Patient Preparation, Main OR, Future State Value Stream Map

With their redesigned future state in mind, the team looked at the current Employee Balance Chart and employed some parallel processing and created this following chart calculating the time that it would take to complete each step of the process. Deliberately incorporated into the process was the collaboration between anesthesiologist and preoperative nurse to allow for joint preparation of the patient. The preparation included the activities of the interview, physical assessment, and blood draw. A formal structure of notification for anesthesiologist was included so that the collaboration could be staged as soon as possible upon the patient's arrival to reduce delays.

Minutes	Clerk Enters Time into SSI and Prints Forms From PCIS	Chart is Given to Assigned RN	RN Gets Patient From Waiting Room	MDA Notified of Arrival	Physical Preparation of the Patient	Family Brought Back to be With Patient	RN/MDA Collaboratively Interview Patient	Implement MDA Orders	Complete Preparation of Patient	MDA Completes Prep of Patient	Surgical Team Interviews Patient	Total Minutes
1	0	0	1	0	1	1	1	1	1	1	1	8
2	0	0	1	0	1	0	1	1	1	1	1	7
3	0	0	1	0	1	0	1	1	1	1	1	7
4	0	0	1	0	1	0	1	1	0	1	1	6
5	0	0	1	0	1	0	1	1	0	1	1	6
6	0	0	0	0	1	0	1	0	0	1	0	3
7	0	0	0	0	1	0	1	0	0	1	0	3
8	0	0	0	0	1	0	1	0	0	1	0	3
9	0	0	0	0	1	0	1	0	0	1	0	3
10	0	0	0	0	1	0	1	0	0	1	0	3
11	0	0	0	0	0	0	1	0	0	1	0	3
12	0	0	0	0	0	0	1	0	0	1	0	3
13	0	0	0	0	0	0	1	0	0	1	0	3
14	0	0	0	0	0	0	1	0	0	1	0	3
15	0	0	0	0	0	0	1	0	0	1	0	3
16												64

Note: The future state Employee Balance Chart has some different heading categories than the current state Employee Balance Chart. The team wanted to represent the improvements as a collaboration of new work methods. The important point was that the overall process was reduced considerably.

Prevent

The team was able to reduce the cycle time by 47% through the creation of parallel processing and elimination of unnecessary steps. In the current state, the RN and the MD each evaluated the patient individually. In the future state, the RN and MD evaluate the patient concurrently, eliminating redundant questioning and eliminating the handoff, known to be a cause of errors, between nurse and physician. This collaboration also eliminates the wastes of waiting and motion (trying to locate the physician) as well as increased capacity to care for more patients in the preoperative area.

Process Step: Operating Rooms

Assess

Waste: Inventory, Motion

Identification: Non-standardized supplies led to increased inventory, motion

Project: To implement 5S in the surgical suite to standardize supplies across all ORs. As an added incentive, the hospital was in the planning process of designing a new surgical services suite that would have 18 operating rooms. The goal was to design the ORs to be able to support any type of patient or service line (i.e., universal). In order to achieve this each room needed to be standardized.

Current State: The surgery suites were identified by service lines, with certain ORs being designated for cardiac cases, while others were always reserved for orthopedic cases; this approach led to service specific supplies being stored in those designated rooms. The surgical services staff, though assigned to designated service lines, had no scheduled responsibility for checking the supplies for par levels or expiration dates; neither did the staff routinely clean the bins that held the supplies. Inventory in the ORs was replenished in a haphazard method according to whoever might be working in the rooms that day. The photos below illustrate the current state of the cabinets. Note that many items were overstocked.

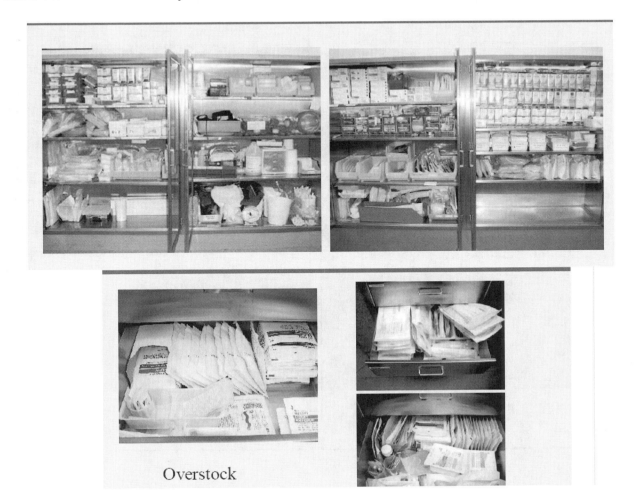

Overstock

Diagnosis

The team decided that a 5S project would help them achieve their goals of workplace organization and universal ORs. The following are few of the Microsoft Excel templates that were used for additional analysis of the proposed areas as well as support for the Treat and Prevent phases.

Tag Worksheet

Purpose: To guide the team in the use of tags for the Sorting activity.

Who should fill it out: Surgical Services 5S Team

Directions: The best way to use this tool is to follow these steps:

1. Fill out the form as completely as possible.
2. Review and modify periodically.
3. Share with the Lean team at the next meeting.

1. Choose team members responsible for design, development, and procurement of the tags. Members from each of the surgical specialties were selected to be on the 5S team. The following specialties were represented: cardiovascular, general, orthopedics, neurology/ophthalmology

2. Determine color(s) to be used for tagging.
The team designed tags and printed them on red paper.

3. Determine the size of the tag and the information required on the tag.
The team selected the following information to be included on the tag:

5S Item Disposition Log

Purpose: To help decide what to do with the tagged items.

Who should fill it out: Surgical Services 5S Team

Directions: The best way to use this tool is to follow these steps:

1. Decide the category in which each tag should belong.
2. Determine the action to take.
3. Use this form along with the Unneeded Items Log (next worksheet).

Category	Possible Action
Obsolete	Sell
	Hold for depreciation
	Donate to a school or charity
	Discard
	Employee Auction
Defective	Return to supplier or vendor
	Discard
Trash/Garbage	Recycle
	Discard
Unneeded in area	Move to holding area
Used at least once per day	Carry with you
	Store at point-of-use
Used at least once per week	Store in area, close to point-of-use
Used at least once per month	Store where accessible and easy to find
Seldom used, must keep	Store out of the way, visually control and create standard for retrieval
No need to keep	Discard
Use unknown	Move to holding area and seek additional input from employees, once input has been received, assign item(s) to one of the above categories

5S Job List

Team Members: _____

Purpose: To designate specific duties ensuring the first 3 S's are adhered to.

Target Area: _____   Date: _____

Job or Activity	SORT	SET IN ORDER	SHINE	STANDARDS	SUSTAIN	Frequency				Notes
						Start of day	End of day	Weekly	Monthly	
Monitor par levels	v							RT		
Monitor cleanliness levels										
Monitor organization										
Monitor inventory levels										

Five Minute 5S Checklist

Team Members: _____

Purpose: To assist the team in completing assigned duties on time.

Target Area: _____   Date: _____

	Standard Time to Perform for _____ (Ex. John)
Sort	The Room Captains will validate that the supplies are in the correct location (1 minute)
Set-In-Order	The Room Captains validate the cabinets are stocked appropriately at the start of the day. (1 minute)
Shine	The Room Captains validate that the cabinets are clean. (1 minute)
Standardize	The Room Captains will audit their respective ORs and each others to validate standardization. (1 minute)
Sustain	The Room Captains will sign off completing the 5S checklist. (1 minute)

Treat

The Surgical Services team assigned room captains for each service line; cardio-thoracic, general, neuro-ophthy-spine, orthopedics, and vascular. Together, the captains identified the appropriate supplies, set the new par levels, and designed the layouts of the cabinets. The captains were then responsible for taking this work to their teams to pilot the design; the time frame of the pilot was two weeks. Following the pilot, the captains reconvened to discuss potential improvements to their overall design. These improvements were then tested following the same pilot plan until a consensus was achieved that the design would meet the supply needs of the surgeons. Once consensus was achieved, the captains made labels, par level checklists, and created a deployment strategy for the audits that would be required to sustain the work. This process took approximately four months. The photos below were part of the pilot project.

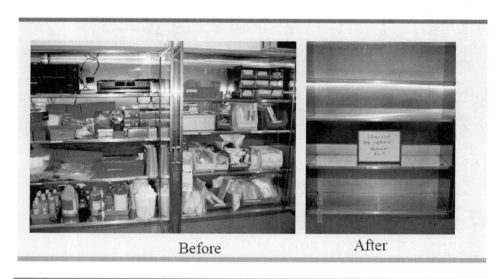

Before   After

Lean   Clean

Prevent

Specialty	Operating Rooms	Cost Savings
Cardiothoracic	14, 15, 16	$4,442.94
General	1,3,4,6,7,8,9,10	$4,614.12
Neuro-Opthy-Spine	5 & 13	$24,501.98
Orthopedics	11 & 12	($5,501.29) *
Vascular	17	$24,613.77
Total		$52,671.52

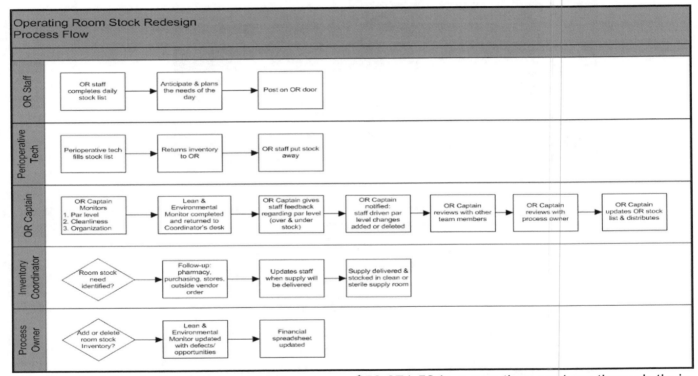

The Surgical Services team was able to secure $52,671.52 in a one-time savings through their 5S project.

Special Thanks for Surgery Case Info: Elizabeth A. Stuart, MSN, ANP-BC, is a nurse practitioner at Saint Joseph Mercy Health System in Ann Arbor, Michigan. Elizabeth, a Six Sigma Green Belt, spent 20 years as an operating room nurse, specializing in cardio-thoracic surgery. She has effectively led Six Sigma projects on improving the process for orthopedic preference cards and OR Restocking. Other project work includes development of both the cardio-thoracic professional model and educational manual. In 2008, Elizabeth achieved board certification as a nurse practitioner and is currently providing pre-anesthetic evaluations for surgical patients in a surgical preparation center.

Process Step: Inpatient Rooms

Assess

Waste: Defect

Identification: Orthopedic patients are at an increased risk for falls as a result of their surgical procedure

Project: To create a visual control system that will identify patients who are at risk for falls

Current State: Patients who have undergone total joint replacement have increased dependency needs and are at increased risk for falls.

Diagnosis

The nurses on 5E (the orthopedic floor at the hospital) recognized that their post-surgical total joint patients were at risk for falls due to their limitations in ambulation. Patients could be in the following ambulation categories: ambulate with hospital staff only, ambulate with assistance of staff or family, or ambulate on own. Patients would be assigned to a category of ambulation after having been assessed by the physical therapist. As the patient progresses through the post-operative recovery period, the physical therapist will 'promote' the patient to advanced levels of ambulation. The greater potential for patient falls arose when neither the patients nor the staff could consistently identify which patients were in which ambulatory category. Patients who need-ed assistance for ambulation were not being recognized and when they attempted to ambulate on their own, would fall.

The 5E staff recognized the need to address the issue of patient falls and formed a multi-discipli-nary team, consisting of a nurse, patient care assistant, physical therapist, physical therapy aide, and an orthopedic surgeon. The team brainstormed various ideas and potential solutions to the problem of total joint patient falls. As a result of this discussion, the team created a Cause and Effect (or Fishbone) Diagram as shown below.

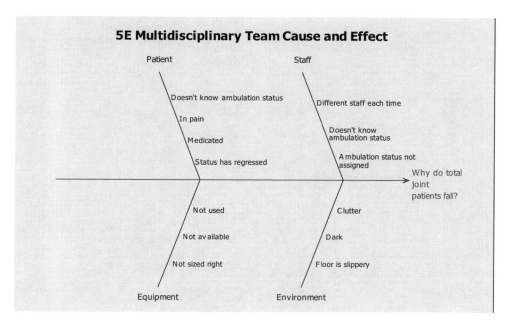

Although the team discussed many of the items on this diagram, they discovered that two of the items, that neither the patient nor the staff could consistently identify the ambulation status, could be resolved through the development of visual controls.

Treat

The team devised a name badge system, whereby the patients would wear a disposable badge that would identify them by their first name, to protect their identity, and by their ambulatory status; the ambulatory status would be designated by stars. The ambulatory status categories are listed below:

- Ambulates with hospital staff only: One star
- Ambulates with hospital staff and/or family: Two stars
- Ambulates on own: Three stars

Educational material was developed and patients, families, and staff were informed of the proposed solution.

Prevent

This solution was piloted on the 5E unit. The preliminary data looked favorable. More importantly, the patients and their families were highly engaged in attempting to "get more stars" on their badge; this encouraged earlier advanced status ambulation. The data indicated that despite patients being promoted to earlier advanced ambulation, the number of falls still decreased by 78.5%; the identification of patient ambulation status was instrumental in decreasing falls.

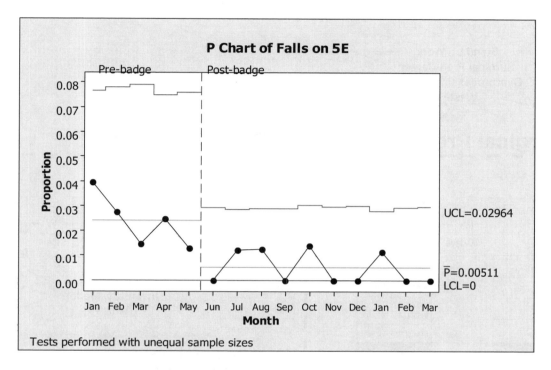

The Surgical Services Team implemented four improvements to their value stream in the areas of (1) Surgical Preparation, (2) Preoperative Holding, (3) Operating Rooms, and (4) Inpatient Rooms. These improvements were focused at eliminating waste to improve patient safety, clinical quality, and operational efficiency. These Kaizens were identified on their future state map on the following two pages. The results from all these improvements were:

Surgical Prep Center
- ✦ Reduced the patient appointment time from 135 to 75 minutes
- ✦ Reduced cancellations from 1.7 to 0.6
- ✦ Retained revenues of $259,000

Preoperative area
- ✦ Reduced cycle time (mostly wait time) by 47%

Operating Rooms
- ✦ Saved $52,671.52

Inpatient Rooms
- ✦ Decreased falls by 78.5%

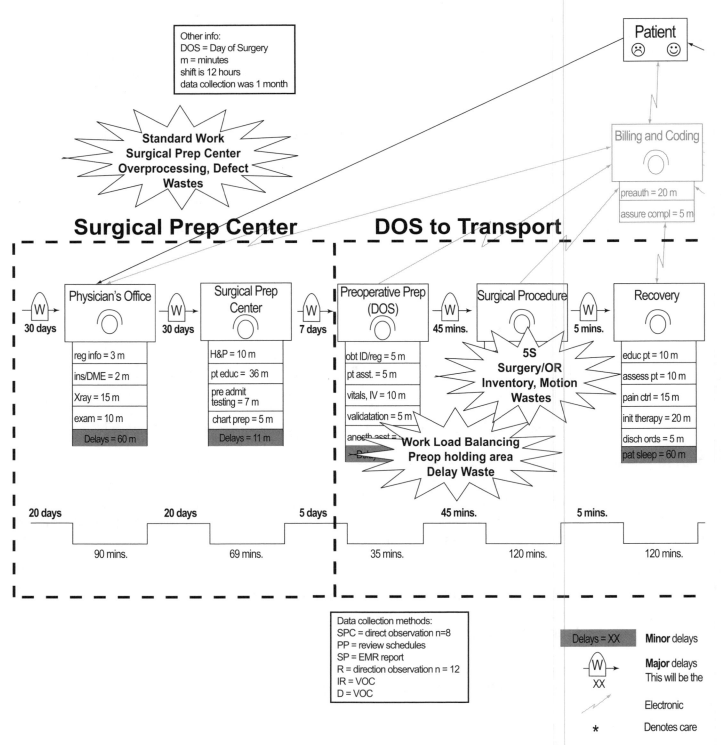

The Total Joint Replacement (Knee) Future State

The team decided to include in the Recovery process box the time that the patient was sleeping (60 minutes) as value-added time.

Value Stream Map for Surgical Services

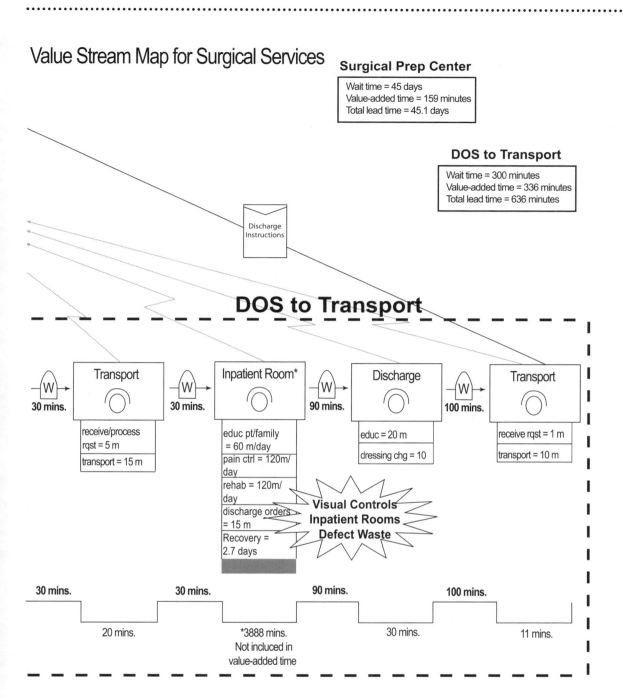

Surgical Prep Center

Wait time = 45 days
Value-added time = 159 minutes
Total lead time = 45.1 days

DOS to Transport

Wait time = 300 minutes
Value-added time = 336 minutes
Total lead time = 636 minutes

DOS to Transport

Discharge Instructions

Transport		Inpatient Room*		Discharge		Transport	
W	30 mins.	W	30 mins.	W	90 mins.	W	100 mins.

Transport
receive/process rqst = 5 m
transport = 15 m

Inpatient Room*
educ pt/family = 60 m/day
pain ctrl = 120m/day
rehab = 120m/day
discharge orders = 15 m
Recovery = 2.7 days

Discharge
educ = 20 m
dressing chg = 10

Transport
receive rqst = 1 m
transport = 10 m

Visual Controls Inpatient Rooms Defect Waste

30 mins.		30 mins.		90 mins.		100 mins.	
	20 mins.		*3888 mins. Not inclued in value-added time		30 mins.		11 mins.

which represent activities within a process that may be non value-added but included in the process cycle times.

which represent significant time delays between one process (or department) and another.
main reason why two processes are not connected on a value stream map.

information connecting current value stream process to another potential value stream or critical process.

pathway and is not included in the DOS to Transport times.

The first round of changes was focused on the elimination of waste and promotion of Lean techniques, such as standardized work (SPC checklist), 5S, and visual cues. Not all improvements are reflected on the times shown on the map (e.g., cost savings due to the 5S project, decrease in falls, etc.). Other Kaizen Events were to be planned to meet the total lead times and value-added times as shown above.

Executive Assistant's Email Case Study

Assess

The senior executive at this hospital selected six staff from the Quality Improvement Department to learn the principles of Lean. The intention was to allow the team to learn by doing, then to train other staff at the facility in continuing additional Lean projects. An administration project was selected focusing on the senior executive email usage.

A staff survey was conducted to get a quick picture of the state of the hospital email system. One staff story from an executive assistant went as follows:

"I feel I probably didn't give enough thought to how Allison's (an Executive V.P.) emails affect me. The more I think about it the more I realize that her emails do overwhelm me and the reason I spend so little time on them is that there are way too many sent to me for me to handle, so I just don't handle most of them. I only address the urgent ones."

A current state value stream map of the email process was developed. The session included senior executives, their assistants, and the quality Lean team. The value-added time for emails per day was determined to be 100 minutes, the total time for the email journey was 10,210 minutes, thus giving a value-added to total cycle time of 0.02% as conveyed in the following value stream map.

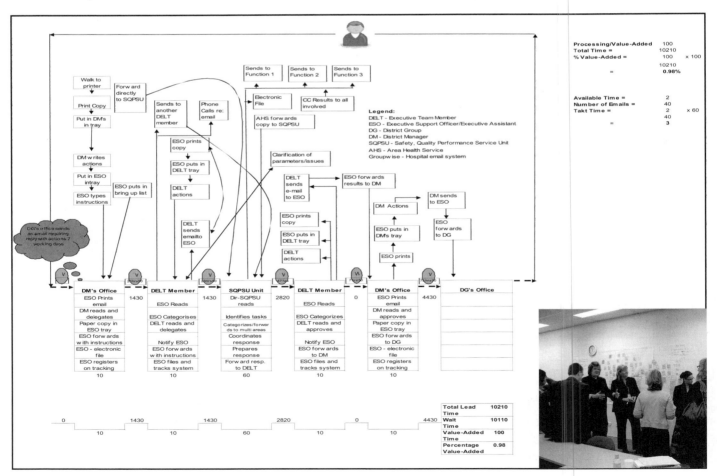

The team collected data to determine how much time was spent on email usage. It gave the executive assistants a log to fill in daily. The log revealed:

53 emails received each day
2 - 3 hrs spent each day

The following illustration shows a breakdown of the time spent on emails by the executive and executive assistant.

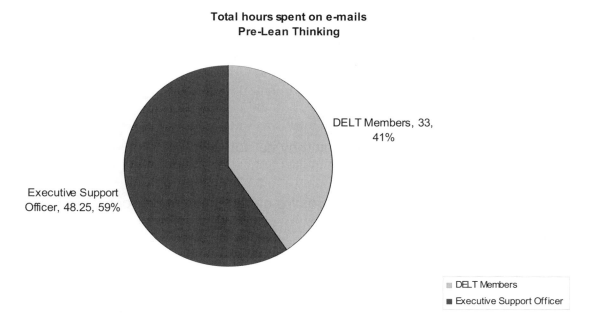

Total hours spent on e-mails
Pre-Lean Thinking

DELT Members, 33, 41%

Executive Support Officer, 48.25, 59%

▪ DELT Members
■ Executive Support Officer

Diagnosis

The team conducted a Waste Walk to highlight wastes in the email process. They found large queue and delays with the email management process, contributing to overproduction and duplication of effort. The following wastes were identified:

Waiting/Delay/Time-In-Queue
Waiting on feedback/reply from sent email
Sitting in Inbox, not actioned
Waiting for executive members/executive assistants to forward

Overproduction
Same email sent to various parties for no real benefit
Same questions asked by many different people
Producing more paperwork than required - including printing emails by several people

Defects/Rejects
Email resent because not sure if sent earlier
Emails forwarded to wrong person for actioning
Incorrect information in the email
Emails received after the deadline date

Motion

Searching for emails within Groupwise as there are too many folders

Printing the email and placing it in the In-tray of executive member and In-tray of executive assistants

Overprocessing

Resending the email because no response received or email sent again in error

Duplication of emails in Groupwise in various folders due to lack of a structured system

Inventory

Stockpile of emails awaiting task completion

Stockpile of emails printed and placed in In-trays or kept in In-boxes

Old emails not deleted or actioned

Transport

Excessive forwarding of emails

Sending documents to executive members that they do not require

Staff Utilization

Executive members and executive assistants unsure of each other's responsibilities in terms of email management

Lack of training in email management

Treat

The Waste Walk and subsequent analysis identified there was no consistent approach to rules and processes surrounding email management throughout the organization. Emails from executive offices were somewhat less of an issue than the next layer down. The team decided (with input from the executive assistants) to set up some simple rules for email distribution. The email rules were distributed to executives and those within the departments for a 30 day trial. The team introduced standardized distribution lists which reduced duplication and waste. Additional email rules were as follows:

To:

Only include staff members in this field who are required to action the contents of the email.

CC:

Include staff who are required to know the content of the email but are not required to action anything directly - FYI (staff members can contribute to the action by liaising directly with the 'To' person. FYI emails should be electronically filed into a separate folder for the executive director to access when available.

BC:

This should only be used in professional circumstances (e.g., distribution lists to employees who should not see other members of the list).

Replies:
General rule should be to reply to sender only, unless requested by the sender to 'Reply All'. (If sender wishes all participants to be included in the reply, must include 'Reply All' at the beginning of the email.)

Subject:
Due date: dd/mm/yy and brief description of contents. If forwarding an externally received email, amend the subject to reflect local rules.

Priority:
High/Urgent - Only to be used when a 24 hrs or less response is required.
Normal/Low - To be used for normal emails.

Prevent

The results of the 30 day trial resulted in the executive sending 33% less emails each day. Also, 30 minutes of time was saved each day by each executive assistant. The before and after results are shown below.

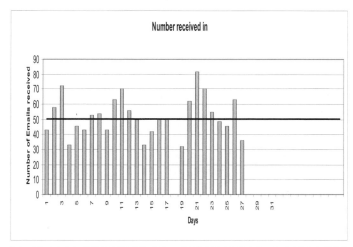

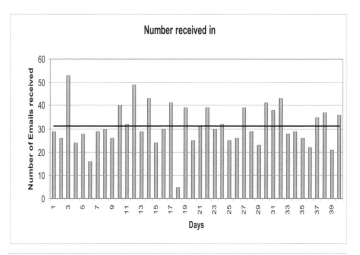

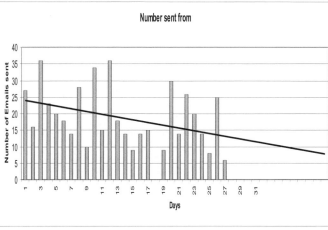

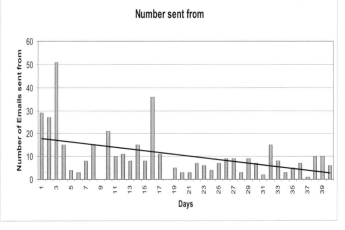

The team developed A3 posters (Storyboards) in each area highlighting their successes and progress. The Storyboards were found to be an excellent communication and engagement tool. The Storyboards focused on promoting the rules and principles around emailing within the organization. The team's Storyboard is on the following two pages.

Email Storyboard (A3 Report)

Theme: Decrease the time spent on email management

Background: No consistent approach to email management; overproduction and duplication of effort; queues and delays in email management; average perceived amount of time spent on emails is 2.6 hrs per day; no guidelines for relievers

Extent: Effects all executive members and executive assistants

Rationale: Time wasted, deadlines required for emails, staff frustration, job sharing, and relief requirements

Goal: To reduce executive assistants total time spent on emails by 30%

Current State Data and Map

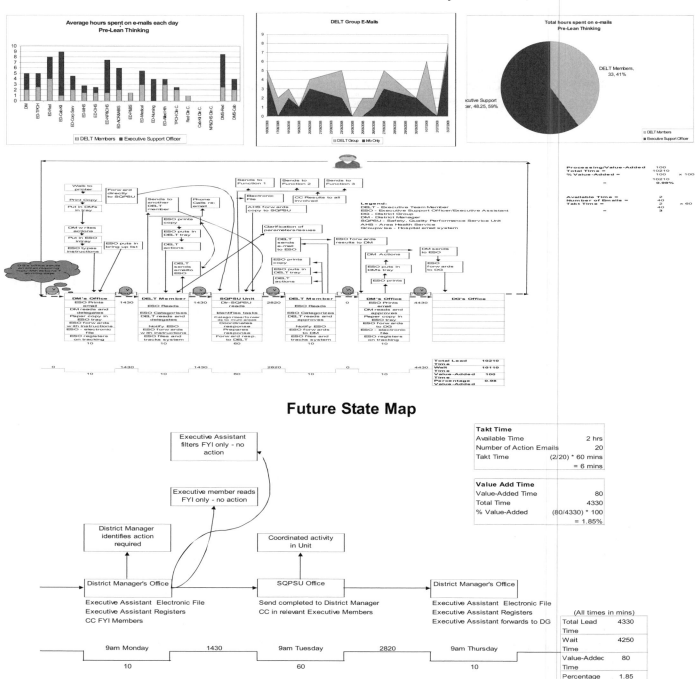

Future State Map

Implementation Plan

What	Who	When	Where
Value stream mapping session	Project team, Assts	7/28	Corporate
Data collection	DELT members, Assts	Weekly	All departments
Future value stream mapping session	Project team, Execs/Assts	8/25	All departments
Reconvene with executive and	Project team, Execs/Assts	8/25	Corporate
Agree on and distribute new email standards	Project team, Execs/Assts	9/15	All departments
Set-up shared email groups	Executive Assistants	9/22	All departments
A3 Storyboard	Project team	9/28	All departments
Measure outcome targets	Project team	9/28	All departments
Display outcomes	Project team	9/28	All departments

An Example of Before and After Data

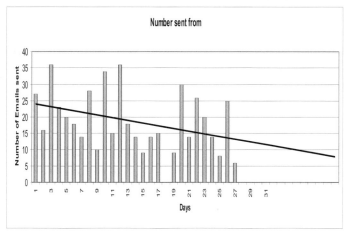

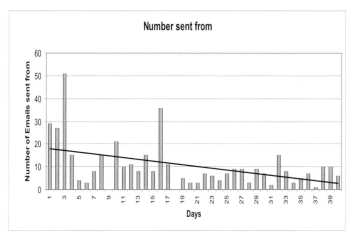

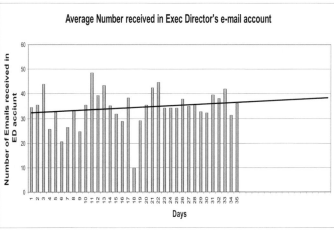

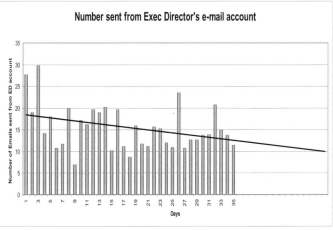

Follow-up
- ✦ Continue data collection weekly then monthly
- ✦ Create visual graphs of pre and post data
- ✦ Share knowledge and experience regarding Lean thinking to inform future decisions related to email processes
- ✦ Roll out new email rules across organization
- ✦ Post all information on intranet in Kaizen Workshop folder

Length of Stay (LOS) for Patients from E-Referral Case Study

Assess

This large Australian acute (900 beds, 420 acute) hospital had undergone a recent restructuring of its sub-acute services and was looking to improve service delivery. In addition, when reviewing its Health Roundtable data (which provides benchmarks on Length of Stay (LOS) and a range of hospital indicators across 110 hospitals in Australia and New Zealand), it discovered a longer than comparable LOS. There was also a concern regarding patient's rights to timely assessment and treatment. The executive of the hospital felt that improvements in waiting times for assessments could be achieved with the right amount of support. Access block (patients waiting in the ED) and ambulance bypass (ambulances unable to bring patients to the hospital due to there being no beds) were also a considerable issue for this hospital. The delay in moving patients from the acute into sub-acute was having an impact on bed availability in the acute facility and was contributing to access block and ambulance bypass.

A Lean team, comprising of the manager of the sub-acute service, patient flow manager, the care coordination team leader, and a service improvement facilitator/project officer was formed. Having this interdisciplinary team, with representation from across the continuum of care, was paramount for any success or lasting improvements to be made. After attending a two day Lean Thinking program, conducted by The Health Round Table, the team continued with an analysis with their staff over the next month.

Assessments Made - The historical process saw multiple assessments and long waits which resulted in the occupation of a scarce hospital bed for longer than the expected hospital LOS.

The referral process was as follows:

1. The team assessed the patient as ready for sub-acute assessment and a sub-acute facility as the discharge option.
2. An electronic referral (e-referral) was generated from the computer system to the sub-acute assessor. Without this e-referral "kanban", patients would not go to sub-acute.
3. The sub-acute assessors completed the assessment on patient. The issue was that patients received multiple assessments before being put on the waiting list and then had to wait 4-7 days on the list before the sub-acute assessment.

Takt time was calculated by summing the total number of e-referrals for the year and dividing by the total number of working days. The following graph (next page) shows the average number of referral per day for each month during (figures calculated on a 5 day working week). The takt time was calculated at 10 e-referrals per day.

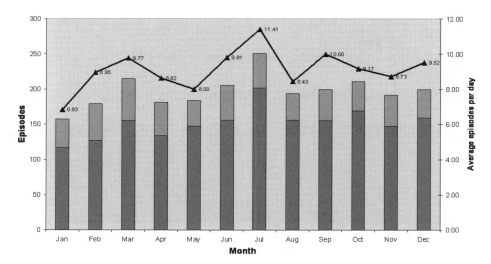

The team set their goal to decrease the Length of Stay for patients from e-referral the sub-acute rehabilitation waiting list by 25% within 3 months. This, in turn, would reduce the overall LOS for patients waiting to be transferred from the acute to sub-acute setting.

An IT database audit revealed that the Average Length of Stay (ALOS) from e-referral to wait listing was 3.66 days with 50% of e-referrals requiring multiple reviews. The time from first review to wait listing for multi-review patients was on average 7.2 days. This was in contrast to those who only had a single review in which case the average waiting time was 0.5 days. Having a family member present at the time of assessment was seen as an important factor in the rehabilitation of the patient. The number of sub-acute assessments where a family member was present was approximately 25%.

The team created a current state value stream map with inter-disciplinary members from both the acute and sub-acute sectors participating. The following is their current state value stream map.

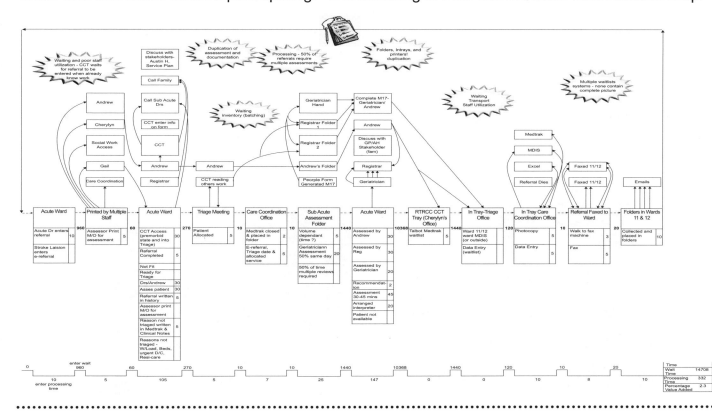

Some of the "light bulb" moments or Kaizen ideas immediately recognized by staff were:

+ Triage of e-referrals effectively happens twice (initially by care coordinator then in a designated meeting)
+ Clinicians report that each e-referral results in multiple assessments at least 50% of the time
+ There was very little sharing of information between sites as each having multiple wait lists

Diagnosis

A Waste Walk was conducted to validate the value stream map. Tasks were observed and questions were asked by the people throughout the walk. The key discoveries made by the team on the walk were:

a) There appeared to be a lot of printers, folders, In-trays with papers, and faxes, where it should be paperless.
b) Many wastes were identified in the Triage process - waiting for reviews, overproduction of information, incorrect processing, and poor staff utilization. Rather than just having one review once the e-referral was made, over 50% of e-referrals required multiple reviews of the same referral. In addition, these additional reviews were carried out by different medical staff. These multiple assessments by medical staff occurred because patients were not medically stable (i.e., the ward put in the referral too early). To further complicate matters, each of the multiple e-referrals also needed to be triaged, so even duplicated e-referrals could have been reviewed and triaged multiple times by the staff.

The team estimated the financial cost of the wastes. Based on the takt time of 10 e-referrals a day, the waste in the Triage process was estimated at $1,023,100 (multi-disciplinary meeting with medical, nursing and allied health at 5 minutes per assessment per e-referral) and the waste resulting from multiple assessments of $910,000. This was based on the time wasted by staff and did not include the waste of excess inventory (paper, printing, and folders).

Treat

The first step in gaining stability with the process was to 5S the acute to sub-acute care coordinator's office. One of the major issues was that if the care coordinator was away then there was no one who knew where to find anything in their office.

The following are before and after 5S photos of the care coordinator's office.

Some of the other key issues with the current state of the office were:

✦ Distinct lack of labels on folders
✦ Key notice board served mixed purposes
✦ Contingency nurse; whom worked in a nearby office, stored boxes of equipment on spare shelves and on top of draws (saline, catheter leg bags, etc.)

There was a dramatic difference post 5S in the Care Coordinators office with folders clearly labeled and now much easier to locate. One of the other key strategies implemented was that in the past the care coordinator walked past eight offices twice daily to pick up the e-referrals (Motion Waste). If the e-referral came to the other office after 3 pm, then it did not get picked up until the next day. The Care Coordinators idea was to move the In-tray into her office eliminating the batching and motion waste.

Some of the key strategies implemented to prevent delays in transfers from acute to sub-acute included:

✦ Having one assessment rather than multiple assessments as well as having assessments conducted by trained nurses rather than consultant medical staff (Work Load Balancing, Standard Work)
✦ Incorporating a seamless process from e-referral to assessment which involved Care Coordinators guiding the e-referral to the appropriate assessment at the appropriate time (when patient clinically ready for assessment) which negated the need for a Triage meeting to discuss referrals (Continuous Flow)
✦ Eliminating some of the repetitive activity and information that was part of the assessments (Mistake Proofing, Standard Work)
✦ Holding back referrals until the patient is medically stable for assessment (Continuous Flow, Standard Work)
✦ Streamlining the completed M17 assessment process to reduce the number of multiple transcriptions (Standard Work)
✦ Eliminating the Triage meeting which was a duplication (Work Load Balancing)
✦ Training Care Coordinators in a nurse assessor role for doing assessments during acute stay (Cross-training)

The following future state value stream map was created.

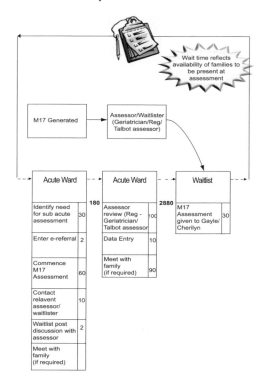

Prevent

Some of the strategies implemented to ensure the long term sustainability of the work included:

✦ Sharing the allocation and wait list between acute and sub-acute (A pull system allowed for care coordinators and ward staff in the acute sector to see who is next on the wait list and begin preparation.)
✦ Improving the e-referral process and subsequent standard form
✦ Training another service improvement facilitator and having both facilitators work in other areas of the health service
✦ Conducting 5S audits weekly
✦ Conducting assessment audits randomly
✦ Integrating the web based e-referral, assessment and waitlist system which allowed for real-time review of total wait list
✦ Reviewing daily all e-referrals
✦ Establishing KPIs for monitoring of all sub-acute referrals

The following were the outcomes:

✦ Reduced LOS for patients requiring inpatient sub-acute service e-referral - waitlist (3.38 days = 65% reduction)
✦ Acute admit - transfer to Sub-Acute (4.37 days = 20% reduction)
✦ Reduced clinician time wasted (multiple assessments - 50% to 12%)
✦ Triage meeting stopped (clinician cost per annum - $1,023,100)
✦ Reduced cost (ALOS reduction = $4,772,040 per annum)

Physician's Office Case Study

We were a busy orthopedic practice trying our best to do quality work and deliver value to our patients. But something was wrong. The patients felt the wait times were too long, the staff was routinely overworked, and the physicians were running on overdrive. Frustration was everywhere. We hoped our Electronic Medical Record (EMR) system would solve these problems, but it only created another layer of confusion. Only by adopting a Lean methodology were we able to fix the entire process and gain real value. Now the staff is empowered to make positive change, and our patients are satisfied getting more care in less time. As a physician I couldn't be happier with the change.

Stephen D. Mendelson, M.D. Orthopedic Surgeon

Assess

A high volume, Orthopedic Surgeon practice in the Midwest implemented an Electronic Medical Records (EMR) solution designed for orthopedic workflows. This solution was designed to better utilize resources, improve communication between medical staff, and provide physicians with fast access to patient medical records and images. While the group experienced notable cost savings around the reduction of paperwork and efficiency accessing medical records, they did not witness improved efficiency related to patient throughput. Improving patient throughput is important because it directly impacts the patient experience - (i.e., less time in the office).

A cross section of the office staff was engaged to develop a current state process map (see page 276), including the office manager, front desk associates, X-ray technicians, medical assistants, practice director, and one of the group's surgeons to determine not only why patient throughput has not improved, but what can be done to improve it. The current state map indicated to the group that the patient/work flow did not change after implementation of the EMR system.

The team, with assistance from an outside Lean-Sigma consultant, realized that eliminating process waste, creating continuous flow, building quality at the source, stabilizing and standardizing processes, using visual controls, and engaging and respecting everyone's contribution were needed to be adopted to improve efficiencies related to patient throughput.

The time between the patient's initial contact with the office to their appointment varied greatly (e.g., 24 hours to one week) which was mainly due to the patient's and/or physician's availability and the patient experience from the time they entered the office until the time they left. Data over a 3 day period, captured from the EMR showed the average office visit was 60 minutes with a standard deviation of 19 minutes . For the purpose of this case study, the team focused on the patient experience for one orthopedic surgeon.

Patient Experience	Visits	Average	Std Dev
Pre-Pilot	136	1:00	:19

The following is the Patient Experience Current State Process Map. The bold, italicized text denotes interaction with the EMR system.

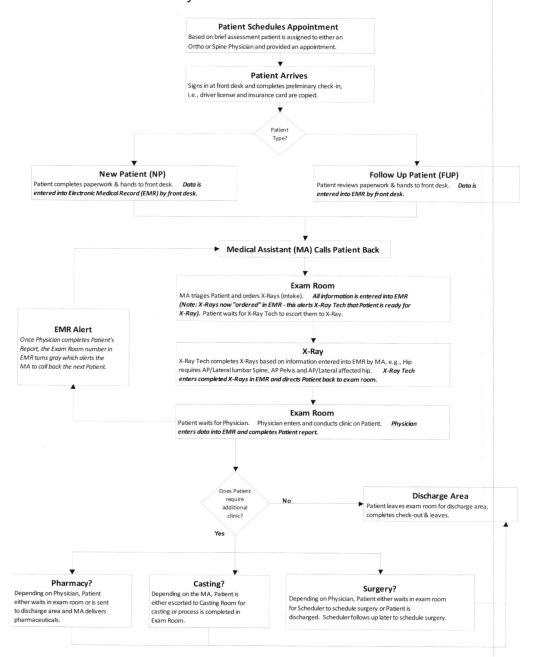

Diagnosis

After mapping out the process and capturing some initial data, the team continued with their Lean analysis of the office and the patient experience. Additional questions that were asked of the staff about the information flow were:

- ✦ Does everyone know the hourly patient target?
- ✦ How quickly are problems and abnormalities in the schedule noticed?
- ✦ What happens when there are problems and abnormalities?
- ✦ Does the patient move smoothly from one value-added step to the next?

To assist in answering the last question - Does the patient move smoothly from one value-added step to the next? - the team created a Spaghetti Map to show the flow of the patient. The triangles represent where delays were occurring in the patient experience as shown below.

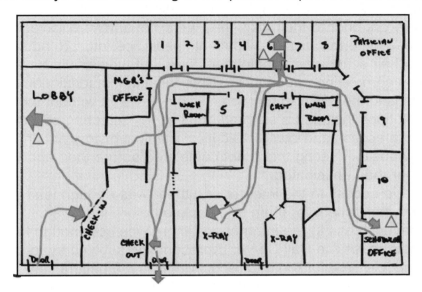

The team was amazed on how much the patient traveled through this process. They also commented that if Spaghetti Maps were completed for the medical assistant, X-ray technician, and physician, then similar type travel would be indicated.

Further discussions with the team members revealed the following:

+ There were variations in each major step of the patient experience, including the operations of check-in, X-ray, exam, and discharge.
+ Operations were isolated (or decoupled) allowing the batching of patients instead of one piece flow from each other. This inherently created the waste of waiting into each step along the way. Small, minor, or incremental wastes often may not seem significant to the staff members, but they do add up.
+ Decoupled operations also made it difficult to notice problems as they happen. When a problem occurred, none of the other work areas (i.e., stations) were aware of it, therefore, the rest of the stations kept working. By the end of the day, the unnoticed problems added up and the subsequent length of the patient stay continually fell short of the target.

Treat

Based on the initial assessment of the process, as well as further diagnosis, the team implemented the following Lean tools:

Introduced a Pull System
Nothing is done by the upstream process until the downstream customer signals the need, e.g., the patient is "pulled" into the X-ray process once an exam room is opened. The EMR becomes the trigger (i.e., kanban or signal). Visually on the computer screen the "room" in the EMR turns gray which alerts the X-ray technician to "pull" the next patient back.

Standard Work

The completed paperwork for each patient varied greatly depending on which representative scheduled the appointment or how prepared the patient was to answer basic insurance and/or medical history questions. Additionally, while most patients have access to the internet and could complete critical paperwork prior to their visit, they were not always directed to the group's website to download necessary forms, e.g., new patient, insurance, etc. To add to this most patients were arriving close to their scheduled appointment time, but then would have to spend an additional 20 to 30 minutes completing paperwork. (Note this time is additional to the EMR captured data). This pattern caused the office to run behind from the start without the ability to catch up. The standard work solutions included a scripted process for gathering critical data:

1. Encourage patient to access and complete critical medical history and insurance forms on the physician group's website. Noting that if not completed before their appointment their office visit would be longer than anticipated.

2. If patient did not have access to the internet and there was enough lead time the forms would be mailed directly to the patient for them to complete before their visit.

3. If patient did not have access to the internet and there was not enough lead time to mail necessary forms to their house the Call Center representatives would try to capture the data immediately or schedule time for them to reconnect with the patient.

4. The final option would be for the patient to arrive 20 to 30 minutes before scheduled appointment to complete necessary paperwork.

Depending on the physician and/or the X-ray technician's experience different types of X-rays were being ordered for similar procedures. For example, a simple knee injury might see 3 to 6 different X-rays ordered depending on the physician and or X-ray technician (overproduction). To minimize this confusion and eliminate potential rework, specific procedures by product line were developed to eliminate any discrepancies surrounding specific X-ray requests, e.g., new hip patient requires AP/Lateral Lumbar Spine, AP Pelvis and AP/Lateral.

Continuous Patient Flow and Physical Layout

To minimize the number of steps and improve patient flow two major changes were made to the office. First, the team decided to move the scheduler's office to the front and place the manager in the scheduler's old office. Second, the team changed the flow of the patient which allowed the patient to be X-rayed before going to the exam room. These two changes minimized the congestion in the hallways thus reducing the number of steps a patient was required to complete during their visit.

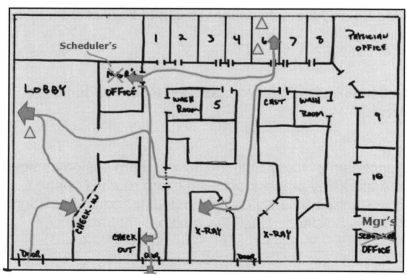

Prevent

The improvements dramatically decrease the amount of time a patient spends in the office, thus improving patient throughput. Before and after results are shown below.

Patient Experience	Visits	Average	Std Dev
Pre-Pilot	136	1:00	:19
Pilot	133	:29	:14

The following is the Patient Experience Future State Process Map.

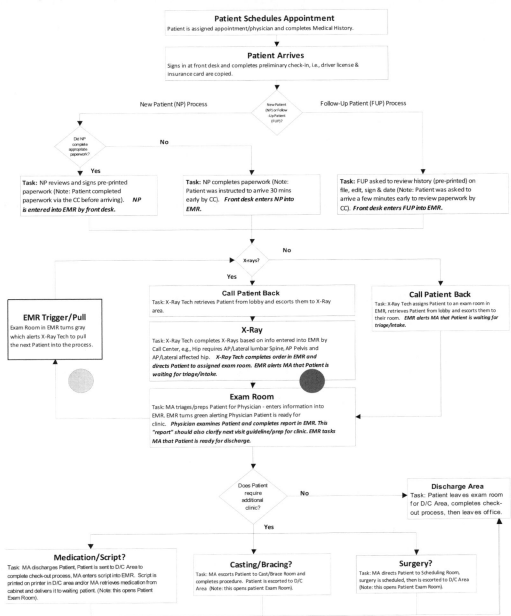

Moving forward the team focused on deploying the future state across all physician clinics, i.e., the Spinal and Ortho areas and the Call Center.

Selecting the Right Kaizen Approach for Your Improvements

There are many ways to define a Kaizen approach for your organization. The typical 3-5 day Kaizen Event, as explained through the Oakview Hospital case study, may not be practical given your specific improvement project, level of Lean or Six Sigma education, and/or staff to support any initiative. The following chart defines three types of Kaizens. Adapt and modify the one that will work best for you.

Types of Kaizen			
	Idea Kaizen	**Kaizen Event**	**System Kaizen**
Also known as:	Point Kaizen, Do-it, Nike Project	Kaizen Workshop, Rapid Improvement Event, Lean Workout, etc.	Also known as: Design, System Integration Project, Kaizen Project, etc.
Goal	Quick, simple change	Improve flow, reduce defects/errors, and work variation	Create flow in situations where change cannot be made in a week
Complexitiy	Easy, quick, "low hanging fruit"	Usually one departmental value stream	More complex/multiple/ intersecting value streams Usually more than one department IT heavily engaged
Focus on	Individual changes	A portion of a value stream or main process	The entire value stream and/or multiple processes
Planning Phase	1 hour to 1 day	1 - 3 weeks	1 - 6 months
Action (Workshop) Phase	1 hour or less	1 - 5 days	1 - 4 weeks
Follow-up Phase	Spot checks, include in internal audits	36-60-90 day follow-up reports	Monthly or quarterly
Changes made	Immediate	Within 2 days of the Kaizen Event week	1 - 4 weeks
Number of people involved on the team (typically)	1	5 - 12	7 - 15
Measure of success	Impact on work environment, reduced stress	Impact on process, improvement departmental Scorecard or other type of measurement	Impact on entire value stream and/or Balanced Scorecard

The following flowchart will assist you in determining a Kaizen approach depending on your type of improvement opportunity. Use this only as a guide.

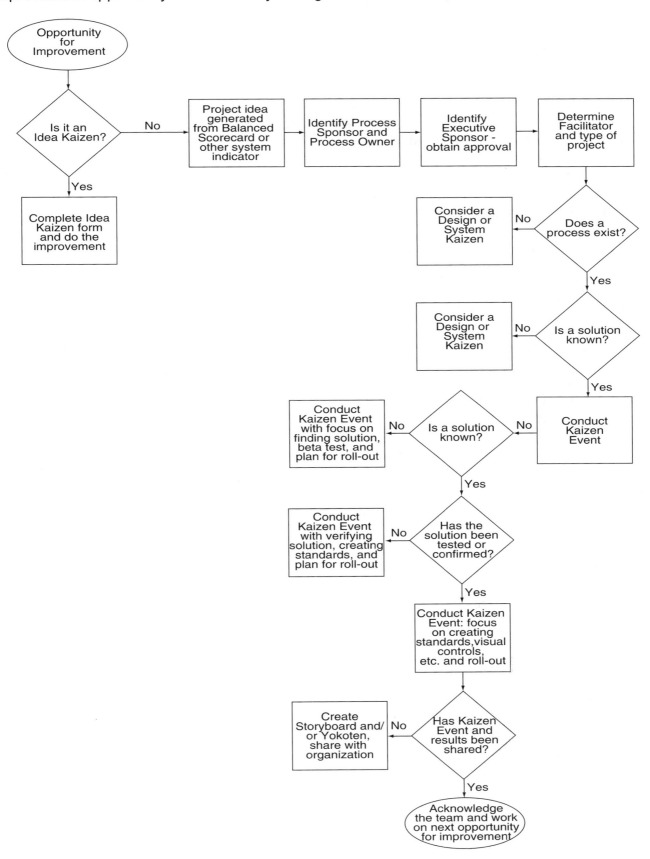

Integrating Lean with your EMR/EMS (Electronic Medical Records/Systems)

Any healthcare process that must be documented on paper presents process challenges. The documents must be completed correctly, approved as necessary, copied to other stakeholders, and stored so that they can be easily found and retrieved. When dealing with thousands of charts that are hundreds of pages long it can be difficult, if not impossible, to find the specific items that are necessary for proper coding, billing, and peer review. Most healthcare organizations are well aware of these difficulties, with the specialty of Medical Information developing its own professional requirements and certifications.

As more healthcare organizations implement an Electronic Medical Record (EMR) system there is a need to design efficient processes that must interact with these systems. Lean is a perfect partner to this type of process change. As the old saying goes, "we do not want to automate a bad process." Implementing an EMR system, which is the natural progression of IT in healthcare, will not automatically improve the Balanced Scorecard measurements as discussed earlier in this book. Processes must be analyzed, reviewed, and improved upon to take full advantage of the benefit that an EMR system can provide.

For example, there are many problems inherent with orders in a paper-based process. Illegible writing, mis-interpretation of writing, incomplete information, lack of signature, lack of date and time, etc. are all "defects" that create rework on the part of clerks, nurses, and other stakeholders. When the order is transcribed into an electronic record, the ordering clinician is responsible for selecting the correct order, modality, dosage, etc. assisted by algorithms built into the program to ensure (for example) that incompatible medications are not selected, or duplicate tests are not ordered. The availability of "Computerized Physician Order Entry" or CPOE, with its clinical decision-making support in the form of built-in pathways or guidelines, is seen as a crucial step towards reducing errors in the ordering process and improving patient safety as the result of clear, correct, and complete orders being delivered in a timely manner.

Likewise, the availability of patient tracking within the Electronic Medical Record system, serves as a visual reference. For example, a large monitor can be placed in a central location in ED so that everyone (staff, that is) can see what patients are present, how long they have been in the ED, and their status (suitably coded, of course, for HIPAA-required confidentiality).

The ability to receive results (i.e., labs, tests, etc.) immediately via the computer system is a superior process to the paper based flow of: department enters and verifies results; reports print on the unit; reports remain in the printer until someone comes to get them; the clinician is contacted or comes by to review the results; the results are eventually placed in the chart (with the possibility of being added to the wrong chart). In the electronic world, as soon as the department enters and verifies the result, it is available via the computer and an alert is posted to the appropriate caregivers that the results are available for review.

There are, of course, some caveats. As computer programs (systems) help us to make decisions about clinical care being a great benefit to patient safety and quality of care, the program is only as good as the information entered; so, we must think about the accuracy and timeliness of data entry, as well as the accuracy and interdependency of the computer modules, when designing or redesigning processes. ***It is important to note that computer systems designed around poor processes will not yield efficiencies.*** And processes that are made to adapt to pre-designed computer systems without regard to patient flow may add extra effort (waste) to the process rather than simplifying it.

Therefore, the application of Lean tools towards an effective process flow should be seen as an important component in the design and implementation of an Electronic Medical Record system.

Applying 5S to Your Emails

The following are some guidelines for implementing 5S to better organize your emails.

1. Sort

+ If you have been gone a few days, or have LOTS of email to go through, sort the senders by name. Tackle your boss's (or Urgent) emails first, then other VIPs, then go down the list in order of importance to your current task load or priority projects.

+ Be ruthless. If you do not need to know it, "red-tag" the item by dragging it over to the "Deleted Items" box. [Added action: If you do not like getting those cute kitten-pictures and the latest urban rumors from your colleagues, take 10 seconds to reply to the sender to say tactfully, "Please do not send them any more." It is a worthwhile investment and most colleagues will appreciate your need to keep your business Inbox for business only.]

+ Ask yourself, does the recipient really need this email? What is it that you want them to do with it when they get it? What makes this email, out of the 80-100 they will receive today, worthy of their limited time? If it is not needed, do not send it. (But, see the note about thank-you emails below.)

+ Be careful of cc's (copy-to) and bcc's (blind copies). Do not add people to the distribution list as a way to let the primary recipient know that you do not trust them to take action, or, if you are setting up a blame-sharing scenario (and they will figure this out without you telling them).

+ Know when to pick up the phone. For any email with more than 3 back-and-forth volleys, consider calling the person to finish the communication. Keep in mind that all communications should not be done by just email. You already know that readers can attribute "tone of voice" to email communications, so if you have got something sensitive or confidential to share, do it in person or by phone.

+ Pick a slower-than-usual week, like a holiday week to begin to Sort your emails. Set aside a couple of hours to go through your emails and see what you can archive - what you can discard - what you can file more appropriately. The investment of time is well worth it.

2. Set-In-Order or Straighten

+ If information sent to you is not relevant, but it is an on-going progress report or something that does not need a response, file it immediately under a helpful heading.

+ If you need to take action on an item, you can: a) Place it in an "action needed by date" folder b) Leave it in your Inbox as a reminder c) Drag it into your Task List - it may convert to a task to which you can add details d) Drag it into your calendar - to add it as a calendar item on the day of your choice or e) Print it and put it in a "to-do" folder. The goal is to keep a clear picture of actions that you need to take, in a way that puts you on or ahead of a deadline - not frantically searching for the original email when your boss or colleague asks you how you are doing on project X.

+ Help recipients know what you want them to do with the email. For example: Put it in the title: Project XXX (please read and provide feedback by Friday), Status of Team YYY (please respond with any questions), Action Plan for Department ZZZ (Urgent - Action Needed by End of Business Day), or Meeting Notes from xx/yy/zz (Review and File).

+ Remember that a lot of people scan through emails using the Preview function. Put the most important things in the top 2 or 3 lines of the email, including an executive summary, action requested, and any deadlines (if not in the title).

3. Shine or Scrub

+ Do you archive your emails? Do not let the computer do it automatically - there may be some long-term projects that you need to keep the running history on, all in one place. When a project is finished, archive the entire folder.

+ If your email Inbox has a restriction on size, you have options:
  a) You can save everything to your hard drive or shared drive (open the email, click on FILE then SAVE AS), and then save any attachments to the same place. There are also applications you can buy or download for free that handle this action, but check with your IT department first.
  b) In MS Office you can create a .pst file that stores on your hard drive or shared drive which looks just like a folder in your mailbox. You can store emails there just as you do in your regular mailbox. Click on FILE, NEW, OUTLOOK DATA FILE. (Get someone to help you if you have never used this, but after you have done it once, it is easy.) It does not usually "count against" your regular mailbox size limitations.

+ If the email is longer than a couple of paragraphs, consider sending an attachment instead. Within the email, use bullet points to draw attention to important issues. Use bolding (sparingly) to draw the eye to essential points or deadlines.

+ If you are sending an attachment or application file, consider sending the .pdf version to save space.

+ Review your email before sending it. Take out any unnecessary verbiage - be concise and at the end of the email, say something like "please feel free to contact me if you have any questions or concerns about the above."

4. Standardize

✦ There is no one way to organize your folders. Folders can be organized by name of the sender; week of the month; project name; etc. A general rule of thumb is to have no more than 3 levels of folders for any one heading - unless you have a perfect memory. The work group or department should have a standard naming conventions for shared files and folders.

✦ Corollary: Most of us still use and receive paper in our jobs. It is a lot easier to find things if your paper filing system matches your email folder structure, so when you try to find your hardcopy master project list for company A in region D related to Project X, it is under the same paper file folder headings as you would find it if it had been sent electronically.

✦ Many time management experts think that you should set a certain time aside each day to read and reply to emails.

5. Sustain

✦ Create an email audit form to review when sending emails, comprised of the checkpoints you want to review before you hit send. An example may be something as simple as the following:

> Check, do all recipients need this email? Check cc's. Phone instead?
> Action requested vs review - clear to all recipients?
> Concise enough? Need attachment?
> OK to go?

✦ Tracking emails feels a bit like "Big Brother is watching you". Use tracking very sparingly; it may be preferred to set (via a flag or rule) a reasonable timeframe for a response and then give the recipient a nudge if they do not get back to you. But, it is a personal preference; do not flag every email as "high importance".

✦ Your email signature/contact info is an essential part of business communication. Do not just sign "Regards, Sue" - if someone needs to call you back or fax you a response, it is very frustrating to have to go searching for the information. The basics include: Name, title, company, mailing address, phone, fax, email, website if there is one. Use with caution: motivational quotes, images that add size to the email, blinking or moving graphics, background stationary, fonts other than web-safe (arial, verdana, courier, times new roman).

There are usually many other options in each email system, such as assigning categories to emails or flagging them with various colored flags, that you can use as well. Remember the overall concept of 5S. It is to organize work to reduce waste. This can be accomplished through the various email controls that are most likely available in your email system.

Consider the same concepts as applied to your Desktop PC file and folder system using Internet Explorer or Mozilla Firefox.

The 5S Desktop (PC) Pocket Handbook - *Using the Power of the Toyota Production System (Lean) to Organize and Control Your Electronic Files and Folders* is a step-by-step guide for the implementation of 5S to all your electronic files. The XP version of Windows Explorer and the Office 2003 software suite were the versions used in creating this handbook. If you have an earlier or newer version than this, there may be slight differences in how a particular step or approach (command string) would be done. Keep in mind the overall goal you are attempting to accomplish, and using your version knowledge, apply that to the particular step or approach.

This handbook is designed to be:

1. **An implementation guide.** This handbook steps you through each phase of the 5S process. Examples are shown to assist you in this process. No two file systems (Desktops) are the same; therefore, use the examples in this book as a guide when you apply that phase or step to your Desktop.

2. **A Lean beginning.** 5S is a fundamental Lean tool and is considered the foundation for additional Lean tool application. Once 5S has been implemented and results have been obtained, there will be a need to integrate more Lean tools into your Desktop environment.

3. **A spark for the department.** Once everyone understands the basic premise of Lean and 5S, then that understanding can serve as a catalyst for a more comprehensive application of Lean tools. (*iLean* and **Lean Office Demystified II** are available books on how additional Lean tools can be applied to your Desktop environment.)

4. **A bridge for improved performance.** It is often stated that the average person at work today has nearly 80 emails to deal with on a daily basis. This, along with the other application files, can at times be overwhelming for the individual. Using 5S for organizing your emails, as well as the other application files, will greatly assist in managing this barrage of information. Implementing 5S to your files and folders will allow for a more stress-free workplace.

Please visit www.theleanstore.com for more information about this book.

Additional Sources for Finding Improvement Ideas in the Healthcare Industry

This following a list of some healthcare organizations that may provide additional assistance in learning more about improvements of patient care and safety in the U.S. and the world.

Advancing Excellence in American Nursing Homes (**www.nhqualitycampaign.org**)
American College of Cardiology (**www.acc.org**)
American College of Surgeons (**www.facs.org**)
Agency for Healthcare Research and Quality (**www.ahrq.gov**)
American Heart Association (**www.americanheart.org**)
American Nurses Association's National Database on Nursing Quality Indicators (**www.nursingworld.org**)
American Society of Anesthesiologists (**www.asahq.org**)
American Society of Health-System Pharmacists (**www.ashp.org**)
Centers for Disease Control and Prevention (**www.cdc.gov**)
Centers for Medicare and Medicaid Services (**www.cms.hhs.gov**)
Health Care Without Harm (**www.noharm.org**)
Hospital Quality Alliance (**www.cms.hhs.gov**)
Institute for Healthcare Improvement (**www.ihi.org**)
Institute of Safe Medication Practices (**www.ismp.org**)
Joint Commission International Center for Patient Safety (**www.jcipatientsafety.org**)
Joint Commission on Accreditation of Healthcare Organizations (**www.jointcommission.org**)
Josie King Foundation (**www.josieking.org**)
Leapfrog Group (**www.leapfroggroup.org**)
National Association of Healthcare Quality (**www.nahq.org**)
National Business Group on Health (**www.businessgrouphealth.org**)
National Coordinating Council for Medication Error Reporting and Prevention (**www.nccmerp.org**)
National Patient Safety Foundation (**www.npsf.org**)
National Quality Forum (**www.qualityforum.org**)
Society for Healthcare Epidemiology of America (**www.shea-online.org**)
Surgical Care Improvement Program (**www.cfmc.org**)
Veterans Health Administration (**www1.va.gov**)

Glossary

5S: A process to ensure work areas are systematically kept clean and organized, ensure patent and staff safety, and provide the foundation on which to build a Lean healthcare system.

5 Why Analysis: A method to assist a team in arriving at the root cause of the problem quickly without statistical analysis. The 5 Why strategy involves looking at any problem and asking: "Why?" and "What caused this problem?" as many times as it requires to get to the root cause.

ACT: The fourth phase of the PDCA cycle. It adopts and updates the necessary standards, abandons the process change, or runs through the cycle again.

Activity: The single or multiple act of taking a course of action.

Assess: The first phase of Value Stream Management for healthcare. It is compromised of the tools and methodologies by which an area or process is evaluated and prepared for detailed analysis.

Assessment: A structured form upon which to analyze a department or area relative to a particular topic.

Baby Boomer: Individuals born between the years of 1946 and 1964.

Balanced Scorecard (or Quality Dashboard): A broad set of categories on which an organization is measured on. These measurements have goals and when a certain category is not meeting its goal, then resources are committed to work on meeting the goal.

Basic flowchart: Standard symbols used to identify all the major steps in a process - usually no more than six steps. Mostly used for the 30,000 foot view for management review.

Benchmarking: A structured approach to identify, visit, and adapt world-class practices to an organization.

Brainstorming: The process of capturing people's ideas and organizing their thoughts around common themes.

Catchball: A process in which ideas are "tossed" back and forth between two groups until a consensus is reached.

Cause and Effect Diagram: A visual representation of the various factors affecting a process.

CHECK: The third phase of the PDCA cycle. It verifies results on actions taken to solve the problem.

Continuous flow: The ability of a process to replenish a single unit of work (or service capacity) when the customer has pulled it.

Check sheet: The visual representation of the number of times an activity, event, or process occurred for a specified period of time.

Control chart: The visual representation of tracking progress over time. Similar to line graphs.

Countermeasure: The short and long term actions taken by the team members to isolate and eliminate the root cause(s) of the problem.

Current state value stream maps: A visual representation of the way information and workflow is occurring presently.

Customer: The next process that requires something to be provided (i.e., data, information, service, material, etc.). The ultimate customer in healthcare is *typically* the patient.

Customer demand: The quantity of product or service required by the customer. Also referred to as takt time.

Cycle time: The time elapsed from the beginning of a work process request until it is completed.

Data: Factual information used as a basis for further analysis.

Data check sheet: A method by which to collect, organize, prioritize, and analyze data.

Deployment flowchart: Standard symbols used to visually convey the people (or departments) who are involved in the process. These flowcharts are helpful if the process being mapped crosses departmental boundaries.

Diagnosis: The second phase of Value Stream Management for healthcare. It is the process to further identify and gather information for adequate measurements to be taken, thus allowing a statement or conclusion to be drawn concerning the nature or cause of the area or process requiring attention.

Distribution Report: A historical departmental or functional listing on the volume of work or service completed within a specific time period.

D-M-A-I-C: The process improvement methodology or roadmap of Six Sigma. D-M-A-I-C stands for Define, Measure, Analyze, Improve, and Control.

DO: The second phase of the PDCA cycle. It develops and implements solutions to a problem.

Document Tagging Worksheet: A form to capture the work elements and steps accurately, as a chart, patient, or document moves throughout an entire process or value stream.

Donald Berwick, M.D.: One of America's leading patient safety advocates and the founder, president, and CEO of the Institute for Healthcare Improvement.

Effective meeting: The efficient use of people's time when they are gathered together working to obtain a desired result.

Employee Balance Chart: A visual display in the form of a bar chart that represents the work elements, times, and workers for each process relative to the total value stream cycle time and takt time (or pitch).

Edward Deming (1900 - 1993): A census consultant to the Japanese government after WWII, famously taught statistical process control methods to Japanese business leaders.

Elevator speech: A brief, comprehensive verbal overview on the purpose and related-activities regarding a product, service, or project.

Ernest Codman (1869 - 1940): A surgeon in the early 1900s who is credited with initiating quality in healthcare.

Facilitator: A person designated in a meeting to ensure everyone stays on task and that everyone contributes.

Failure prevention analysis: A technique that allows the Kaizen team to anticipate problems before the implementation of a solution.

First-In First-Out (FIFO): A work-controlled method to ensure the oldest work upstream (first-in) is the first to be processed downstream (first-out). This could be a raised flag or an email alert.

Fishbone Diagram: See Cause and Effect Diagram.

Flash report: The weekly communication of the Balanced Scorecard's critical measurements to management allowing them to keep abreast of the trends, as well as call attention to any significant changes that may require immediate action.

Florence Nightingale (1794 - 1875): A compassionate nurse who cared for the poor and indigent as well as for soldiers in the Crimean War; she is known as the founder of modern day nursing.

Flow: The movement of material or information.

Flowchart: Standard symbols used to visually represent a type of operation, process, and/or set of tasks to be performed. Synonymous with process map.

Forming: The first stage of team development. It involves reviewing the project, establishing team roles, determining meeting times, and ensuring the right members are on the team.

Frequency chart: A visual representation of the number of times an activity, event, or process occurred for a specified time period.

Future state value stream map: A visual representation on the application of the various Lean tools as applied to the current state value stream map.

Gantt Chart: A table of project task information and a bar chart that graphically displays the scheduled tasks and progress in relation to time.

Heijunka (same as Leveling): The balancing of work amongst the workers during a period of time both by volume and variety.

Heijunka box: A physical device similar to a group of mail boxes dedicated to holding the work units or kanban cards for that day (or week).

Henry Ford: An American car manufacturer, who in the early 1900's, started mass production of the Model T, using continuous flow assembly line (conveyor belts). Henry Ford created production efficiencies through standardizing work methods.

Hippocrates (470 - 370 BC): Known as the "Father of Medicine" in the Age of Pericles. "First, do no harm", from Hippocrates continues throughout the ages.

Histogram: The visual representation that displays the spread and shape of the data distribution.

Idea Kaizen: A quick and easy method to document and solve a simple problem with little or no management approval.

Impact Map: A method by which a team can identify the solutions that will most likely have the greatest impact on the problem with the least effort.

Individual cycle time: The rate of completion of an individual task or single operation of work; for example, drawing blood, writing an order, dispensing a medication to a patient, etc.

Industry benchmark: A peer or competitor standard by which one can be judged.

In-process supermarket: A physical device between two processes that stores a certain quantity of work or service capacity that, when needed, is pulled by the downstream process.

Interim containment actions: The activities that will immediately isolate the problem from your customer. This may require additional resources, manpower, etc. and many times is considered a band-aid until permanent countermeasures can be put in place.

Interruption: The stopping of a process without notice.

Joint Commission on the Accreditation of Healthcare Organizations (JCAHO): A non-profit organization that sets standards for healthcare facilities and issues accreditation to those facilities that meet those standards.

Just-In-Time (JIT): A system to supply work (data, information, etc.) or service (patient care) at precisely the right time, in the correct amount, and without error.

Kaizen: "Kai" means to "take apart" and "zen" means to "make good". Kaizen is synonymous with continuous improvement.

Kaizen Event: A focused group of individuals applying Lean tools to a specific area within a certain time period.

Kaizen Event Scorecard: A visual record that conveys the results of the improvements. It will provide the team with the necessary data in which to make corrections if trends are negative and the improvements are not going as expected.

Kanban: A card or visual indicator that serves as a means of communicating to an upstream process precisely what is required at the specified time. In Japanese, kanban means "card", "billboard", or "sign".

Key Performance Indicator (KPI): Agreed upon numbers by an organization that will reflect how well the organization is meeting its overall goals. Key performance indicators are typically long-term considerations for an organization.

Lean: The the tools and concepts, along with the philosophical approach, derived from the Toyota Production System to eliminate all waste or non value-added activities from a process while improving flow.

Lean Chronicle: The record or narrative description of the activities that comprise the Lean-Sigma Kaizen (or continuous improvement) Event.

Lean healthcare: The application of the Lean tools and practices to the healthcare industry.

Lean-Sigma: The combination of Lean tools with Six Sigma placing emphasis on the data collection and control phases of Six Sigma.

Leveling (same as Heijunka): The system that balances (allocates, distributes) the volume and variety of work among the staff during a period of time - typically a day.

Meeting Information Form: Written communication that details time, place, location, action items, etc. for an effective meeting to occur.

Metric: A specific number (data) that is utilized to measure before and after improvement initiatives.

Mistake proofing: A system designed to ensure it is impossible to make a mistake (or error) or produce a defect. Also known as poka-yoke.

Norming: The third stage of team development. At this point, team ground rules are being adhered to, communication is occurring without disruptions, progress is being made toward the objective, and everyone is contributing in a positive way.

Observation: A way to collect information about a process by watching and documenting on how people do their jobs.

Observation Guide: A printed form that provides space for recoding information about the process being analyzed.

Opportunity flowchart: Standard symbols used to display the process and categorize between value-added from non value-added activities.

Pareto Chart: The visual representation in a bar chart format that lists the issues of the problem in descending order of importance.

Paynter chart: A visual representation of defects over time relative to the subgroups derived from the Pareto chart.

Performance measurements: The measurable indicators that can be systematically tracked to assess progress made in achieving predetermined goals and using such indicators to assess progress in achieving those goals.

Performing: The fourth stage of team development. It involves diagnosing and solving problems with relative ease, making constructive self-changes, achieving project milestones earlier than anticipated, and coaching other team members.

Permanent countermeasure: The activities that modify or create a process standard. These changes will ensure that the root cause(s) of the problem will not occur under similar circumstances.

Physical layout (Lean): A self-contained, well-ordered work area that optimizes the flow of patients and work.

Pie chart: A circular chart divided into sectors, illustrating relative magnitudes, frequencies, or percents.

Pitch: The time frame that represents the most efficient and practical work (or patient) flow throughout the value stream.

PLAN: The first phase of the PDCA cycle that identifies and analyzes a problem. It establishes the foundation upon which the team resources will be allocated.

Poka-yoke: It is Japanese for mistake proofing. It is derived from "poka" - inadvertent mistake and "yoke" - avoid.

Prevent: The fourth phase of Value Stream Management for healthcare. It is comprised of creating the necessary processes to control and sustain the improvements implemented in the previous phases as well as sharing the knowledge.

Problem solving: A team working together, following a structured process, to remedy a situation that caused a deviation from a norm.

Process: A sequence of tasks (or activities) to deliver a product or service.

Process flowchart: Standard symbols used to represent a process in detail. It will provide a detailed visual listing of all the major and sub-steps in a process.

Process map: Standard symbols used to visually represent a type of operation, process, and/or set of tasks to be performed. Synonymous with flowchart.

Project Prioritization Worksheet: A listing of the main areas of concern relative to the significant factors that are important to the organization.

Pull: A system in which nothing is produced by an upstream (supplier process) until the downstream (customer process) signals the need for it. This enables work to flow without detailed schedules.

Push: Work is pushed along regardless of need or request.

Queue times: The amount of time a work unit or service request must wait until it is released.

Resistance: The opposition of an idea or concept.

Root cause: The origin or source of the problem.

Round robin: A technique in communications whereas one idea from each person is obtained in a circular manner, until everyone has stated their idea.

Run Chart: The visual representation of serial data points over time.

Runner: A designated function for someone to maintain value stream pitch integrity.

Sakichi Toyoda: Developed the first automatic power loom in 1902, allowing it to visualize defects and stop the machine whenever a thread would snap.

Scatter and concentration plots: The visual representation of data to study the possible relationship between one variable and another.

Scribe: A person designated in a meeting to take notes.

Set-In-Order: The second activity in the 5S system. This will ensure items are properly stored and placed in the correct location.

Sequence table or chart: A matrix which shows each value stream pitch as grouped work elements, when it is required, by whom, and in what quantity.

Shine: The third activity in the 5S system. This involves cleaning everything thoroughly and ensuring cleaning is part of the audit process.

Six Sigma: A customer-focused statistically based process improvement methodology for reducing defects based on process improvements. The objective of Six Sigma is the achievement of 3.4 defects or errors out of every million-defect opportunities for error.

Sort: The first activity in the 5S system. This involves the weeding out of items within the target area that have not been used for a period of time or are not expected to be used.

Spaghetti diagram: Standard symbols used to trace the path of a part, document (electronic), person, or service through all its phases.

Standardize: The fourth activity in the 5S system. This involves the creation of documents/rules to ensure the first 3 S's will be done regularly (and made visible).

Standard work: Establishes and controls the best way to complete a task without variation from the original intent. It is the basis for all continuous improvement activities.

Standard Work Combination Table: The visual representation displaying the sequential flow of all the activities related to a specific process.

Standard Work Chart: The visual representation on the sequence of work being performed.

Status Reports: Communicates the status of the project that was defined in the Team Charter, on a regular basis to management.

Storming: The second stage of team development. It involves team members realizing that the task is different and/or more difficult than they first imagined. Impatience about the lack of progress and inexperience on group dynamics has some team members wondering about the entire project.

Storyboard (A3): A poster-size framework for displaying all key information of a Lean-Sigma project. Storyboards can be 8.5" x 11" or can be poster size.

Structured brainstorming: A defined method in which each team member contributes his or her ideas in order.

Sunset Report: A document that contains a summary of what was learned from the project.

Supermarket: The system of storing a certain level of in-process work or service capacity to be pulled by the downstream customer when there is a difference in the cycle times of the process(es).

Sustain: The fifth activity in the 5S system. This involves the process of monitoring and ensuring adherence to the first 4 S's. Many times this will be a regular audit.

Takt time: The pace of customer demand. Takt time determines how fast a process must run to meet customer demand.

Task: A single event or activity within a process.

Team champion: The person who has the authority to commit the necessary resources for the team.

Team Charter: A document detailing the team's mission and deliverables to ensure strategic alignment.

Team leader: The person designated to run the day-to-day or week-to-week activities of the team and ensure action items are evenly distributed.

Timekeeper: A responsible team member that ensures the scheduled meeting times (start, stop, topics) are adhered to.

Timeline: A visual representation of key events within a particular time period, arranged chronologically.

Total cycle time: The rate of completion of a process, or group of tasks, that have a common element. It is calculated by adding up the individual cycle times for that process or value stream.

Total Quality Management (TQM): A comprehensive and structured approach to organizational management that seeks to improve the quality of products, services, and customer satisfaction through ongoing refinements.

Touch point: The direct and/or critical contact between a service provider and the customer.

Training plan: The specific actions to educate the process worker.

Treat: The third phase of Value Stream Management for healthcare. This involves the application (implementation) of Lean tools to the process or area.

Unstructured brainstorming: A method in which team members contribute their ideas as they occur (or come to mind).

Value stream: The actions (both valued-added and non value-added) that are necessary to deliver a product or service to a customer.

Value Stream Management (VSM): A proven, effective, and disciplined step-by-step methodology for understanding and applying the principles and practices of the Toyota Production System (i.e., Lean) to improve processes within an organization.

Value stream map: A visual representation of the material, work, and information flow, as well as the queue times between processes for a specific customer demand.

Visible pitch board: A bulletin board, whiteboard, etc. displaying the pitch increments and associated work.

Visual control: A system (i.e., signs, information displays, maps, layouts, instructions, alarms, poka-yoke or mistake proofing devices, etc.) designed to ensure a process produces what is expected, and if not, what must happen.

Visual production board: A physical device at the process location that displays the work requirements for the day (typically), as well as being updated every hour or two.

Visual metric: The display of measurements.

Voice of the Customer (VOC): A process used to capture (via direct discussions, interviews, surveys, focus groups, observation, reports, logs, web questionnaire, etc.) customer (internal or external) requirements and then using that data in providing the customers with the best in class service.

Walter A. Shewhart (1891 - 1967): The statistician at Western Electric credited with developing the PLAN-DO-CHECK-ACT (PDCA) cycle in 1931.

Waste: Anything that adds cost or time without adding value. The seven most common wastes are: 1) Overproducing, 2) Waiting, 3) Transport, 4) Overprocessing, 5) Inventory, 6) Motion, and 7) Defects. Many times you will see an 8th waste added, that being People Utilization.

Waste audit: The method of analyzing a process in comparison to the seven (or eight) wastes.

Waste walk: The project team members visiting the process area and subsequently identifying the waste on the current state value stream map.

Work load balancing: The optimal distribution of work units throughout the value stream to maintain takt time or pitch.

Yokoten: It means "best practice sharing" or "taking from one place to another" in reference to what had been learned from an improvement project.

Index

List of the Forms and Worksheets Contained in this Book

The following forms and worksheets are available at **www.theleanstore.com** as a Microsoft Excel spreadsheet for you to customize:

1. Kaizen Event Preparation Schedule - 3 Weeks Before Event
2. Kaizen Event Preparation Schedule - 2 Weeks Before Event and 1 Week Before Event
3. Kaizen Event Daily Review
4. Kaizen Event Scorecard
5. Kaizen Event Daily Schedule - Days 1 - 3
6. Kaizen Event Daily Schedule - Days 4 - 5+
7. Idea Kaizen Form
8. Checklist for Creation of a Balanced Scorecard
9. Hospital Balanced Scorecard
10. Project Prioritization Worksheet
11. Distribution/Volume Report
12. Distribution Report
13. Takt Times for ED
14. Cycle Time Table
15. Team Charter
16. Meeting Information Form
17. Status Report
18. Effective Meeting Evaluation Worksheet
19. Brainstorming for pre-Value Stream Mapping
20. Readiness Guide for the Assess Phase
21. Waste Audit 1
22. Waste Audit 2
23. Waste Audit 3
24. Waste Audit 4
25. ED/Inpt Delay Worksheet
26. ED/Inpt Delay Worksheet Summary
27. Document Tagging Worksheet
28. Voice of the Customer (VOC) ED/Inpt Survey
29. 5 Why Analysis
30. Readiness Guide for the Diagnosis Phase
31. Sort Inspection Sheet
32. Tag Worksheet
33. 5S Item Disposition Log
34. Area Map and Arrow Diagram Worksheet
35. Criteria Checklist for Set-In-Order
36. Criteria Checklist for Shine
37. Initial Shine Plan
38. Control Point Worksheet
39. Five Minute 5S Checklist
40. 5S Job List
41. Standard Training Matrix
42. 5S Audit Form
43. Supply Survey Form
44. Supply Order Form
45. Standard Work Chart
46. Failure Prevention Analysis Worksheet
47. Impact Map
48. Gantt Chart Worksheet
49. Readiness Guide for the Treat Phase
50. A3 Report - Storyboard
51. Yokoten Worksheet
52. Readiness Guide for the Prevent Phase

Additional Books to Assist Your Lean Healthcare Journey

The following books and products are available at **www.theleanstore.com**.

Lean Healthcare: 5 Keys to Improving the Healthcare Environment
This book is the first in the industry to offer real solutions and practical advice for improving patient and non-patient care processes, as well as reducing costs. Included in the book are over 20 forms, worksheets, and guidelines for you to use as a workbook as you implement your 5S portion of a Lean or Six Sigma project. Key learning features of this workbook include: 40+ digital photos demonstrating Lean and 5S projects, identification of who should be doing what part of the 5S activity, detailed procedures ensuring each 5S step is done thoroughly, starter tips providing valuable insights from Lean Sensei, and quotes from various leaders throughout the world.

The New Lean Healthcare Pocket Guide (XL) - Tools for the Elimination of Waste in Hospitals, Clinics, and Other Healthcare Facilities
The New Lean Healthcare Pocket Guide is the collection of input from healthcare professionals and Lean Sensei. It provides easy-to-use and easy-to-understand tools, methods, and concepts based on the world-class Toyota Motor Company. *The New Lean Healthcare Pocket Guide* is designed for use as a quick and easy reference as you learn and implement Lean tools. The tools of 5S, continuous flow, cycle time, document tagging, error proofing, goals and outcomes, Just-In-Time, kanbans, takt, pitch plus all the other Lean tools are thoroughly defined, as well as providing the necessary steps to implement that tool. There are over 20 case studies presented throughout the book demonstrating how that tool was used in various healthcare settings. Many of the case studies and examples presented in the *Value Stream Management for Lean Healthcare* book are also included in this pocket guide to assist you in standardizing your training materials. Also, over 20 photos of Lean healthcare practices are included in this new version!

The New Lean Healthcare Training Set
The New Lean Healthcare Training Set is a comprehensive package to allow a facility to standardize their Lean or Six Sigma training. The numerous healthcare examples and case studies presented throughout this training package will allow the participants to better understand how Lean can be applied. The Set allows you to teach the topics contained in *The (New) Lean Healthcare Pocket Guide,* as well as with numerous examples from the *Value Stream Management for Lean Healthcare* book, all explained on the Note Pages of the Facilitator's Guide. *The New Lean Healthcare Training Set* will allow you to:
1. Communicate a standard approach to applying Lean in healthcare
2. Learn from other healthcare facilities that have shared their Lean success
3. Conduct Kaizen Events using the 3 S's of Stabilize, Standardize, and Simplify
4. Summarize the Lean healthcare training by conducting a Lean Healthcare Jeopardy game

The Value Stream Management for Lean Healthcare Training Set
The Simply Lean Pocket Guide
Lean Office Demystified II
The 5S Desktop (PC) Pocket Handbook
The 5S for the Office User's Guide
The Lean Pocket Handbook for Kaizen Events

Also, new and exciting eTools are now available to meet your Lean Desktop initiatives!